A.P. Martinich *Thomas Hobbes*
Roger Middleton *The British Economy since 1945*
W.M. Ormrod *Political Life in Medieval England, 1300–1450*
Richie Ovendale *Anglo-American Relations in the Twentieth Century*
Ian Packer *Lloyd George*
Keith Perry *British Politics and the American Revolution*
Murray G.H. Pittock *Scottish Nationality*
Murray G.H. Pittock *Jacobitism*

continued overleaf

Please note that a sister series, Social History in Perspective, is available covering the key topics in social and cultural history.

British History in Perspective

Series Standing Order: ISBN 0-333-71356-7 hardcover/ISBN 0-333-69331-0 paperback

You can receive future titles in this series as they are published by placing a standing order. Please contact your bookseller or, in case of difficulty, write to the address below with your name and address, the title of the series and the ISBN quoted above.

Customer Services Department, Macmillan Distribution Ltd
Houndmills, Basingstoke, Hampshire RG21 6XS, England

Conquest and Colonisation

The Normans in Britain, 1066–1100

Revised Edition

Brian Golding

palgrave
macmillan

First edition 1994
Reprinted 1996, 1998
Revised edition 2001

Published by
PALGRAVE
Houndmills, Basingstoke, Hampshire RG21 6XS and
175 Fifth Avenue, New York, N.Y. 10010
Companies and representatives throughout the world

PALGRAVE is the new global academic imprint of
St. Martin's Press LLC Scholarly and Reference Division and
Palgrave Publishers Ltd (formerly Macmillan Press Ltd).

ISBN-13: 978-0-333-96152-0 hardback
ISBN-10: 0-333-96152-8   hardback
ISBN-13: 978-0-333-94717-3 paperback
ISBN-10: 0-333-94717-7   paperback

This book is printed on paper suitable for recycling and made from fully managed and sustained forest sources. Logging, Pulping and manufacturing processes are expected to conform to the environmental regulations of the country of origin.

A catalogue record for this book is available from the British Library.

Library of Congress Cataloging-in-Publication Data
Golding, Brian.
    Conquest and colonisation : the Normans in Britain, 1066–1100 / Brian Golding.–Rev. ed.
        p. cm. – (British history in perspective)
    Includes bibliographical references and index.
    ISBN 0-333-96152-8
        1. Great Britain–History–William I, 1066–1087. 2. Great Britain–History–William II, Rufus, 1087–1100. 3. Normans–Great Britain.
    I. Title. II. Series.

DA197 .G65 2000
942.02'1–dc21   00-053073

Printed in Great Britain by the MPG Books Group,
Bodmin and King's Lynn

CONTENTS

PREFACE

For over nine hundred years the Norman Conquest has been a subject of discussion and debate. Of Sellars and Yeatman's two memorable dates in history, 1066 remains the only one that still readily comes to mind, and is still instantly recognisable. Regarded by contemporaries as expressing the will of God, a divine judgement on an errant king and nation, the Conquest has for the most part continued to be interpreted in quasi-moral terms. So, for seventeenth-century historical commentators, Stuart government was defined within the context of the 'Norman yoke', an alien autocracy that had long subverted pure Anglo-Saxon institutions of free government: a reading which Freeman was to develop in the nineteenth century when he implicitly compared Victorian parliamentary democracy, typified by Gladstone, with the *witenagemot* persuaded by the rhetoric of earl Godwine. Alternatively, the Anglo-Saxon state has been regarded as administratively and militarily, if not morally, backward, a kingdom on the edge of a Franco-centric 'Western civilisation' that needed the Norman dynamic as a catalyst for its own internal development and external expansion during the medieval period and beyond. Like most colonisers, the Normans devalued the achievements of the culture they conquered, and the justificatory, and circular, argument for their success was that they 'won' because they were 'superior'. Later historians have too often implicitly, and sometimes explicitly, colluded in this analysis.

Yet the historiography of the Conquest does raise important issues of national identity on both sides of the Channel. How did the mid-eleventh-century English perceive themselves? Was there a clearly defined *gens Normannorum*? and how did the Normans, if they were a distinct race, relate themselves to a wider Francophone culture? Our answers to these questions are inevitably determined by our own contexts and contemporary cultural conditions; each generation inevitably constructs its own history of the Conquest. Nevertheless, there does seem to be one historiographic constant. However much historians might argue over whether or not the Conquest was a 'Good Thing', or over the extent of 'cataclysmic' change consequent upon 1066, there has been, since the twelfth century, general agreement that assimilation between Normans and English was speedily achieved, and that the Conquest occasioned no permanent, long-term disjunction. Chroniclers, often themselves of mixed race, stressed continuity; the author of the *Dialogue of the Exchequer* wrote that by his time (*c*.1170) English and Normans were indistinguishable. Thus the Conquest was subsumed into the teleological flow of English history: it became part of the national heritage – and 'Heritage'. Thus it has come about that those most potent symbols of alien dominion, the great stone castles of Anglo-Norman England, are now part of the central core of monuments which not even the most philistine and market-led administrator has yet suggested should be alienated.

This account of the Norman Conquest is intended as a synthesis of recent scholarship within the context of an interpretation which argues that the Norman penetration of England, and to a lesser extent of Wales and Scotland also, before 1100 proceeded fitfully, and was by no means assured of success until the 1070s. The interaction of native and colonising influences was highly intricate. It had begun years before 1066; it would only be fully realised during the reign of Henry I. The first sections of this book examine the background to the Norman invasion, and the course of military conquest that began at Hastings. It then discusses the process of colonisation, before analysing the impact of the Normans in three central areas of English society: government, military organisation, and the Church, before concluding with an attempt at an overview of the assimilative process and the emergence of an Anglo-Norman England.

Notes and bibliography have necessarily been kept to a minimum and are intended to provide no more than pointers to further discussion. Where essays in journals have recently been republished in a collection, that reference has generally been given.

ACKNOWLEDGEMENTS

In writing, I have contracted many debts, to historians living and dead. Above all, my gratitude and thanks are due to my friends and colleagues at the Battle Conferences on Anglo-Norman Studies. Many will find their insights reflected here; I hope not too distortedly. The Conferences' founder, Professor Allen Brown, did more than anyone this century to foster research on the Conquest: controversial and inspirational, his influence remains profound. His heir as conference organiser, Marjorie Chibnall, has encouraged and supported me, as she has so many other colleagues. To others, too, I owe much: to Professor Christopher Holdsworth and Mr John Gillingham for their careful criticisms, and to Drs Janet Burton and Tessa Webber, who have also read drafts, and to my Special Subject students over more than a decade, who have stimulated, criticised, and advised. I thank them all.

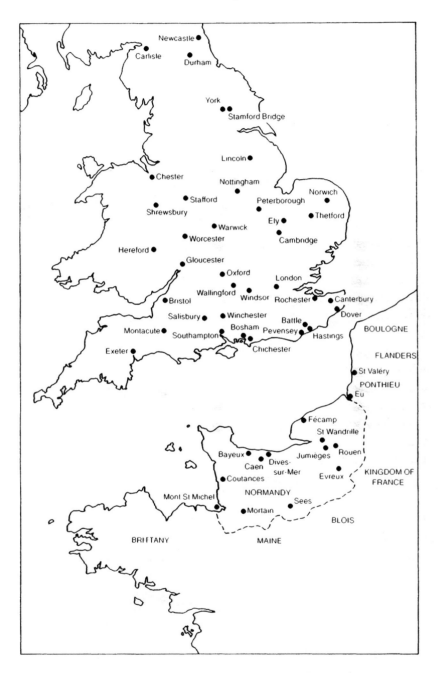

Map 1 England and Normandy in the second half of the eleventh century

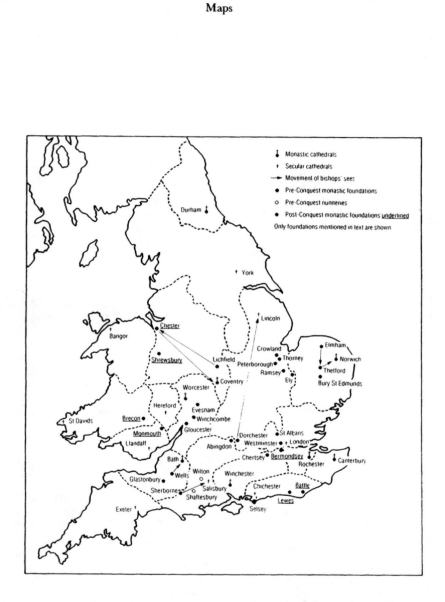

Map 2 The Church in post-Conquest England and Wales

Map 3 The Normans in Wales, 1066–1100

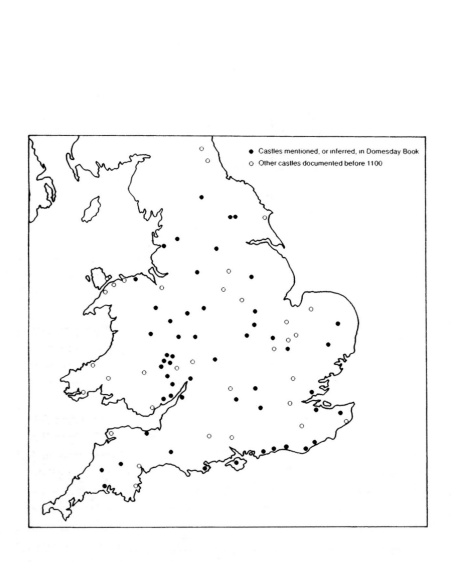

Castles mentioned, or inferred, in Domesday Book
Other castles documented before 1100

Map 4 The castles of early-Norman England and Wales

1

THE SOURCES

For most contemporary chroniclers the Norman Conquest was a quarrel in a far-away country between people of whom they knew nothing. Few noticed it: those that did sometimes got its date wrong. Hardly surprisingly, only Anglo-Saxon and Norman writers were concerned with events leading to Hastings, and its aftermath: their interpretations were inevitably coloured either by the despair of defeat or by the triumph of victory.[1] On one thing alone they were united: in assessing this trial by battle neither blamed the referee – God's judgement was unquestioned.

The author of the 'D' version of the Anglo-Saxon Chronicle believed that the Normans were granted victory at Hastings 'because of the sins of the people'.[2] This northern chronicle (which ends in 1079) is the fullest native account of the first stages of the Conquest. The date of its compilation remains unclear, there are some indications that it was written very shortly after 1066, others to suggest a much later date: certainly its author was most interested in events in northern England and Scotland. Only one other version of the Chronicle records events beyond the battle of Stamford Bridge. The 'C' Chronicle ends just before Hastings, though its entries for 1065 and 1066 may have been written after the Norman success: the Peterborough ('E') Chronicle continued to be produced until 1154. But there were other versions, now lost, of which the most important was that used by the Worcester chroniclers, Florence and John, early in the twelfth century. The textual interrelationships

1

of the Anglo-Saxon Chronicles are too complex to be rehearsed here, but taken together, though they present differing regional perspectives, they are united by a sense of loss and resignation to the will of God.

The Anglo-Saxon Chronicle had begun as a court-centred chronicle of Wessex and it never entirely lost its 'official' or quasi-official status. This 'establishment history' could not readily survive the change of dynasty in 1066. Hastings had deprived it of its *raison d'être*. With the passing of the old order it needed a new function, and to some extent found it as a history for the defeated. It is no coincidence that it was last produced at Peterborough, one of the centres of English political and cultural resistance. But it also reflected new realities and its famous critique of William I's reign in 1087 suggests a growing acceptance of the new masters. In truth, the Chronicle was now marginalised, its very language that of the conquered, its chief value a source for other histories, whose interpretations reveal the growing cultural assimilation between Norman and English.

Though the Chronicle withered away, English historical writing continued, indeed flourished, during the century after the Conquest. In part this was inspired by what James Campbell has termed 'defensive nostalgia', the desire to maintain Anglo-Saxon cultural traditions in the face of Norman indifference or contempt; in part it was the consequence of a felt need to provide histories that were lacking or to reinvent those which had disappeared.[3] That there were gaps in English history, particularly for the Anglo-Saxon period, is made explicit in William of Malmesbury's preface to his *Gesta Regum* ('Deeds of the Kings'), which was intended to remedy this deficiency. Though many post-Conquest histories were of individual monasteries, or they were hagiographies, often of con-temporary or near-contemporary figures, works such as Coleman's *Life of Wulfstan of Worcester* or Eadmer's *Historia Novorum in Anglia* ('History of Recent Events in England') became wider surveys of recent English history. Eadmer is concerned to provide a historical context for Archbishop Anselm's career, particularly his struggles for the primacy, and in treating of Canterbury's fortunes since the time of Dunstan he considers the impact of the Conquest on both the cathedral and the nation. In northern England a *Historia Regum* ('History of the Kings') was produced, traditionally attributed to Symeon of Durham, who certainly wrote a history of his church. The latter is a glorification of St Cuthbert and his community; it stresses continuity and stability in the face of political change, while the *Historia Regum* is an eclectic composition using sources both English and Norman. One of these was a now-lost version of the Anglo-Saxon Chronicle produced at Worcester. This was also used by John of Worcester in his *Chronicon ex Chronicis* ('Chronicle of Chronicles'). These local chronicles were normally commissioned within the monastery. Bishop Wulfstan ordered John to write at Worcester; the history of Durham was seemingly undertaken at the command of its prior, Turgot. Their purpose was to underline the legitimacy of their churches and saints against the challenge of the Normans.

Across the Channel there was, not surprisingly, a different perspective on the Conquest. For William of Poitiers the English who fell at Hastings 'rightly incurred their doom'; for William of Jumièges their death was divine punishment for the alleged murder of Alfred, Edward the Confessor's elder brother, by the Godwine faction in 1036. In their works, particularly that of William of Poitiers, we see that unashamed triumphalism and self-confidence, typical of eleventh-century Norman historians, which Dr Loud has so sensitively analysed.[4] As Orderic Vitalis informs us, both William of Poitiers and Jumièges dedicated their works to William after he became king of England in the hope of his favour. It is, then, in the double context of self-assured *Normannitas* and the search for lucrative patronage that their accounts must be set.

Of the two works, the *Gesta Normannorum Ducum* ('Deeds of the Dukes of Normandy') of William of Jumièges was much the more widely circulated. William was a monk of the ducal monastery of Jumièges and began the first stage of his history in the early 1050s, the second part (including the Conquest) was produced between 1067 and 1070 and, as Dr van Houts has suggested, may have been inspired, or even commissioned, when King William was present at the dedication of the new abbey in July 1067.[5] The *Gesta* was an abbreviation and continuation of the early eleventh-century Dudo of St Quentin's *De Moribus et Actis Primorum Normannorum Ducum* ('Concerning the Customs and Acts of the first Dukes of Normandy'). Like Dudo's work its purpose was to affirm the legitimacy of the dynasty, and though it never enjoyed any official status at the court of the Norman dukes – indeed, William states explicitly that he did not belong to the court circle – it was probably the most influential of the Norman chronicles. Further interpolations to it were made after 1092 (the new version being dedicated to William II Rufus), by Orderic Vitalis after 1113, and finally by Robert of Torigni.

William of Jumièges compared the Normans favourably with the Romans and Greeks, from whom he traced their descent, but he did not so self-consciously proclaim his knowledge of classical authors as his slightly later contemporary, William of Poitiers, who completed his elaborate panegyric, the *Gesta Guillelmi Ducis Normannorum* ('The Deeds of William, Duke of the Normans'), *c.*1077.[6] No manuscript now survives, and the published text is based on that destroyed in the Cottonian Library fire in 1731. This manuscript was incomplete and ended in 1067, though the *Gesta* certainly included events to 1071. It reflects both its author's background and his intentions. William was born in Normandy and his family perhaps had Beaumont connections; he became a knight, till he left to study at Poitiers, where he established himself as a distinguished classical scholar. Professor Davis has presented a persuasive hypothesis that on his return to Normandy William became a protégé of Odo of Bayeux, through whom he may have gained preferment at St Martin's, Dover. It may be, too, that he shared Odo's fall in 1082 – at any rate, for all his fulsome eulogy of King William he never rose higher than archdeacon of Lisieux, and very few manuscripts of the *Gesta* appear ever to have been produced.

The intertextual relationships between William of Jumièges and William of Poitiers have long been recognised. They contain much common material, and there are also some verbal parallels, especially in their descriptions of events before the Conquest, but which was dependent upon which remains unclear. It is even possible that they used a common source. Their relationship to the third, and most controversial, Norman account of the events of 1066, the *Carmen de Hastingae Proelio* ('Song of the Battle of Hastings') is yet more complex. The status of the *Carmen*, the sole manuscript (discovered in 1826) of which is incomplete, remains most questionable.[7] It was long believed to be the epic poem which, according to Orderic Vitalis, was written by Guy, bishop of Amiens, before Matilda joined her victorious husband in England in the spring of 1068, and which was dedicated to Archbishop Lanfranc. Professor Davis has argued that it was a 'literary exercise' composed during the second quarter of the twelfth century in 'one of the schools of northern France or southern Flanders'.[8] Thus, either it is the earliest surviving source for the Conquest or it has little merit as a primary source whatsoever, postdating as it would both Orderic and William of Malmesbury. The recent research of Dr van Houts has placed the *Carmen* in a wider context of poems apostrophising the victorious duke, often explicitly comparing him, as does William of Poitiers, with ancient heroes. These poems were written by clerics, many from outside Normandy, in the hope of reward. Van Houts argues (to my mind convincingly) that the *Carmen* is the most substantial of these poems to survive, that the author was indeed Guy, who was then active at the court of King Philip I of France, and that it was written between Lent and the beginning of Autumn 1067.[9] But, of course, to establish the authenticity of the text is not to accept its veracity. The *Carmen*, like William of Poitiers' *Gesta Guillelmi*, is indeed a 'literary exercise' demonstrating Guy's familiarity with the classical tradition: it is not an eyewitness account of events leading to Hastings and William's coronation.

If the *Carmen* is the most debated of Conquest texts, the Bayeux Tapestry remains the most analysed: a recent bibliography runs to well over a hundred pages.[10] In part, the interest the Tapestry has inspired since the eighteenth century can be attributed to its unique survival as a pictorial embroidered narrative. Similar embroidered hangings are recorded in documentary sources, including one said by Baudri de Bourgeuil to have hung in the chamber of Adela, daughter of William I, and which also portrayed the events of 1066, though clearly on a much smaller scale. There is now general acknowledgement that the Tapestry was produced under the patronage of Odo, bishop of Bayeux, almost certainly before his fall from favour in 1082. He, rather than Duke William, his half-brother, is frequently the central figure in events portrayed; his vassals are given prominence; his cathedral city is presented as the venue for Harold's oath to William. It also seems certain that the Tapestry was planned, and presumably worked, in England, and there is compelling evidence that the abbey of St Augustine's, Canterbury, a house patronised by Odo, was closely involved in the design.[11]

More controversial is the question as to where the Tapestry might have been displayed. It has been argued that the work is too 'secular' for display in Bayeux cathedral and that it was in any case too small to have been viewed effectively there, yet the first reference to the Tapestry, in 1476, refers to its hanging in the nave on the feast of relics and the week thereafter.[12] Moreover, the work's secularity does not necessarily preclude its display in an ecclesiastical setting, given that the story it presents is a strongly moral one depicting the punishment of a perjured warrior. If the Tapestry was shown in a secular building then it is most likely to have been in Odo's palace at Bayeux, though it has recently been suggested that it may have been taken from place to place for temporary display in both England and Normandy.[13] However, it is hard to suppose that a work so explicitly in praise of Odo would have enjoyed widespread appeal, at any rate after 1082.

The problem concerning the display of the Tapestry raises another question, that of the work's 'audience'. For whom was it intended and what message was it meant to convey? While we should beware of seeing, as has one recent commentator, a 'hidden agenda' within the Tapestry that subverts its narrative through its marginal references in order to advance a reading that is Anglo-Saxon rather than Norman, it is true that the Tapestry is at times both ambiguous and ambivalent.[14] Harold is by no means wholly vilified and is presented throughout as an heroic fighting man. Moreover, he is consistently styled *rex* ('king'), an appelation that most Norman commentators would have denied. Though it is perhaps going too far to suggest (as has John Cowdrey) that it had an assimilative function and was intended for a mixed audience of military men with shared values in households 'where French and English rubbed shoulders', the Tapestry remains a subtle, multi-layered narrative that still asks as many questions as it answers.[15]

By the time Orderic Vitalis produced his compelling account of the Norman Conquest, in his *Ecclesiastical History*, 1066 was over half a century away; England and Normandy were united under what contemporaries perceived as the benign and just rule of Henry I, whose elder brother, Robert, late duke of Normandy, lay secure in prison.[16] During the intervening years the political landscape of England and France had been transformed, the political centre of gravity fundamentally shifted. The duke of Normandy remained the nominal vassal of the king of France in a relationship that would resonate throughout the medieval period: the fact that he was now also king of England had created unresolvable tensions. Orderic, therefore, wrote with the benefit and distortion of hindsight. He also wrote long after the military subjugation of England – though not of Scotland or Wales – was complete, when the process of colonisation and assimilation was well advanced. Indeed, his own life testified to that integration. In the moving autobiography written as an epilogue to his history, he tells how as a young boy he was sent 'as an exile' to Normandy, where he entered the monastery of St Evroul.[17] He felt his isolation keenly – he did not even understand Norman French – but here he found stability and peace. The *Ecclesiastical History* was begun at the command of his abbot, Roger, and seems originally to have been intended primarily as a history of St Evroul, but its scope was gradually expanded to encompass the history of England and Normandy within the framework of a universal history. Orderic never questioned the legitimacy of Norman claims to the English throne, but he could never condone what he perceived as the illegitimate plunder of the country that followed. This attitude to the Conquest, that reaches its climax in the great set-piece that is Orderic's construction of King William's death-bed speech, is apparent throughout his work, which is permeated with sympathy and understanding for the defeated.[18] Indeed, at times, most notably in his account of the life and death of Earl Waltheof, that he wrote at the request of the monks of Crowland and which is interpolated into the *History*, his studied ambivalence is replaced by more overt support for the English.

The *Ecclesiastical History*, which Orderic finished in 1141, never enjoyed a wide circulation. By contrast, William of Malmesbury's

Gesta Regum became one of the most widely disseminated histories in medieval England.[19] Like Orderic, William was born of mixed parentage, but a generation later, *c*.1095. Unlike Orderic, William entered an English, not a Norman, monastery. However, Malmesbury abbey could not escape Norman influences and William's first abbot was a monk, Godfrey, from Jumièges. William is unquestionably the greatest of the twelfth-century English historians. Though the *Gesta* was completed by 1125 it was begun many years earlier, certainly well before 1118, and may well have been commissioned by Henry I's queen, Matilda, a patron of Glastonbury. William later revised the *Gesta* and also produced a sequel, the *Historia Novella* ('The History of Recent Events'). He was widely read and also travelled extensively in his search for materials, visiting many English ecclesiastical centres, including the great archive repositories of Worcester and Glastonbury. His intention was to write, as it were, a new Bede for the twelfth century; for him, as for the majority of his contemporaries, histories served to inspire readers with a desire to emulate the good or to avoid the bad. For William, as for Orderic, the history of the Conquest has essentially a moral and didactic purpose. Just as Bede, on whom both so much relied, saw the Anglo-Saxons as the necessary instruments of the divine purpose in the salvation of the British, the Normans were used by God to reform the Anglo-Saxons. But if the conquerors allowed their self-interest to override that function they were to be condemned. The conquered, particularly those who bore no responsibility for perfidy in 1066, were to be pitied. But William also wrote, he tells us, 'for love of my country'.

For all these contemporary, and near-contemporary, historians of the Conquest, then, the Norman victory provided a framework for their own preoccupations. The analysis of its dynamic was secondary. The Conquest they constructed could be used to illustrate their classical expertise; it could serve to demonstrate the valour of a patron; it could reveal the deep purposes of God. After William of Malmesbury, the Norman Conquest no longer had immediate relevance for historians. The chroniclers of Angevin England wrote within a very different political context. There were other cultural influences too.[20] Around 1140 a Norman clerk, Gaimar, wrote his

Estorie des Engleis ('History of the English') for a literate lay woman, Constance, the wife of Ralph fitzGilbert and herself of English stock. This is a vernacular verse romance history presenting the history of Britain from its legendary foundation by Brutus. Much of the more recent content of the *Estorie is* derived from the Anglo-Saxon Chronicle, but romanticised. Here, then, history slides into romance: a Norman clerk writes for an English woman, translating an English source into Anglo- Norman.

No one saw the problems of interpretation of recent history more clearly than William of Malmesbury. The prefaces with which he began each of the five books of the *Gesta Regum* indicate that he was fully aware of the difficulties and potential pitfalls of historical scholarship. Some histories, and he cites in particular the tenth-century chronicle of Aethelweard, are accurate but badly written. In rehearsing events long-past, the historian necessarily relies on earlier works whose veracity cannot always be established. Sources are confused and contradictory; in some instances the historian has no sources at all. In writing contemporary history there is often a tendency to avoid criticism of the misdeeds of the powerful, through fear, and conversely to flatter and even invent to gain approval. In writing the history of the court, a historian (like William) who is far from the events he describes has little knowledge. Of course, William did not always follow his own advice. He could be credulous; he admits that there are diplomatic omissions in his treatment of the reigns of William. II and Henry I.

When William introduces Book Ill of the *Gesta*, which deals with William I's reign, he recognises that Norman historians have been too uncritical, while the English have been over-condemnatory through racial hatred. Claiming to represent both sides, William writes that he will walk a middle path, giving praise where due and blame, though gently, where necessary. Yet this measured moderation is itself a literary device, a product of the blurring of the frontiers between Norman and English that is characteristic of the early twelfth century. He is as much the creature of his time as William of Poitiers. But he should have the last word: 'But the time will come when the reader will judge of such things for himself.'[21]

2

PRELUDE TO THE CONQUEST

England and Normandy, 991–1042

In 991 King Aethelred II of England made an agreement, brokered by the pope, with Duke Richard II of Normandy. Peace was sworn and they promised not to shield each other's enemies. In 1002 this alliance was strengthened by the English king's marriage to Richard's sister, Emma, though this did not apparently prevent an English invasion of the Cotentin (recorded by William of Jumièges alone) shortly afterwards, presumably as a preemptive strike against Viking raids that might be launched from Norman bases. Relations between England and Normandy continued uncertain for the remainder of the reign, and some later sources suggest negotiations took place between King Swegn of Denmark and Richard II as the former planned his attack on Aethelred.[1]

The marriage of Aethelred and Emma occasioned the first substantial Norman settlement of England, and Emma's later marriage to Cnut (Aethelred's Danish successor) ensured the continuance of a Norman presence. Indeed, according to Orderic Vitalis, it was through Emma that the Normans 'won power in England'.[2] Of her Norman companions virtually nothing is known, though there are tantalising hints. Both the Anglo-Saxon Chronicle and John of Worcester record that in 1003 a Frenchman, Hugh, whom Emma had placed over Devonshire as her reeve, surrendered (perhaps willingly) Exeter to Danish raiders, which suggests that the

Norman settlers' loyalty to the English regime could not be assumed. The father of Ralph the staller, a leading figure at Edward the Confessor's court, may have been a follower of Emma, while a woman companion, Matilda, married Aelfgar of Worcester. Herluin, who was probably a Norman (though conceivably a Fleming), accompanied Bishop Brihtheah of Worcester to Germany when they took Cnut's daughter, Gunnhild, for her marriage to the German emperor in 1036. He was rewarded with the manor of Lapworth (Warwickshire), held at the Conquest by his son, Baldwin.[3] Merchants from Rouen enjoyed favourable trading privileges in London, and probably elsewhere. Cnut made grants of English manors, such as Brede (Sussex), to the great Norman ducal abbey of Fécamp, which must have brought Norman monks on a regular basis across the Channel, and it is at least possible that this grant was intended as the first stage of a policy of defending the vulnerable south coast by installing Normans in the region. Later, King Edward was to give the port of Steyning (Sussex) to Fécamp, and Eustace of Boulogne, it has been suggested (most recently by Professor Stafford), was intended by Edward to secure the south-eastern littoral against the possibility of Viking raids launched from Flanders, perhaps using Dover as headquarters.[4] At the same time, Cnut and Emma's Norman chaplains went on to be rewarded with bishoprics in Scandinavia, and English-produced manuscripts were being presented to Norman prelates and monasteries: one psalter given by Emma to her brother, Robert, archbishop of Rouen, ended up in the library of St Evroul, where Orderic, writing nearly a century later, said it was still in almost daily use.[5]

In 1013 Edward and Alfred, sons of King Aethelred, sought refuge with their uncle, Duke Richard II, from King Swegn of Denmark's invasion of England. After a brief return to England, by 1017 they were back in Normandy, where they were to remain until 1035. According to Norman sources they were treated with honour by both Richard and his successor, Robert; their sister, Godgyfu, was married to Drogo, count of the French Vexin. How far this respect was translated into action is difficult to assess; the dukes cannot have been under any delusions about the difficulties of any projected return to England. William of Jumièges, and later William of Malmesbury, wrote that Robert planned an invasion in the *aethelings'* support in 1033 or 1034, but was foiled through adverse winds. At about the same time, Edward is found witnessing a charter in favour of Fécamp as *rex*. In another, seemingly genuine, he granted land in Cornwall to Mont St Michel, perhaps in gratitude for Robert's attempt to place him on the throne in 1033, or perhaps in advance of it. Here he styles himself *rex Anglorum* ('king of the English').[6] Moreover, it would appear that relations between Normandy and Cnut remained tensely ambivalent till the latter's death, in spite of his marriage to Emma. All this would suggest that Edward may have been seen as a king over the water, and that he was regarded by his Norman hosts rather as the exiled Stuarts in France some eight hundred years later, sometimes as an embarrassment, sometimes as a pawn, sometimes as a legitimate king.

Edward the Confessor and the Pre-Conquest Norman Settlement

When Edward did finally come into his own, in 1042, though not, as Norman sources would have us believe, as a result of Norman support, there can be little doubt that Norman settlement in England accelerated, and that the main reason for this was Edward's desire for support against the growing power of Earl Godwine of Wessex and his family. However, we need to keep a sense of proportion here. Edward's court was international in composition; those who came offering service and looking for reward could all be of use in royal power politics. Lotharingians, Bretons and, initially, Danes, all had their place. Moreover, the alleged leaders of a 'Norman party', Robert, the former abbot of Jumièges, and Ralph of Mantes, the son of Edward's sister, Godgyfu and Count Drogo, though they may have arrived earlier in the reign, had to wait for their rewards: Robert was not made bishop of London till 1046: Ralph first witnesses as *dux* ('earl') in 1050. Nor does the Norman settlement appear to have been officially sanctioned by Duke William, even if he had the power at this date. Ralph came to England not as a Norman, but as the king's nephew.[7] It has been plausibly suggested that his first power-base was the east midlands; he married an east Mercian, Gytha; their son was called Harold, which reflects Anglo-Scandinavian rather than Norman sympathies. It was probably only after the exile (from which he never returned) of Godwine's wayward eldest son, Swegn, in 1051, that Ralph was installed as earl in the west midlands, where he was optimistically intended, as an experienced border soldier of the Vexin, to hold the troubled Anglo-Welsh frontier. Other Norman settlers in Herefordshire, such as Osbern Pentecost and Richard fitzScrob, may have been Ralph's vassals in the Vexin. Ralph was not the only settler with royal connections from across the Channel to make good. Robert fitzWimarch, a Norman–Breton, is said in some sources to have been a kinsman of the king; so too, according to William of Malmesbury, was Osbern, the brother of William fitzOsbern, a royal chaplain, and later bishop of Exeter.[8] Ralph the staller may have been present in England from birth. Robert (later 'of Rhuddlan') was brought to Edward's court by his father, Humphrey of Tilleuil. Here he received military training and knighthood before returning to his Norman home.[9] These settlers were an important, but not the paramount, element at Edward's cosmopolitan court of the late 1040s. It is questionable, however, how far these men, composed of Edward's kin and individual place-seekers, constituted a 'faction', or consciously prefigured the post-Conquest Norman settlement, though in the heightened political tension of 1050–2 it was easy for a pro-Godwine source like the *Vita Aedwardi* (the 'Life of King Edward') to portray Robert of Jumièges as a Machiavellian party leader. If there was a party at court it was Godwinist.

At the end of 1050 the influence of Godwine and his sons appeared as strong as ever. Through the intercession of the Godwinist archbishop Ealdred of York, Godwine's son, Swegn, had been recently pardoned for the abduction of the abbess of Leominster and the murder of his cousin Beorn, and the earldoms of southern and central England were securely in family hands. But on the death of Eadsige, archbishop of Canterbury, he was replaced, not by the monks of Christ Church's nominee, another Godwine kinsman, but by Robert of Jumièges. According to the, admittedly biased, *Vita Aedwardi*, Robert now became openly hostile to Godwine, but this may have owed less to rivalries between Normans and English than it did to tenurial disputes in south-eastern England between the archbishop of Canterbury and Godwine, as earl of Kent. In the spring of 1051, Robert went to Rome to collect his *pallium* (i.e. the archiepiscopal pall, worn as mark of office). He returned in June, but outright hostilities did not break out till later that summer. Edward had already sanctioned the building of castles by Normans in earldoms controlled by the Godwine family; Osbern Pentecost built one in Herefordshire, Earl Swegn's territory; Robert fitzWimarch one at Clavering (Essex), in Harold's; while a third was at least projected at Dover, in Godwine's own earldom. This was to be placed in the hands of Eustace of Boulogne, who had married the widowed Godgyfu, Edward's sister.[10] According to the 'E' version of the Chronicle, in September Eustace visited Edward and 'told him what he wished'. While returning home *via* Dover Eustace became engaged in a skirmish between his own forces and the garrison there. This precipitated open conflict. Eustace complained to the king at Gloucester; Godwine and his sons mobilised their forces; but the Earls Leofric (of Mercia) and Siward (of Northumbria) urged caution, and the hearing of the dispute was deferred to a later date at London, though Swegn was immediately outlawed. But before the matter could come to judgment, Godwine and his sons, realising that their support was ebbing away, fled, Harold and Leofwine to Ireland, the others to Flanders.

The dispersal of the Godwine faction gave Edward a unique opportunity to reconfigure the political landscape. The vacated earldoms were allocated to Ralph of Mantes; Aelfgar, the son of Earl Leofric; and Odda of Deerhurst; while a Norman, William, was appointed to the bishopric of London. Godwine, meanwhile, appealed to the count of Flanders and the king of France for support. Though this was not forthcoming, after several setbacks the family were able to return in the late summer of 1052 and force their acceptance back into the king's government. This counter-coup did not result in the eviction of all the Normans but only, as the Chronicle puts it, of those who were 'unjust', so Osbern Pentecost, with his companion, Hugh, had to abandon their Herefordshire castles. They moved north to fight for King Macbeth of Scots against Earl Siward and Malcolm Canmore (the son of king Duncan, who had been killed by Macbeth in 1040): there, in 1054, they were killed. Another Norman in Herefordshire, Richard fitzScrob, remained, however. So, yet more surprisingly, did Earl Ralph, though he had profited from Swegn's forfeiture of the earldom of Hereford and had led the fruitless naval defence against Godwine's return. Robert fitzWimarch also survived to be present at Edward's deathbed in 1066. Three Norman bishops also fled 'with their Normans'. Archbishop Robert and Bishop Ulf of Dorchester never returned, though William of London soon came back.

Given these varying fortunes it seems harder still to argue that there was a coherent *Norman* faction at Edward's court. Men like Osbern Pentecost were adventurers looking to establish themselves wherever the opportunity arose. Norman priests similarly offered more peaceable, but no less necessary, services. Neither group should be seen as an advance guard of the Conquest. Had Godwine believed that they collectively posed a serious threat to his family's influence they would all have been expelled when he returned in triumph; equally, had they been in England in an 'official' capacity, it is hard to believe that Duke William would not have protested at their treatment, or that the Norman sources would have passed over these events, as they do, in silence.

The Offer of the Crown?

By 1052, therefore, Normans had been settled in England for half a century. Some benefited from kinship with the king, others from the service they offered him, all from Edward's obligation to Normandy for the refuge the dukes had offered for nearly thirty years of his life. But did this sense of gratitude lead to an offer of the crown? Norman sources, especially William of Poitiers, were insistent that it did. Most modern historians have seen a connection between the political unrest of 1051–2 and a promise of the succession to the throne, which, it is argued, either precipitated Godwine's rebellion, or was a consequence of it. Yet was this promise ever made? Can we concur with Galbraith's forthright statement that the alleged offer of the throne was an 'absurd pretext' for naked aggression, or that the account of Harold's perfidy is a 'cock-and-bull story'?[11]

William of Jumièges, the earliest Norman source, writes succinctly that Archbishop Robert of Canterbury conveyed the offer of the throne from Edward to Duke William. This was later confirmed by Earl Harold, who pledged fealty and gave many oaths. William of Poitiers is, as usual, much more circumstantial. He adds that the offer was confirmed by leading men of the kingdom, including 'archbishop' Stigand (who had not been appointed to the post by 1051), but omitting the central player in the drama, Harold, from his list. Godwine is also said to have given two hostages from his family. These were taken back to Normandy by Archbishop Robert. Later (in 1064 or 1065) Harold was allegedly sent to ratify the arrangement. He swore to support the duke's cause at Edward's court, and to use all his power to help William to the throne on the king's death. Meanwhile, he promised to maintain a garrison of William's *milites* ('soldiers') at Dover castle, and to place other garrisons in castles as William directed. This 'alliance' was seemingly to be cemented by a marriage between Harold and one of William's daughters. Edward's promise and Harold's confirmation were the basis of Norman claims: Harold's treachery the cause of the Conquest. But William of Poitiers was prepared to use other justifications. William had an hereditary right to the English crown through Emma: Edward had promised the crown in gratitude to the Normans for their assistance in 1042. Yet, though occasionally William did claim kinship with Edward, as he did in a charter for St Martins-le-Grand, London, *dei dispositioni et consanguinitatis hereditati Anglorum basileus* ('by the will of God and hereditary kinship emperor of the English'), he must have known such a claim was extremely weak, and not surprisingly this card was rarely played.[12] Nor did William aid Edward to the throne in 1042, though the returning exile was accompanied by a small Norman entourage.

That the account of the offer of the crown is emphasised by the Norman historians is not, of course, surprising. Neither is the silence of contemporary English sources, and even the Bayeux Tapestry, with studied ambiguity, leaves the promise and the *nature*, though not the event, of Harold's oath, to be inferred by its readers. Although the Norman sources are inconsistent and sometimes contradictory, a chronology of events can be constructed on their basis. Most historians who accept that an offer was made agree that this occurred between mid-Lent, when Robert was elected archbishop, and late June 1051, when he returned from Rome after having collected his *pallium*. During this time he could have conveyed the offer to William. This was, it is suggested, the prime cause of Godwine's rebellion, which was sparked off by the conflict at Dover with Eustace of Boulogne shortly afterwards. Though English sources are silent on the offer, one, the 'D' version of the Chronicle (followed by John of Worcester), records that William himself came to England, seemingly at the end of 1051, 'with a great force'. Edward received him 'with as many companions as suited him and let him go again', while John adds that they were entertained honourably and returned laden with gifts. The silence of the other sources, including the Norman, and the circumstantial evidence that William was facing grave unrest in his duchy at this time have led some to argue that this entry is an interpolation, but all who accept its reliability assume that William's visit was to receive the offer of the throne in person.[13]

There is one other English source which needs consideration. Writing at the end of the century, the Canterbury monk, Eadmer, presented a different interpretation of the events of 1051 and the Conquest.[14] He tells of a serious (though unspecified) quarrel between Godwine and Edward, which resulted in Godwine's exile until after the death of queen Emma (March 1052). The other nobles, desirous of peace, urged reconciliation but the king, who was suspicious of Godwine, only consented if he were given hostages, Wulfnoth (Godwine's son) and Haakon (his grandson, the son of Swegn). These were sent to Normandy for safe-keeping. Harold later wished to secure their release and, in spite of Edward's reluctance, set out for Normandy. On meeting William, the duke revealed that Edward had promised the throne to him while Edward was in exile. He suggested that Harold pledge support, garrison Dover for him, and make a double marriage (Harold to William's daughter, Harold's sister to one of William's vassals). In return, a hostage would be freed and Harold richly rewarded; the second hostage would be released when the terms of the agreement had been met. Harold duly swore and took his nephew home. On Edward's death, William demanded first Harold's sister and then fulfilment of the other promises. Harold refused: his sister had died; he had garrisoned Dover; he could not promise the kingdom as it was not his to grant. This story retains some of the elements found in William of Poitiers, who may have been their source. Other features are impossible to credit, such as the alleged offer of the throne while Edward was still in exile. The whole account may be an attempt to describe unpalatable events from an English perspective, sidestepping the main issue of the offer, but it should still be taken seriously.

Before considering the credibility of these various accounts it is necessary to establish some contexts. Succession disputes were nothing new. The death of Cnut, in 1035, had been followed by five years of uncertainty during which one claimant, Alfred, son of King Aethelred, had been killed; Alfred's brother, Edward, had mounted an unsuccessful invasion the following year; two other claimants, Harold Harefoot and Harthacnut, bitterly contested the throne. Even after Edward's accession, in 1042, he was gravely troubled by the ongoing machinations of his mother, Emma, and the dynastic ambitions of Magnus of Norway. Until a strict principle of primogeniture evolved, dispute was almost inevitable between claimants, all of whom might consider themselves king-worthy, but none of whom had an exclusive right. Moreover, rules of succession were steadily evolving. Dr Williams has shown how, by the tenth century, the kingdom of Wessex was regarded as indivisible and hereditary, though there was also a bias towards primogeniture.[15] This did not preclude the occasional appearance of a *sub-regulus* ('under-king'), the anticipated heir, who might be appointed to this position of authority during his father's lifetime – it should, perhaps, be remembered here that Harold is so styled by John of Worcester. But the appointment of a single ruler normally involved a choice between candidates, and herein lay potential danger. Support needed to be obtained from the leading magnates, the *witenagemot*, and though the Old English monarchy was never elective the consent of powerful lords and thegns was increasingly regarded as both necessary and prudential. One thing we are never told is how these men would react to an illegitimate heir. Certainly, in the ninth century, bastards of the royal line were denied the succession: William's bastardy, combined with his but distant ties of kinship, may well have rendered him ineligible. But the choice of successor, within the parameters of kinship, lay with the king, who could bestow the crown either by a *post obitum* grant (i.e. a grant to take effect after the grantor's death) made *inter vivos* (i.e. between living principals), or by a death-bed bequest, the *verba novissima* ('last words'). In both Normandy and England the former was regarded as irrevocable if made in due legal form before witnesses, though in England it could be revoked if it was later included in the testamentary device known as the *cwide*, since the latter *could* be amended if required. Alternatively it could be superseded by the *verba novissima*.[16] William of Poitiers did not deny that Edward had made a *verba novissima* bequest to Harold, but he denied its validity, for in Normandy a *post obitum* grant was in no circumstances revocable. But in any case it is doubtful that Edward's alleged grant to William was strictly a *post obitum* bequest, since this required the recipient to enter upon the benefice immediately, while the donor retained an interest in it till death.

In examining the question of the Norman succession we need to answer two related, but distinct, questions: was an offer legitimate, and, more controversially, was there an offer at all? As just observed, by the mid-eleventh century succession to the throne was regulated by three criteria: kinship; the choice of the reigning king; the approval of the magnates. William's kinship with Edward was remote: it was no better than that of Swegn Estrithson of Denmark and considerably weaker than that of Edward *aetheling*, the son of Edmund Ironside, who had fled to Hungary in 1017, or Ralph of Mantes; it was arguably weaker than any claim Eustace of Boulogne might have. Indeed, only Earl Harold, amongst the 'serious' contenders, had a weaker claim by blood, though his sister's marriage to Edward created an extremely close kinship tie by marriage. No wonder Norman sources made little of William's rights in this respect. If an offer of the throne was made it required ratification by the *witenagemot*. As we have seen, William of Poitiers states that this occurred before Robert of Jumièges set out for Rome in 1051, taking the offer and Godwine's hostages with him. But, apart from the erroneous reference to 'archbishop' Stigand, this confirmation excites suspicion. Why should Godwine have agreed to an arrangement that was potentially so damaging to his family's ambitions? He was not at this point in a weak position – his rebellion shortly afterwards would not have been ventured had he not thought he could win. Why, for that matter, should any of the *witenagemot* have consented to a Norman heir? Moreover, the taking of hostages – and there are strong arguments for thinking that hostages were required at some point – is far more likely to have occurred during the negotiations at Gloucester, when the tide turned against Godwine, as surety for his appearance at the London trial; indeed, John of Worcester says just this. The only time when Edward could realistically have expected assent for his succession plans would have been following the Gloucester negotiations, and most probably between Godwine's flight and his triumphant return the following year.

We should now turn to the offer itself. By 1050 it must have been clear that a succession crisis was inevitable. Indeed, it has been argued that Edward's reluctance or incapacity to father an heir had been known since the mid-1040s and that, therefore, all were aware from an early date of problems ahead. The difficulty in 1050, as in 1066, was not an absence of possible claimants but that none commanded universal support or had much to recommend them. Names were almost certainly being canvassed: according to Adam of Bremen, Edward considered Swegn Estrithson as a possible successor; it is likely that some voices, perhaps that of Robert of Jumièges, were heard in favour of William. But in 1051 William himself was hardly in a position to think of expanding his territory. In March the count of Anjou occupied Le Mans, thereby strengthening his influence in Maine, the vital strategic buffer state between Anjou and Normandy. By the summer the position had worsened as Geoffrey of Anjou moved into Bellême. Though by the end of the year William had captured the two towns of Alençon and Domfront, his position remained far from secure, and was to worsen steadily in 1052. It is unlikely that Edward seriously thought William a viable candidate for the English throne. We should now reconsider the alleged visit of William at the end of the year. In the accounts given in the 'D' version and John, it is William who is presented as the client, Edward as lord. He is 'received with as many of his companions as suited' the king, and John has pointed out that the Anglo-Saxon word normally translated as 'received' is *underfeng*, a term that carries connotations of overlordship and which seems to indicate that William became Edward's man, a suggestion apparently reinforced by William of Poitiers' reference, at one point, to Edward as William's *dominus*.[17] This episode is usually interpreted as William agreeing to become the vassal of Edward in return for the kingdom. But there may be another explanation. At the end of 1051 Edward must have appeared stronger than he had ever been: the Godwine family had fled, the nation was at peace. By contrast, William's position was weak. If William did come to England he may have done so to gain support at home from the English king; perhaps, too, he was concerned to rebuild bridges weakened by diplomatic developments across the Channel.

An understanding of the crisis may lie in the tangled and obscure politics of the territories between the two growing powers of Flanders and Normandy. In 1050–1 Duke William had married Matilda, the daughter of Count Baldwin V of Flanders. This marriage, first projected in 1049, linked the two principalities. Shortly afterwards Tostig, Godwine's son, married Baldwin V's half-sister, and it was to Bruges (in Flanders) that Godwine fled in 1051, while Baldwin provided support for his new relatives in their successful bid to return to England in 1052. Such alliances could not have been welcomed in all quarters, perhaps above all in the counties of Ponthieu and Boulogne. These were vulnerable small states between the 'super powers'. Ponthieu had taken advantage of earlier Norman weakness to encroach on Normandy's north-eastern frontier. In 1052 Count Enguerrand of Ponthieu was killed fighting for William of Arques in his rebellion against the duke. His successor, Guy, joined the alliance against William only to be captured at the battle of Mortemer. On his release he became a vassal of the duke. Eustace of Boulogne, though he is not known to have taken an active role in the rebellion, gave refuge to Count William of Arques after the latter's castle finally surrendered to Duke William. Across the Channel, Edward may have been equally worded by the Norman–Flemish alliance. Relations with Flanders had been ambiguous during the reign. Flanders was a convenient bolt-hole for rebels and exiles. Osgod Clapa had earlier found refuge there, as did Swegn during his exile from 1047 to 1049. In 1048 a substantial Viking fleet had raided the south-east coast from Flemish harbours and then withdrawn there to sell its spoils, and in 1049 Edward agreed to Emperor Henry III of Germany's request for a sea blockade of Baldwin during the latter's rebellion against imperial authority.

Edward and Eustace had therefore a common interest in keeping Flanders and Normandy apart. This may have underlain Eustace's visit to the English court in 1051. It is likely that a discussion of the defence of the Channel was on the agenda; by installing Eustace at Dover Edward would kill two birds with one stone: he would establish a faithful member of his family in a strategically sensitive base controlling both sides of the Channel, while at the same time reducing Godwine's authority in the south-east. By inserting Eustace and trustworthy Normans in Godwine's spheres of influence the king could limit the power of the Godwine family. But such a policy does not necessarily imply a Norman alliance: Earl Ralph and the others were loyal to Edward, not William, and in any case both Edward and Eustace had every reason to distrust William. There was no incentive, and many disincentives, to make William an offer of the throne at this time.

But whether or not an offer was made, by 1054 Edward was ready to consider another possible successor, Edward *aetheling*, exiled in Hungary since his father, Edmund Ironside's death.[18] His recall was almost certainly the purpose of Archbishop Ealdred's lengthy visit to Cologne to meet the Emperor Henry III. This achieved little immediately, but in 1057 Edward arrived in England. It is possible that his return had been orchestrated by Harold, who was certainly in Flanders in late 1056, and may have travelled on to Germany.[19] According to John of Worcester, Edward returned at royal command, and the king had determined to make him his heir.

Unfortunately, the proposed heir died before he could meet King Edward. The reason for his death, and why he was not apparently allowed to see the king, have been the subject of considerable debate ever since. The 'D' version of the Chronicle voices this uncertainty: 'we do not know for what reason it was brought about that he was not allowed to see . . . King Edward'.[20] Harold stood to gain by the exile's promotion, unless he was already thinking of the crown for himself (which is possible). William, by this time secure in Normandy, would have seen any claim he might have had cut out by the nomination of an heir with closer ties of kinship, but there is little he could have done about it. It has been suggested that Edward refused to see the claimant in order to register his disapproval of this reversal of his pro-Norman strategy, but this explanation seems unlikely on two counts. First, if that was the case, then the recall of Edward must have been against the king's wishes, and it is unlikely that Harold, however dominant in court, could act so independently: Edward was still no cypher. More significantly, after Edward of Hungary's death, his son Edgar was named *aetheling* by the Confessor. The precise implications of this honorific have been debated, but it was only given to those who were considered throne-worthy; such men had a privileged legal status second only to that of the king, and, according to Dr Stafford, the term was only applied to the sons of those who had reigned.[21] Whatever the meaning of Edward's nomination, therefore, it certainly seems to have brought the young Edgar clearly into the picture as a probable successor.

At the same time, the field of possible successors was narrowing. Edward *aetheling* had just died, so too had Earl Ralph, leaving a minor as his heir. It was unlikely that Edgar *aetheling* would come of age before the King's own death: William and Harold were, for different reasons, becoming the most likely beneficiaries of the succession problem, *faute de mieux*. The years between 1057 and Harold's visit to Normandy in 1064 (or, possibly, 1065) witnessed the growing power of Harold in England, culminating in his victories over the Welsh, and the steady expansion of William's control over Normandy and its bordering states. Both men were probably already manoeuvring for the English crown.

The Norman sources agree that Harold visited William in order to confirm the earlier offer of the crown. But, again, they need to be questioned in the light of the near-universal silence of English chronicles. Tantalising as ever, the Bayeux Tapestry offers a slightly different version of events. Harold is shown leaving England at, it would appear, the behest of Edward. He rides with his companions, taking hawks and hounds, embarks at Bosham and 'arrives in the land of count Guy', i.e. of Ponthieu – there is no mention of any shipwreck. He is captured, taken to Beaurain, where the two men confer, but what about – Harold's ransom or the succession? 'Rescued' by Duke William, Harold is surrendered by Guy. He then rides with William on his Breton expedition, distinguishes himself on campaign, and is given arms by the duke. Controversy persists as to whether this indicated his knighting or a pledge of fealty, or both. The two men journey to Bayeux, 'where Harold made an oath to William', though the Tapestry is vague as to its purport. On his return to England Harold is shown in an attitude of submission to Edward, and virtually all are agreed that the king is portrayed as reprimanding his earl. Here is a problem. If the Tapestry shows Edward both sending Harold on his mission and reproving him on his return, Harold must have failed the king in some way. But if Edward had sent him to confirm the offer of the throne, then, if the Norman sources are to be believed, he would have no cause for complaint, the mission would have been satisfactorily accomplished. Can an alternative scenario be suggested? The *Vita Aedwardi* makes oblique references to Harold's freedom with his oaths. It also refers to Harold's meetings with 'the princes of Gaul'. Harold studied them and 'noted down most carefully what he could get from them if he ever needed their services in any of his projects'.[22] This diplomatic activity – and we should remember Harold's earlier visits to Flanders, and perhaps to Germany – is corroborated by William of Poitiers, who writes that Harold spent a great deal of money in order to bring powerful *duces* and *reges* to his cause. Is the king of France and, possibly, the German emperor, referred to here? We have only Norman sources to indicate that Guy captured Harold: as Professor Barlow has pointed out, at one point William of Poitiers says merely that Harold was in *danger* of being captured.[23] Harold's visit to Guy could have been premeditated. Though Guy of Ponthieu had been a vassal of William's since the defeat of 1054, that does not mean that he was not still afraid of the power of his mighty neighbour. Guy may have been forced to hand over Harold as a diplomatic guest, not a prisoner, *force majeure*. In the hands of an unscrupulous captor, Harold had little option but to swear an oath, but for what? Oaths were a familiar feature of the late eleventh-century political landscape in France, but their implications were often ambiguous. They could be interpreted as a ritual reinforcement of vassalage, but alternatively they might be exchanged between equals with no assumptions of superiority, as Dudo of St Quentin explicitly made clear when he described the oath made by Duke Rollo of Normandy to the French king in 911. 'Political' oaths on relics were not unknown, but as Dr Stafford puts it, 'it was not an obligatory part of eleventh-century hospitality'.[24] At the same time an agreement of this magnitude, whereby the English throne was pledged to the Norman duke, would surely demand the giving of hostages, but in fact William released one of the two hostages he had held since 1051. Is it possible that Harold set out on a diplomatic mission to powerful French princes, and at the same time hoped to arrange for the release of his relatives? To gain their (and his own) freedom he might have been prepared to swear what was not his to grant, the throne. Such an *ultra vires* act would have occasioned Edward's reprimand.

What has been argued above is an expression of honest doubt concerning the validity of the Norman sources: it is an hypothetical alternative reading of sources and events. The recent work of Dr Garnett provides a valuable reassessment of the development of Norman propaganda in the years after 1066.[25] Initially there is ambiguity in descriptions of Harold's status. An early charter in favour of Regenbald, the king's priest, refers to Harold as *rex*, as too, of course, does the Bayeux Tapestry, consistently. Yet by 1086 the story is clear. William and his tenants-in-chief hold manors whose history is referred back to the time of King Edward, and Harold is no longer *rex* but *comes* ('earl'), or more tellingly, *invasor* ('usurper'). Yet just occasionally the mask slips and we read that William 'conquered the kingdom'. Administrative sources suggest that a clear and consistent interpretation of William's legitimacy took time to develop; by contrast, the Norman chroniclers, William of Jumièges and William of Poitiers, were already advancing 'moral' justifications for the conquest by the early 1070s. The sources on which we rely were written with the advantage of hindsight and in the aftermath of Norman victory. On the Norman side they were propagandist justifications of an illegitimate seizure of the English throne; on the English side they were interpretations that avoided the issue of the succession, for the chroniclers were well aware that Harold's claim was as flimsy as that of William. It has been argued that since there was no need for the Norman chroniclers to advance legalistic justifications for the Conquest following victory at Hastings, their version of events should be accepted as trustworthy in the main. But there was an occasion when these arguments could have been useful. As William sought approval for his invasion from the pope, such material could well have been submitted in his support. A promised crown, a perjured lord, these were issues that might appeal to an ecclesiastical judge. Whether they were a faithful representation of the facts is open to doubt. In the fraught atmosphere of a royal court faced with a succession crisis, the possibility of a Norman succession was almost certainly discussed; it was probably raised informally by Edward, perhaps as a bargaining counter in the tortuous domestic politics of 1051–2, but that it was given formal reality must remain unproven. William was but one among many more or less unsatisfactory candidates. In 1066 Norman legitimacy depended on the sanction of battle, the ultimate judicial ordeal.

3

THE NORMAN CONQUEST, 1066–1100

The Norman Invasion

By the end of 1065 Edward had probably been ill for some time. The magnates who gathered for the consecration of the new Westminster abbey during the Christmas festivities must have guessed that they would soon need to elect a new king. The crisis could not have come at a worse time. A few weeks earlier the Northumbrians had finally risen against the harsh rule of their earl, Tostig. His appeal to Edward and to his brother, Harold, to restore him to authority had been turned down. As a consequence he had broken with Harold, and fled to take refuge with his wife's family at the court of Flanders. Only Edgar *aetheling* had close kinship ties with the dying king. Some may have considered his claim, as William of Malmesbury reports; William even at one point suggests that Edgar was nominated by Edward.[1] After Hastings, the surviving native magnates were prepared to back Edgar *faute de mieux*; Brand, the incoming abbot of Peterborough, was so rash as to send to Edgar for confirmation of office. But it must have been obvious to the majority both before and after Hastings that Edgar was too inexperienced a figure to provide a rallying point.[2] That left Harold and, if the Norman chroniclers are accepted, William. There is no indication that any voice spoke out for the duke, though that does not mean that Harold's succession was greeted with unanimous acclaim. The Norman chroniclers, hardly surprisingly, stress that many opposed his election; they are corroborated by the *Life* of Bishop Wulfstan of Worcester, which reports how he travelled north to rally support for the new king.[3] Harold was duly consecrated, most probably by Archbishop Ealdred of York, who had longstanding ties with the house of Godwine, while Stigand, archbishop of Canterbury, though himself a Godwine protégé, was probably too damned by his flouting of so many canonical laws to be entrusted with the coronation, whatever Norman propagandists and the Bayeux Tapestry might allege. Norman writers did not, nor could they, deny Harold's consecration, though they did their best to denigrate it. As well as bringing up Stigand's unsavoury reputation, William of Poitiers claimed that only a few nobles were present at the elective *witenagemot*, but even if true it is doubtful if this was a valid objection. The Bayeux Tapestry, ambiguous as always, continues to style Harold as *rex* after his coronation, so too does William of Poitiers, though much less consistently, since elsewhere Harold is reviled as an usurper and traitor to Edward's true successor, Duke William.

In Normandy, a decision to invade came early in 1066, either when it became clear that Harold would not cede the throne to William, or when it seemed that William could take advantage of Harold's shaky position. According to Orderic, Tostig travelled from Flanders to Normandy and promised his support for an invasion of England. There may be some truth in this. The Anglo-Saxon Chronicle tells how Tostig spent the winter in Flanders at St Omer with his wife 'and all those who wanted what he wanted'. Tostig's wife was the aunt of the Countess Matilda; he and William had a common enemy in King Harold. Though he may not have entered into a formal agreement with William, and was probably ready to offer his support to whichever of the claimants he felt had most chance of success, it is certainly possible that he alerted William to the possibilities of invasion. William next held councils (according to Orderic, with Tostig's encouragement) to discuss policy. Though the sources are unclear, and the most circumstantial are the latest in date, it is likely that a meeting of the duke's 'inner council' was followed by a broader-based assembly at which misgivings were voiced. William fitzOsbern probably acted as chief ducal negotiator. Military preparations for the invasion went on through the early months of 1066. William's army was assembled by summons throughout the duchy and it may well be that magnates made individual bargains, based on their resources, as to the number of men they would bring. They had also to provide ships. The contributions made by most of the leading magnates in this venture are detailed in the *Ship List*, which is almost certainly a near-contemporary text. Their obligations were substantial. Robert, count of Mortain owed 120 ships, his brother, Odo of Bayeux, 100, while William fitzOsbern, Hugh of Avranches, Roger of Montgomery and Roger of Beaumont accounted for 60 ships each, but more vessels than were owed were provided according to means. William's wife gave the flagship, *Mora*, which is depicted with its decorative figurehead in the Bayeux Tapestry. It is most likely that the magnates prepared their ships and assembled knights on their own estates before gathering at Dives-sur-Mer.[4]

Support, both divine and earthly, was purchased. English lands were promised to William's followers, and to a number of abbeys including St-Valéry-sur-Somme and Fécamp, whose land in Steyning (Sussex), which the abbey claimed as a grant from Edward the Confessor, was confirmed, conditional on the expedition's success.[5] A diplomatic mission was also sent to Rome to obtain papal support for the invasion. Orderic Vitalis states that this was led by Gilbert of Lisieux, though it has recently been suggested (by Dr Garnett) that Lanfranc, abbot of St Stephen's, Caen, prepared the case against Harold.[6] William of Poitiers relates how a treaty was signed with the Emperor Henry IV, who promised German aid if requested, and also that Swegn of Denmark offered assistance.

No medieval battle and the events leading to it is better documented, or more analysed by modern commentators, than Hastings and, despite the fact that nearly all contemporary or near-contemporary sources record events from the victorious Normans' perspective, their course is in little doubt, and only a few details, such as the chronology and site of the 'Malfosse incident', remain uncertain. It is unnecessary, therefore, to recount them in any detail.[7] For six weeks the invasion fleet waited, initially at Dives-sur-Mer and then much further to the north-east at St-Valéry-sur-Somme in Ponthieu. The reason for the move is debated. Both William, of Poitiers and Orderic imply that the ships were blown up the Channel, and William certainly mentions considerable problems: a failure of supplies; the loss of ships in a storm; desertion by some of the ducal forces. From Dives the invasion was perhaps intended to be launched towards the Solent and thence to Winchester; Harold's fleet was patrolling off the Isle of Wight, protecting this approach to Southampton and Winchester. A move along the coast, whether or not involuntary, might confuse the waiting English; the crossing from St-Valéry to the Sussex coast was also appreciably shorter. It can be suggested that the Norman fleet was dispersed by storms, but that it was William's decision to sail so far up the coast – St-Valéry is well over a hundred miles from Dives – to take advantage of a short crossing into the heartland of Harold's patrimony in Sussex. Harold obviously anticipated a Norman invasion from the early summer of 1066 and he kept his land and sea forces mobilised along the south coast. Only in early September did the logistical problems of provisioning his army and navy oblige him to disband them. On arrival in London he heard of the surprise arrival of King Harold Hardraada of Norway, who had invaded (with Tostig's support) on his own account into the Tyne estuary. His army was reassembled and marched north to York, where the battle of Stamford Bridge resulted in an overwhelming victory. Hardraada, the last of the Viking kings, and Tostig were both killed. However, their earlier crushing defeat of the Earls Edwin and Morcar at Fulford Bridge and the very speed with which Harold had led his forces had depleted and exhausted his army. The landing of William at Pevensey on 1 October compounded his problems. Harold had really no option but to move to Sussex, where his ancestral lands were being ravaged, as soon as possible. Moreover, he probably hoped to repeat the success of a surprise assault, so effective at Stamford Bridge, against the Normans. He might even have considered a night attack. This was a high-risk strategy. Both the Anglo-Saxon Chronicle and, in more detail, John of Worcester, describe how Harold fought before the whole of his army was assembled. This was due in part to William's own surprise tactics immediately prior to the battle, when he was able by rapid manoeuvre to select a favourable battle ground, but in part also to Harold's rush south without waiting for all reinforcements to come in. Moreover, had Harold been able to delay, William's position would have become less tenable, established on a narrow bridge-head as winter approached and supplies dwindled, and with extended communication lines to Normandy. There had already been hints of unrest amongst his forces during the long wait for embarcation; further inactivity might have brought heightened tensions in William's camp.

From Hastings to Westminster

On 13 October, when Harold arrived at the ridge along which the town and abbey of Battle now extend he found William already drawn up on Telham hill to the south. Battle was joined the following morning and lasted till dusk. Its outcome was several times in doubt. After a long period of Norman cavalry charges and stubborn infantry defence from the English the deadlock was broken, when the Bretons on William's left wing turned in flight. They were pursued by a section of the English forces; William himself was reported killed. Had Harold at that point committed the whole army to a counter-attack it is likely that William would have been defeated; Harold's failure to take the initiative, and the recovery of William's forces, allowed the latter to advance onto the ridge. English resistance was gradually weakened, and it is likely that the Norman cavalry turned, at least once, in feigned retreat to lure the defenders down from their positions. Towards the end of the day Harold was killed, seemingly incapacitated by an arrow wound and then cut down by cavalry. His death marked the end of organised resistance, a few survivors mounted a last-ditch defence but the battle was by now irretrievably lost; Harold and his brothers, Gyrth and Leofwine, were dead, as were the greater part of his forces.

Of their names we are largely ignorant. Domesday contains some references to those who fell fighting William. We know that Ailric, the chamberlain, fought in a naval battle against William, perhaps defending the invasion shore.[8] Some survivors were outlawed. Eadric, Edward the Confessor's steersman and Harold's thegn, was outlawed to Denmark with Alwi of Thetford, Ringolf of Oby and Abbot Aelfwold of St Benet's Holme, who had been responsible for the defence of the east coast.[9] Another thegn of Harold who was presumably present at Hastings, Skalpi, hung on to his land in 1066, only to lose it when he went north, where he died at York in outlawry. We are also uncertain of the composition of Harold's forces. Though the majority of those identified in Domesday as falling at Hastings were *liberi homines* ('free men'), at the heart of Harold's army were the household retainers, the housecarls, of the king and his lords, as well as thegns performing their military duties. Some of Harold's army may have been made up of peasants; the Bayeux Tapestry certainly shows some of the English as poorly armed. William of Poitiers reports that a large force had been sent to aid the English from Denmark, though how much credence should be given to this statement is doubtful since the king of Denmark also claimed the English throne. According to William of Malmesbury the majority of Harold's forces were made up of stipendiaries and mercenaries, but he had very few soldiers 'from the provinces', which is often interpreted as forces of the fyrd. It is interesting that William distinguishes between stipendiaries and mercenaries. The former were soldiers retained on a permanent basis and paid primarily in cash, and were probably to be identified with the housecarls, while the latter were hired temporarily for specific campaigns.

In modern times a claim to descent from those whose names are inscribed on the Falaise roll as serving on the Norman side at Hastings carried a social cachet similar to that of a Daughter of the American Revolution, but only about thirty-five have been positively identified as 'companions of the Conqueror'.[10] Virtually all were leading members of the Norman aristocracy: we know nothing of their mounted vassals, let alone the names of those who made up the substantial forces of Norman infantry and archers. The Penitential of Erminfrid of Sion clearly indicates that priests also took part in the battle. Remigius, later bishop of Dorchester, seems to have been active on the field, while the role of Odo, bishop of Bayeux, is unclear. He was certainly present (like Geoffrey, bishop of Coutances) at Hastings and his role is glorified in his Tapestry, but whether he actually fought must be a matter of doubt. Though the names of few of those who fought for William at Hastings are recorded, the chroniclers indicate that there wēre many non-Normans present, and Domesday Book shows that landholders from most of the principalities of northern France as well as Flanders were settled in the conquered land. It seems likely that Eustace of Boulogne played a prominent role, as the *Carmen de Hastingae Proelio* indicates, though this was understandably downplayed by the Norman sources, written after Eustace's revolt in 1067.[11] William of Poitiers mentions Bretons, French, Aquitanians, and men from Maine amongst William's forces. Orderic Vitalis refers also to men from Burgundy 'and other peoples north of the Alps', while the *Carmen* states that there were men from Sicily and southern Italy. Most fought, like the Normans, in the hope of reward from William's 'well-known generosity' (William of Poitiers), but others had ties of kinship or shared common interests. The largest group were the Bretons, so reviled for their cowardice at Hastings by William of Poitiers. Alan the Black and Alan the Red of Penthièvre were related to William. They and their vassals fought for the Normans and were well rewarded, particularly in the honour of Richmond (Yorkshire). Others were recruited from the marcher lands of Brittany; they saw their interests best-served by their more powerful neighbour and had supported William's cause in his intervention in Breton affairs in 1064. The Aquitanian force was mainly Poitevin and was probably led by Aimeri of Thouars, who is included in his compatriot William of Poitiers' list of those who were most worthy of praise in the battle. Like the lords of Penthièvre, Aimeri was a kinsman of the duke; like them he had a common interest in defending his frontier against the ambitions of the count of Anjou.[12]

After Hastings William rapidly made to secure the ceremonial, ecclesiastical and commercial 'capitals' of the realm, at Winchester, Canterbury and London. Archbishop Stigand surrendered at Wallingford, swearing to be William's man. His prompt submission may have been one factor guaranteeing his temporary survival. He continued to exercise his archiepiscopal functions – he almost certainly co-officiated at William's coronation; he consecrated Bishop Remigius in 1067; he attended royal councils, where he sometimes witnessed before Archbishop Ealdred. Another reason for his survival may be that he had played a leading role in royal administration, and could not thus readily be discarded. Shortly afterwards, the remaining lords of Anglo-Saxon England, Archbishop Ealdred, Edgar *aetheling*, the Earls Edwin and Morcar, along with the leading men of London, similarly submitted, commending themselves to the victorious duke, who swore that he would be a good lord to them. Such submissions indicated their recognition of William as legitimate king. Dr Nelson has drawn attention to the Normans' apparent reluctance to accept their duke's promotion. Certainly they feared that William's authority over them would be substantially enhanced and, according to William of Poitiers, only consented at the prompting of the Poitevin, Aimeri of Thouars, when they realised that their own wealth and lands would be increased by the coronation of their lord. In other words, their claims would only be legitimised through William's.[13] Though the Anglo-Saxon Chronicle implies that had the English submitted earlier the Norman ravages would have ceased, the Chronicler goes on to assert that the Normans continued their spoliation till William's coronation (on Christmas Day, 1066) by Archbishop Ealdred, who probably used the very same coronation *ordo* ('order') as employed for Harold. The penitential ordinance of Erminfrid makes it clear that a state of *publicum bellum* ('legitimate war') still obtained between Hastings and Christmas. Normans who killed during this period would still have to perform penance but it was mitigated. After the coronation, however, only rebellious English were denied the new sanctions of royal protection.[14]

The Rebellious Years

The battle of Hastings made the Norman conquest possible, but the real process of subjugation was long-drawn-out, and for many years uncertain. Until 1070 the Norman hold on England was but tenuous, and success could not be considered complete until 1075. The early years saw resistance to conquest across England, and it was only lack of coordination and the ultimate failure of Scandinavian assistance to materialise that saved the new regime. Accounts of the disturbances of these years are confused in the extreme. Chroniclers seldom agree on either their sequence or their nature. To contemporaries, as to William, they must have seemed bewildering and threatening, an ever-changing pattern of alliances, a new rebellion flaring as soon as one was extinguished. The chroniclers of the early twelfth century wrote with the benefit of hindsight, but they too inevitably simplified their accounts and wrote after the details had been forgotten. Modern historians, trying to make sense of these years, are obliged for clarity to separate out the strands of rebellion; to discuss, for example, resistance in the south-west in isolation from unrest on the Welsh marches, or the northern rebellions without reference to those in the fenlands; yet such an approach is distortive, for it fails to take account of the interplay between the rebellions that was potentially so dangerous for William.

Victory at Hastings, followed by the rapid seizure of Canterbury, Winchester, and most importantly, London, enabled William to establish a reasonably secure base in the south-east with little cost. But his success owed as much to the disunity of the surviving English leaders as it did to overwhelming military supremacy. The comparative ease of the autumn campaign, the apparent submission of the native aristocracy, combined with an intention to create a genuine Anglo-Norman state in partnership with them, may have persuaded William that he could safely make a triumphal return to Normandy in the spring of 1067. In solemn procession at Rouen (the seat of the archbishop) and Fécamp (where ducal palace and monastery adjoined), his English captives and looted treasures were displayed. By so doing he associated the two ecclesiastical *foci* of ducal power in his victory. Odo of Bayeux was left in Dover and William fitzOsbern in Winchester as his representatives, perhaps taking over the ranks of earl previously held by Harold and his brother Leofwine.[15] By this time the military resettlement of the southern shires had begun. The majority of the Godwine family

estates lay in this region, and were available for immediate distribution; the area was militarily sensitive, controlling as it did the
Channel, and it was here that the power base of the English kings
had been for generations. But most leading Englishmen were
seemingly confirmed – for a price – in their lands and offices.
Though taken to Normandy by the king, Edwin, Morcar and
Waltheof retained their positions as earls of Mercia, Northumbria
and the southern-midland shires respectively. Diplomatic marriages
were arranged. None was of greater significance for the future than
that of the king's own niece, Judith, to Earl Waltheof, while the
failure to carry through the proposed marriage between Earl Edwin
and William's daughter was, according to Orderic, the catalyst for
Edwin's rebellion. In the Church, Stigand remained Archbishop of
Canterbury. All the indications are that William wanted minimal
disruption and to reinforce his claim to legitimacy by a policy of
business as usual. This policy failed. The king and his magnates
were marching to different tunes. It was all very well for the king to
take crown lands and those of the Godwine family, and clearly some
land which had been held by those who fell in 1066 could be
speedily reallocated, but there was certainly not enough to satisfy
both the conquerors and the surviving aristocracy. No king, however
politically able, could hope to balance these claims. Most of the
contemporary chroniclers suggest that English resistance began
through resentment at baronial, not royal, oppression. Orderic
Vitalis explicitly blames William fitzOsbern and Odo, and oppressive lords who ignored royal orders.[16] As important was William's
underestimation of longstanding hostilities within the country, and
between England and her neighbours. Anglo-Norman penetration
of the north was to be severely hampered by provincial rivalries,
extending back more than a century; the king soon realised that
England could not be secure unless Wales and Scotland were
neutralised; the Danish kings presented a real threat, albeit one that
was ultimately thwarted. Even Ireland was dangerous. In 1068 and
1069 sons of Harold, who had taken refuge with Diarmait, king of
Leinster, launched major raids in the south-west, which, though
repulsed, indicated the continuing fragility of the Conquest.

1066 was followed by several years of what was, in essence,

guerrilla warfare, backed up by sporadic raids mounted either by English survivors, such as the sons of Harold, or more threateningly, by the Danes. Both the Evesham and Abingdon chronicles tell how rebels against Norman rule, exiles and robbers, hid in woods and islands from which they emerged to attack passers-by. The Abingdon chronicler also records how the abbey's tenants joined in rebellion against the Normans, though it is not specific as to where or when (Freeman's suggestion that they went to help Hereward in his fenland rebellion is untenable), which suggests that there was a greater level of discontent across the whole country than we allow for in concentrating on the well-documented risings. How much this was coordinated resistance, how far opportunist lawlessness, is hard to determine. Above all, the introduction of the *murdrum* fine testifies to these unstable times. In legislating that all Frenchmen who settled in England after Hastings should be in the king's peace, William proclaimed himself their protector in an alien land. The author of the late twelfth-century *Dialogus de Scaccario* ('Dialogue of the Exchequer') knew the dangers, and attributed the introduction of *murdrum* directly to English attacks on the hated Normans. There was nothing new in the legal concept, but William restricted its meaning, from secret killing in general, to apply only to Normans. By imposing a fine of 46 marks, to be paid by the lord of the dead man (or of the land where the crime took place, there is some uncertainty on this point) if the perpetrator was not speedily arrested, and then, if he could not pay, raising the sum from the hundred, William was both encouraging his lords to protect their vassals, and placing a financial burden on the native community.[17]

Several English leaders, lacking resources and fortified bases, found guerrilla tactics the only viable response to Norman might. At least two rebel commanders, Eadric 'the wild' and Hereward, were thegns whose own estates had been expropriated.[18] Eadric has been plausibly identified with the bishop of Worcester's helmsman and leader of his military forces. As such he was a powerful figure in the west midlands. According to Orderic, he made his peace with the king in 1067 but soon afterwards attacked Hereford with Welsh support. In 1069 (again in alliance with the Welsh) he turned his attention to Shrewsbury, but this rising, which was potentially hazardous, linking as it did English and Welsh forces, was put down by William fitzOsbern. John of Worcester states that Eadric surrendered in 1070, and in 1072 went with William on his Scottish campaign.

The first major rising, however, occurred in Kent in the summer of 1067 and was focused on Dover, centre of the oppressive Odo's operations. According to William of Poitiers, the Kentish rebels appealed to Eustace of Boulogne for assistance, and together they mounted an unsuccessful assault on Dover castle. Eustace fled home in disgrace (though he was reconciled with William in the mid-1070s). Why he should have become involved in this escapade is far from clear – the suggestion that he wished to claim the throne for himself is impossible to substantiate – but it is possible that he was looking to establish himself in Kent, with all the military and commercial advantages that that implied for Boulogne. Moreover, Edward the Confessor had intended him to garrison Dover in 1051. He may have felt that he had rights in the region, which were being thwarted by the settlement of Odo of Bayeux and his supporters, like Hugh de Montfort in Kent, while it has also been recently suggested that he had been disappointed in his hope of obtaining the lands of his wife, Godgyfu, and his step-son, Earl Ralph of Hereford.[19] At the same time as Eustace raised rebellion in Kent, and potentially more seriously, English malcontents are reported by William of Poitiers to have invited King Swegn of Denmark to claim the throne for himself. This worrying development may have persuaded William to return to England at the end of 1067.

Next year there was trouble at Exeter, seemingly in response to increased taxation, but it may be significant that Gytha, Godwine's widow and Harold's mother, was based in the city; resistance may well have focused round her and have been co-ordinated with a raid launched from Ireland on the south-west by three of Harold's sons. Part of this force went to Bristol, where an attack was beaten off, and when the invaders retreated to north Somerset they were defeated by a local force led by Eadnoth the staller, who was killed. The men of Exeter, meanwhile, attempted to rally support from the region, but there is little evidence that assistance came from elsewhere in the south-west. However, the townspeople put up a spirited resistance against William's forces and only surrendered after an eighteen-day siege. Gytha fled to Flanders with a large store of treasure, but the burgesses were treated surprisingly leniently, perhaps, as Round suggested, because the king was anxious to gain support in the south-west.[20] In a response which was to become characteristic, William built and garrisoned a castle, which he placed under Baldwin fitzGilbert. Then, after moving into Cornwall, doubtless as a show of strength, he returned to Winchester.

In the summer of 1069 the sons of Harold again made a raid from Ireland, this time with over sixty ships. The details of this expedition are obscure and a reconstruction of events conjectural, but it would seem that on landing at Exeter they proceeded to ravage Devonshire. They were joined by supporters in Devon and Cornwall but Exeter remained loyal and held out against their siege. At the same time, and probably linked with this offensive, the men of Dorset and Somerset rose against Robert of Mortain's new castle at Montacute. This siege was relieved by a force recruited from London, Winchester and Salisbury and led by Geoffrey of Coutances, who was, along with Robert, the chief landholder in Somerset. At Exeter the garrison broke out from the siege and the rebels fled. Caught unawares in the Taw estuary by Count Brian, the Breton who seems to have had overall responsibility for the defence of the south-west, Harold's sons fled back to Ireland. The south-western rebellions of 1068 and 1069 share many characteristics with other native risings. They were led by Harold's own family, which attempted to coordinate resistance across the region, but for whatever reason they failed to command universal support. Exeter supported them; Bristol remained loyal to the new order. Later Exeter was loyal and held out against rebels from its hinterland. The first assault on Exeter used English forces, so did the army that relieved Montacute, and that which caused Harold's sons to flee in 1069. In short, there was no coherent strategy of resistance, Harold's memory commanded no more loyalty here than William. But above all, William survived by the building and garrisoning of castles in vulnerable places. These were to be the focal points of defence, and later, centres of outward colonisation.

But far more serious disturbances than in the south-west broke out when the Earls Edwin and Morcar, finally realising that they stood to retain little from loyalty in the face of the acquisitiveness of the Norman lords, rose in alliance with Bleddyn of Gwynedd. At the same time rebellion flared in the north. William moved to Warwick, in the Mercian heartland, built a castle and went on to Nottingham, where another castle was raised. In the face of this display of strength the Mercians capitulated. They were followed by the men of York. Malcolm king of Scots, who had sent aid to the northerners, negotiated peace and William returned south, building more castles in the east midlands as he went.

Early in 1069 rebellion again broke out in the north.[21] At Durham the new commander, Robert of Comines, was massacred with a large force of knights, and the same fate befell the castellan of York. But it was not merely these military disasters that so concerned the king, it was the fact that in the north, as nowhere else, there was the potential for a dangerous anti-Norman coalition made up of Edgar *aetheling*; the native Northumbrian aristocracy; Malcolm Canmore, king of Scots; and, most seriously, King Swegn of Denmark. By the spring that coalition looked to be in place. The English exiles moved south from their Scottish base and besieged York. Only the rapid arrival of William himself relieved the garrison. William built a second castle, and placed his most experienced commander, William fitzOsbern, as its castellan. In September Archbishop Ealdred died. His role as mediator between the old and the new after 1066 was considerable; he was the most influential of the English clerics, and his departure may well have prompted his compatriots, freed from his moderating counsels, to a final revolt. At the same time, a large fleet led by Swegn's sons and comprising, if Orderic is to be believed, not only Danes, but numerous forces from Poland, Lithuania, Saxony and Frisia, landed, first at Dover, where they perhaps hoped to take profit from Kentish support. Beaten off, they moved up the east coast, where they attacked Ipswich and Norwich, but were repulsed on both occasions. In the Humber estuary they were met by the northern rebels and together they mounted an attack on York, which was devastated. However, at this point, rather than pressing home their advantage the rebels dispersed, and the Danes retreated with their plunder to the Lincolnshire side of the Humber. Here they were flushed out by the king and fled back into Yorkshire. While William crossed to Staffordshire to put down another rising, the counts of Eu and Mortain were left to deal with the Danes. Soon afterwards William himself re-crossed the Pennines, occupied York, and then proceeded to search out and destroy the rebels and the Danes, who by now had retreated to their ships. The 'Harrying of the North' had begun. The Danes made peace with William. According to John of Worcester the king gave them leave to plunder the coastal regions so long as they did not actually engage in hostilities with the Normans. Such a surprising arrangement may be fanciful, or it may be part of a wider treaty whereby the Danes released Norman prisoners taken in their attack on York. William kept Christmas at York. That winter the economic infrastructure of the north was destroyed. There would be no recovery for generations.

But even now 'pacification' was not complete. William had to move west to Chester and Stafrord once more, in order to crush recurrent risings in Mercia. Only then could he return south to pay off his soldiers at Salisbury and to keep Easter at Winchester. The Easter court of 1070 in many respects marks the conclusion of the military stage of conquest. The country was now apparently secure from internal disorder, and Norman authority had been extended to the Welsh and Scottish frontiers. There were still powerful external threats, but only now must it have appeared that the Norman Conquest of England was irreversible. Such an achievement was duly and ritually celebrated. The king was crowned by cardinal legates from Rome, and it is probably at this time that one of them, Erminfrid, imposed the penances on the king and his army for the death and destruction they had caused. This at once expressed ecclesiastical disapproval for the slaughter while at the same time legitimising the new order[22] Peace with the Church was cemented by the deposition of Archbishop Stigand, and the appointment of new bishops and two archbishops, Thomas to York and Lanfranc to Canterbury.

By 1070 William must have realised that his policy of creating a genuine Anglo-Norman state was unrealisable, and from now on change would be by imposition not consensus. It is only at this point, according to Orderic, that wholesale reallocation of honours took place, with the consequence of further unrest. The risings of 1070 and 1071 were the result of resented appropriations at all levels. This accounts for the rebellion of the Earls Edwin and Morcar, and for that of a disinherited thegn, Hereward. Once again, the crisis was heightened by Danish involvement. King Swegn himself is said by the Chronicle to have arrived in the Humber in the spring of 1070 and to have made an alliance with the local people. The Anglo-Saxon Chronicle stresses the serious nature of this attack, twice saying that the people expected the Danes would conquer the country. But this time the focus of unrest was to be the Fens, around the great abbeys of Peterborough and Ely, not the north. The chronology of events is even harder to reconstruct here, since the sources, particularly the *Liber Eliensis, Gesta Herewardi,* and Gaimar are so muddled and imprecise. The leader of the English rebels was Hereward. He is known to have held land of the abbey of Crowland and to have earlier been exiled, though in which reign is uncertain. He may also have held land in Warwickshire of, amongst others, the bishop of Worcester. Late sources suggest that he was a kinsman of Abbot Brand of Peterborough, by whom he was said to have been knighted. This account may be a garbled reference to a tenurial relationship with Peterborough; certainly the Anglo-Saxon Chronicle refers to Hereward and his followers as the 'men' of the abbey. If so, perhaps his career as a monastic thegn was similar to that of Eadric at Worcester. Certainly Brand's death, in November 1069, seems to have triggered the revolt. Brand was replaced by the warlike Norman Turold, who already had a reputation as an unsympathetic abbot at Malmesbury, whence he was transferred. Brand had, of course, come out for Edgar *aetheling* in 1066, and the abbey was long to continue a stronghold of the native culture. Moreover, there were some connections with the north. A Peterborough monk, Aethelric, had been appointed bishop of Durham in 1042, and when he resigned in 1056 he had been replaced by his brother, Aethelwine, also a monk of Peterborough. Aethelwine's activities during the northern rebellion were at best ambiguous, and in 1069 he fled Durham and was outlawed. At the same time his brother was taken to Westminster to face unspecified charges. He seems to have been held in custody at Westminster abbey till his death in 1072.

A catastrophic raid on Peterborough was launched from Ely, the centre of Danish operations, by the Danes and Hereward. However, the Danes soon made an agreement with William, and returned with their loot to Scandinavia: Turold entered the abbey, but Hereward and the English rebels remained at Ely, which was sympathetic to their cause, and where the abbot was a nominee of King Harold. In 1071 the rebels were reinforced by the arrival of fresh forces, including Earl Morcar and Bishop Aethelwine of Durham. It is possible that Edwin was also present, but more likely that he was killed while trying to rally support for the cause somewhere in northern England. Hereward's last stand soon entered legend, but the essential elements of the story indicate that after a siege King William gained the surrender of the Isle of Ely, perhaps by threatening the monks with the confiscation of their property outside the isle and with the imposition of a Norman abbot. Aethelwine was sent into the custody of the abbot of Abingdon; Morcar was captured and imprisoned; Hereward apparently made his peace and was re-seised of his lands. William probably realised that Hereward's resistance was a futile gesture without Scandinavian support. It may be significant, as Freeman suggested, that it was just at this time that Eadric 'the wild' seems to have surrendered, also recognising that without the Danes the cause was hopeless. Gradually the rebels were being worn down: both Eadric and Hereward are said to have come to terms with the new regime. They, like their followers, must have seen that further resistance was pointless and it was better to try to retrieve something from the wreckage by judicious surrender. For William the real prize was the removal of the troublesome brothers, Edwin and Morcar.

The Revolt of 1075

The last great revolt William had to face in England was also the most serious. In 1075 Ralph de Gael, earl of Norfolk, Roger de Breteuil, earl of Hereford, and (probably) Waltheof made an alliance against the king. The motives behind this curious troika's rebellion remain obscure, and it is doubtful if they had a coordinated programme. Nevertheless, in uniting Norman, Breton and English malcontents they posed a serious threat and added a new dimension to unrest. According to the Anglo-Saxon Chronicle, Ralph had a Breton mother and an English father, Ralph, born in Norfolk, and it has been suggested that the latter, usually known as Ralph the staller, was himself the son of an English mother and a Norman follower of Queen Emma. Both Ralph I and Ralph II are styled Ralph *anglicus* ('the Englishman') in Breton charters. By the 1060s Ralph I was well established in Edward's government, with extensive estates concentrated in East Anglia, and he would appear to have held the lordship of Gael in eastern Brittany. Surviving the Conquest, he extended his authority in East Anglia and was created earl shortly after 1066, when he may have taken over the role previously held by Gyrth Godwineson. Ralph II may have spent his early career in Brittany, and in 1065 he is found supporting Conan against Duke William. Nevertheless, in the late 1060s he was in England, apparently a loyal follower of William, and he succeeded his father, *c.* 1069, as earl of East Anglia.[23] Roger de Breteuil succeeded his father, William fitzOsbern, as earl of Hereford in 1071. William's authority had been considerable, both in the west midlands and in the Wessex heartland. Roger's power was perhaps more limited, as the king turned to other regional administrators such as Abbot Aethelwig of Evesham, and Roger may also have been resentful of the imposition of royal sheriffs in a region where their writ had seemingly not previously run. The role of Waltheof in thew rising is murkier. He was venerated as a saint at Crowland; John of Worcester, Orderic Vitalis and, more ambiguously, William of Malmesbury asserted his innocence. But his earlier career should not have inspired confidence. He had been too young to succeed his father, Siward, as earl of Northumbria in 1055, but seems later to have been granted comital authority in Northampton and Huntingdon. After Hastings he was one of the captives taken to Normandy but was, soon after, restored to power, though the building of a royal castle at Huntingdon perhaps indicates William's concern to curb his power. In 1069 he joined the northern rebellion but soon surrendered. He returned to power, was regranted the earldom of Huntingdon, and was married to Judith, a kinswoman of the king. In 1072 he became earl of Northumbria: he was, therefore, by far the most powerful of the Anglo-Saxon survivors.

According to the Anglo-Saxon Chronicle, the plot was hatched at the feast celebrating the marriage of Earl Ralph to Roger of Breteuil's sister, which the king had arranged – though John of Worcester wrote that William had forbidden it. Ralph and Roger are identified as the ring-leaders, persuading the Bretons to join them and (by implication) Waltheof and the unidentified bishops and abbots who were also present. Their appeal to Denmark for naval assistance, perhaps using Waltheof's Danish connections in these negotiations, made the plot yet more dangerous. Orderic's account is fuller. In an imaginary speech the rebels rally support by claiming that William is a tyrant; a bastard with no legitimate claim to rule – it is hard to imagine two of his tenants-in-chief, who had profited more than most from the Conquest, using such words; his followers had been poorly rewarded; his opponents, including Conan of Brittany, poisoned.[24]

Ralph's attempt to gain support in East Anglia failed, and after a long siege of Norwich castle he escaped by ship, going on to Denmark to press the rebels' cause. His wife defended the castle for a long time but a powerful force led by a number of prominent magnates, William de Warenne, Richard fitzGilbert, Geoffrey of Coutances and Odo of Bayeux, finally forced her surrender. Ralph's English lands were forfeit. Exiled with him were his Breton followers, while others were mutilated. These were men whose allegiance was to Ralph rather than to William, whose vassals they had never been. Ralph returned to his Breton lordship, where he continued resistance by seizing Dol and holding it, with other Breton rebels, against both the duke of Brittany and King William. Meanwhile Roger continued the fight. He raised a force in the west but his attempt to break out of his Herefordshire heartland was foiled by as powerful a group of loyalists as had opposed Ralph in the east: Bishop Wulfstan of Worcester, Abbot Aethelwig of Evesham, Urse d'Abitot and Walter de Lacy. The calibre of this defence force witnesses to the seriousness of the rebellion, it also accounts for its failure since the rebels were unable to mobilise more than limited local support. In spite of Lanfranc's urgings, Roger refused to surrender till it was too late. When he did submit he was deprived of his lands and imprisoned for life.

The Danish force did arrive but by now it was futile. It was one of the most powerful Scandinavian invasion fleets ever assembled, with 200 ships led by Cnut (son of King Swegn) and Earl Hakon. Bishop Walcher of Durham, on reporting peace in the north to Lanfranc, who was coordinating defence against the rebels, was told by the archbishop that the Danes were coming and that he should garrison his castle. But, as so often, nothing materialised. The Danes sacked York Minster (yet again) and retreated to Flanders, where Cnut's father-in-law, Robert I, ruled. Waltheof had early fled to William in Normandy, revealed the plot and attempted to bribe his way out of trouble, but on his return to England the king arrested him. By Christmas it was all over, but Waltheof was held till the following May, when he was convicted and beheaded at Winchester.

In its involvement of Norman, Breton, English and Danish elements the rebellion was potentially disastrous for William's regime. The earldoms of Roger, Waltheof and Ralph stretched in an almost unbroken line across England from the Welsh border to the North Sea, where a junction could be effected with a Danish fleet. From his bases in eastern Brittany Ralph could easily threaten the Norman frontier. The stakes were clearly high enough to risk all-out revolt. All leaders probably felt to some degree outsiders, deprived of their fair share of the spoils. Ralph and Waltheof were representative of the old order. The former, though his position and estates were confirmed by William, owed them ultimately to his father and King Edward. Waltheof also looked back to earlier days and his father's inheritance: neither had a history of unbroken loyalty to the Norman regime. Roger, at first sight, had less reason to complain, but he too had a diminished authority. Dr Lewis has suggested that all wished to restore their fathers' substantial earldoms, that were based on pre-Conquest boundaries, and that this concern is reflected in their aim, as reported by Orderic, to divide the kingdom in three with one (unspecified) becoming king, the others *duces* ('earls').[25] In Herefordshire, William fitzOsbern's power had been great, though not untramelled. He farmed the royal estates and held many of those formerly belonging to Earl Harold and sheriff Alwine. By taking over Harold's lands and responsibilities and by farming royal manors Earl William's authority was considerable, if never formalised.[26] No royal sheriff was appointed. Such freedom was denied his son, who probably felt undervalued and under-rewarded, particularly as the king looked increasingly critically at Roger's exercise of royal powers. The intrusion of royal sheriffs into Roger's territory was perhaps the last straw.[27] Some of Roger's tenants remained loyal to the king, others were brought down in his disgrace. The Book of Llan Dâv relates how three tenants, whom William fitzOsbern had enfeoffed at Monmouth, surrendered with Roger and forfeited their lands along with many others, and the *Vita* of St Gwynllyw tells how three Norman knights fled to the court of Caradog ap Gruffudd of Gwynllŵg after 1075. It has been plausibly suggested that Earl Roger had earlier aided Caradog in his victory at Rhymni over Maredudd ab Owain of Deheubarth in 1072, and that ties of allegiance were called upon three years later.[28]

Waltheof's part in the rebellion has been attributed to his failure to exert royal authority in Northumbria and, in particular, to collect taxes. Professor Kapelle is perhaps too apt to attribute all northern unrest to resentment of high taxes, and the fact that no expedition was launched against Northumbria argues against this interpretation.[29] Nor is there evidence that he had earlier negotiated with the king of Scots and Edgar *aetheling*, who returned to Scotland in 1074, for support. A more likely reason may have been a feeling that he too was losing out. Orderic Vitalis says explicitly that Waltheof was killed because the Normans coveted his wealth and large honours – he had accounted for Edwin's rebellion in similar terms.

The 1075 rebellion marks a watershed in the Conquest. Though troubles in the north would still cause great difficulties and result in the death of Bishop Walcher in 1080, this was the last rising in which the English had a major active interest. Troubles would now come from within the ruling family and from rebellious Normans. Indeed, in 1088 William Rufus would rely on his English supporters to get him out of trouble. After 1075 Anglo-Saxon survivors realised that cooperation with the new regime was the only viable way forward. This was partly, of course, because there were now no significant English leaders left. Edgar had been neutralised, Waltheof along with the other English earls was dead. At the same time, the rebellion led to a major redistribution of lands that was as great as any since 1066. We cannot know how far those who benefited from the earls' disgrace, such as Roger Bigod or Richard fitzGilbert in East Anglia, or Walter de Lacy in Herefordshire, were already being used as counterweights to the earls' influence, but it is indisputable that they owed their great influence after 1075 to the king's patronage.

By 1076 native resistance to Norman rule had come to an end. The reasons for failure are manifold. Perhaps most important, though there were rebellions in all regions of the country, from Exeter to Durham, from Dover to Cumbria, they were uncoordinated. Though there are some indications that rebels in different parts of the country were in some contact with each other there was no overall strategy and too many conflicting interests. No single leader acceptable to all emerged; rivalries between the insurgents could be bitter, as the betrayal of Earl Edwin to the Normans by some of his men reveals. Moreover, the rebels never comprised the majority of the native population. Orderic Vitalis noted that many English feared God and honoured the (new) king. Copsi, though not his vassals, was loyal in the north, and paid with his life. Bishops, townspeople, prominent native *milites* and many of the common people, all for doubtless different reasons, supported the new regime. If there was little unity amongst the rebels, neither was there a single coherent programme for rebellion. Some resented high taxes; others, like Edwin and Morcar, fought to retain their status; Edgar looked for the crown. Moreover, the same unpredictability of the risings, and the maddening way in which they flared up all over the kingdom, that gave them considerable nuisance value, also meant that they could be countered individually. The only two risings which could have toppled the regime were the northern rebellion of 1069, which brought together English, Scots and Danes, and that of 1075, which similarly saw English,

Normans, Bretons and Danes in alliance. But it was the attitude of external allies that sealed the fate of the English rebels. Welsh princes, the kings of the Scots, of Denmark and of Ireland, Eustace of Boulogne, were all prepared to intervene in the troubled kingdom, but their agenda differed from that of the native rebels, they had no interest in restoring the house of Wessex, even if a suitable candidate was to hand. Indeed, it was immaterial to them whether a Norman or an Anglo-Saxon occupied the English throne. Denmark, in the last resort, proved a broken reed. Swegn had no real designs on the kingdom, there was no danger of a revival of Cnut's empire, he and his forces were above all concerned, as they always had been, for booty. The risings taught William two lessons: that he could never assume the loyalty of the surviving Anglo-Saxon aristocracy, and that to ensure his survival in England he must intervene across the frontier into Wales and Scotland.

The Normans in Wales

The assaults on England's Celtic neighbours can be interpreted as an expression of the Norman imperial dynamic, they can also be seen as defensive measures to secure the frontier, rather as Duke William had brought neighbouring regions, like Ponthieu or Bellême, into clientage to secure the duchy of Normandy. These interpretations are not, of course, mutually exclusive. Nowhere in Britain did the Norman invaders make greater use of internal dissensions than in Wales.[30] Lacking political and geographic unity, Wales had always been a divided country; its princes subject to no supreme authority. Alliances and frontiers shifted with kaleidoscopic rapidity. Periodically a prince would emerge, like Gruffudd ap Llywelyn of Gwynedd in the mid-eleventh century, to control several regions, but such control was always ephemeral. Violent instability was furthered by complex inheritance systems. Even the boundary with England was scarcely fixed; Offa's Dyke, though it made a demarcation of sorts, recognised as both a legal and psychological frontier, was crossed from both sides by expansionists, and the 'debatable lands' of the marches were, throughout the

49

Anglo-Norman period (and long beyond), an extraordinary racial, linguistic, and administrative mix.

The frontier with Wales had been unstable since the rise of Gruffudd ap Llywelyn in 1039. Attempts to curb his threat to the stability of the English marcher shires, especially Herefordshire, had met with mixed success. The introduction of Edward the Confessor's nephew, Ralph of Mantes, as earl of Hereford in 1050 signalled the first stage of Norman colonisation in this region. In spite of innovative military strategy, the building of castles at strategic points, including Hereford, and the use of cavalry forces, Ralph was ignominiously defeated in 1055 by a coalition of Gruffudd, Aelfgar, the disgraced earl of Mercia, and Irish supporters.[31] He was unable to prevent further disaster the following year, when the new and warlike bishop of Hereford was killed, along with the sheriff. Ealdred, bishop of Worcester, took over the administration of Hereford diocese, and on Ralph's death, in 1057, he was succeeded as earl by Harold Godwineson. He and his men were given substantial estates in the march to bolster their insecure position. This settlement prefigured post-Conquest arrangements and the rule and powerbase of William fitzOsbern.

In part at least, Anglo-Norman policy in Wales was shaped by earlier developments and claims. A Wales divided into rival and unstable princedoms was not necessarily advantageous to England, as these quarrels could spill across the border. On the other hand, a powerful Welsh prince controlling much of the region was even more of a threat to the border. Too often, moreover, English rebels had fled into Wales for refuge and support. As recently as 1055 Aelfgar of Mercia had threatened the whole of the west midlands by his alliance with Gruffudd. William's first need, therefore, was to ensure that Welsh leaders did not take advantage of a disturbed England to encroach eastwards. Did he also aim at conquest to integrate Wales into his kingdom? For two centuries Wessex kings had claimed overlordship in Wales.[32] Certainly Welsh princes on occasion paid tribute, they attended the English kings' courts, and in seeking English aid in their own power struggles inevitably emphasised their client status. In 1056 the Anglo-Saxon Chronicle records that even the powerful Gruffudd swore to be a loyal under-king of Edward the Confessor, and, after the former's death, both English and Welsh sources agree that Bleddyn and Rhiwallon were installed as client kings in north Wales by Edward. Earl Harold, the victor over Gruffudd, seems to have attempted to take part of south-east Wales for himself: had he survived, these lands might have been permanently lost to the English crown. Claiming legitimate succession to Edward implies that William also assumed Edward's and his predecessors' claim to overlordship in Wales. But this did not necessarily involve conquest and territorial expansion: clientage did not necessarily mean total subjugation. As Professor Davies emphasies, this was a political not a constitutional relationship.[33] The dynamic behind Anglo-Norman penetration of Wales before the Edwardian Conquest came essentially from the barons, not the crown, and though, on occasion, kings did involve themselves across the border, their intentions were normally pragmatic responses to military emergencies rather than carefully considered programmes of annexation.

The Norman invasions of Wales were directed from three centres; Hereford, Shrewsbury and Chester. Hereford, the headquarters of the unfortunate Earl Ralph in Edward's reign, was put under the control of William fitzOsbern, perhaps as early as 1067, and though he did not possess the entire shire his authority remained considerable until his death in 1071. His first priority was defensive: by establishing great lordships between Wales and England to hold back the incursions of the Welsh in alliance (once again) with Earl Edwin and Eadric 'the wild', who threatened both Hereford and Shrewsbury. In the latter, Roger of Montgomery was installed, while at Chester, where William himself built a castle during his northern campaign, Hugh of Avranches became earl, after the short rule of Gerbod the Fleming.

Consolidation of control along the Marches was achieved in usual Norman fashion. Castles were built, towns laid out, monasteries founded. At Hereford the castle was rebuilt by William fitzOsbern. In the process, the church of St Guthlac was isolated within the new defences. A new urban centre, to which the market was moved, was established to the north of the *burh* ('defended town'), the land being obtained from the bishop in exchange for rural properties, together with a new church. To encourage settlement, French merchants were given lucrative privileges, modelled on those of fitzOsbern's Norman frontier town at Breteuil, where he had similarly laid out a fortified *bourg* with associated church.[34] A similar development is found at Chepstow and Monmouth. On the northern Welsh March, Hugh of Avranches, earl of Chester, founded a new town at Rhuddlan, adjacent to his castle. Here there had once been a Mercian *burh* until taken by Gruffudd ap Llywelyn. By 1086 there was a little urban community, complete with church and mint. Outside the towns land was typically held by the earls' vassals in compact castleries. Men like Warin the Bald, William Pantulf or Robert of Rhuddlan were to spearhead the Anglo-Norman drive to the west, under the watchful, if benevolent, eye of the crown.

There is no evidence of a central coherent plan for settlement and conquest west of Offa's dyke. The king may have encouraged settlement or conquest but left the barons he had appointed along the frontier to get on with it. Punitive or defensive raids into Welsh territory shade gradually into aggressive incursions for booty and territorial gain. Advance was to some extent conditioned by events elsewhere. Until fitzOsbern's death in 1071, Normans moved rapidly into south-east Wales. Thereafter, and especially following William's son Roger's unsuccessful rebellion in 1075, which brought him down, along with several of his vassals in Wales, the process slowed. Similarly, the fall of Roger of Montgomery, in 1101, reduced the advance into mid-Wales. But progress, however fitful, there certainly was. By the death of William I, south Wales west to the Usk was in Norman hands, and further west there had been some additional penetration.[35] By the late 1070s, indeed, it is likely that coins of William were being minted at Cardiff. In mid-Wales the Normans were also well established and had even made tentative forays into Ceredigion and Dyfed. In the north, Chester had proved an excellent base for expansion westwards along the coast. Between Chester and Rhuddlan considerable settlement occurred, while beyond, Robert of Rhuddlan in turn moved on towards Gwynedd. By 1078 he was at Deganwy on the Conwy, and in Domesday he is recorded as holding this region for the king. Domesday also reveals that he held 'Nort Wales', i.e. Gwynedd, for

£40 per annum, a relatively nominal payment, which may be the annual tribute paid to William previously by the native claimant to Gwynedd, Gruffudd ap Cynan, whom Robert had captured and imprisoned. The status of Robert's farm ('annual payment') is debated, but it seems reasonable that this sum was regarded as a quid pro quo for Robert's endeavours to conquer Gwynedd for himself.

For, as suggested above, William I generally allowed his magnates to pursue their expansionist activities in Wales without interference. He had more pressing business on both sides of the Channel, and in any case his claim to overlordship in Wales was somewhat different from his claim to England. So long as friendly native rulers and Norman adventurers acknowledged his ultimate authority and paid tribute, so long as the border remained secure, William was seemingly happy in a passive role. William I led only one expedition into Wales, in 1081. Yet that penetrated in the far south-west to St David's, where a small royal castle may have been established. William's visit, optimistically described by a Welsh chronicle as a pilgrimage, was a show of strength designed to impress his authority in the country at its ecclesiastical heart.[36] It was a symbolic act of lordship, nothing more – the chief political event of the mission was the recognition of Rhys ap Tewdwr as ruler of Deheubarth in south Wales in return for his fealty and an annual tribute of £40. Robert in the north, Rhys in the south, Norman and Welsh both made their renders to William. With little exertion, and above all by taking advantage of Welsh internecine conflicts, William had succeeded not only in removing the Welsh threat to the west midlands, but in extending control to a degree unprecedented.

The first generation of the Norman conquest of Wales was inevitably more piecemeal than that of England. After William I's death there are indications of a more coordinated policy. William Rufus, together with his brother, Robert, may have led a small and unsuccessful expedition in 1091, William of Malmesbury blaming its failure on the unfamiliar terrain and poor weather conditions. A Breton, Hervé, was appointed bishop of Bangor the following year, the first cross-Channel bishop of a Welsh diocese, though Herewald, bishop of Llandaff (1056-1104), was probably English. At the same time, further advances took the Normans ever deeper into Gwynedd; in the south a castle was built at Cardiff, which enabled the conquest of Morgannwg, while Bernard de Neufmarché established himself at Brecon, where in 1093 Rhys ap Tewdwr was killed in a skirmish with Norman settlers. His death opened up new opportunities and brought new dangers. Led by Earl Roger of Shrewsbury and William fitzBaldwin, the Normans moved almost unopposed into Dyfed and Ceredigion, and Arnulf, Roger's son, was established at Pembroke, while Philip de Briouze moved into Radnorshire. But the very success of the Norman advance brought temporary nemesis. With overextended supply lines, the forward bases and castles were exposed to fierce Welsh counter-attacks. In 1093 Robert of Rhuddlan was killed in a skirmish with Gruffudd ap Cynan of Gwynedd, while in Powys and Dyfed the Normans were thrown out of all but their most fortified strongholds. In 1094 Roger of Montgomery died, his son lost Montgomery itself in the following year. This prompted royal intervention which achieved nothing, and in 1097 William Rufus tried again, with equally inconclusive results. Worse was to come in 1098, when Hugh of Montgomery was killed. How far the anti-Norman reaction was a coordinated resistance movement organised from Gwynedd is debatable, but by 1100 the Normans had been driven back in the north to Conwy, and their bishop, Hervé, had fled from Bangor; in the south-west, much of Dyfed had been lost, though Pembroke was held. Only in the south-east were the settlers reasonably secure. When the advance began again it would be with new men, like the Clares, for many of the leading families who had ventured into Wales were now in disgrace, notably Robert de Bellême and his brother Arnulf of Pembroke, while the death of Earl Hugh of Chester in 1101, without an adult male heir, further limited comital authority in the north.

The Normans in Scotland

Far more dangerous than Wales to the Anglo-Norman state was Scotland. Tension between the two kingdoms had existed for generations, and was bound to increase as the Scotto-Pictish kings expanded southwards to meet the ambitions of the Wessex kings pressing northwards.[37] The inevitable flashpoints were the border buffer states of Lothian, and to a lesser extent (because marginally more integrated into the English kingdom), Northumbria on the east, and Cumbria on the west. These debatable lands are the clue to Anglo-Scottish relations throughout the eleventh century.[38] In 973 Edgar of England and Kenneth of Scotland had come to an agreement at Chester whereby Lothian was ceded to the Scots while Edgar's rights to Northumbria were confirmed. John of Worcester would write, decades later, that Kenneth was one of the kings who rowed Edgar on the Dee, interpreting this as a picturesque symbol of submission, but in reality Edgar needed Kenneth's support if he was to make good his claim to Northumbria against the Danes, and the meeting at Chester was an agreement between equals with shared interests in opposing Cumbrian and Viking incursions. It was to the advantage of the Wessex dynasty and its chroniclers to stress the frequent submission of Scottish to English kings, and in the same interests for Anglo-Normans to emphasise this vassalage to enhance their kings' claim to overlordship; in fact there is little evidence of formal submission or, conversely, overlordship. This is not to say that an English king did not welcome a relatively weak and submissive northern neighbour, that the king of Scots was not sometimes beholden to him and that some sort of acknowledgement of his suzerainty may not have followed as a *quid pro quo*, but it was not a structural or essential element of the relationship between them.[39]

This complex connection is nowhere better illustrated than during the reign of Malcolm III Canmore, whose reign, straddling the Norman Conquest of England, reveals a unity in Anglo-Scottish history unaffected by 1066. Brought to the throne by Edward the Confessor in 1054, after a successful campaign, led by Earl Siward of Northumbria, to expel Macbeth of Moray, his position was not secure until the defeat of a northern faction led by Macbeth's son in 1058. Malcolm, then, began his career as a client of the English king. He had his powerbase in the old Scotto-Pictish heartland, but by marrying the widow of Earl Thorfinn of Orkney and Caithness he neutralised any Scandinavian threat to the far north of his kingdom and furthered the integration of Orkney into his realm. Relations with England grew more ambiguous as his strength increased. Cumbria was, as so often, the problem. The region stretched from Strathclyde in the north to Stainmore (a strategic crossing through the Pennines into north Yorkshire) in the south. Since 1018 the Scots had held Cumbria, whence Northumbria could be seriously threatened. Seemingly, in the late 1040s, Siward, taking advantage of unrest in Scotland following Macbeth's seizure of power, had captured southern Cumbria (south of the Solway) and placed it in the hands of a member of the native Northumbrian house of Bamburgh, Gospatric. In so doing, he had temporarily removed a danger to Northumbrian security, but ensured future disorder. When Malcolm launched his first raid on Northumbria, in 1058, it was almost certainly to recover Cumbria: he was to die for the same cause on a similar expedition in 1093.

In 1061, however, Malcolm did regain the disputed province, and Earl Tostig made no apparent attempt to recover it. Perhaps this acceptance of a *fait accompli* underlay Malcolm's support for the deposed earl in 1066; perhaps, too, he hoped to profit from instability south of the border to extend his rule into Northumbria, at least north of the Tees. The defeat, first of Tostig and Harold Hardraada, and then of Harold Godwineson, altered the balance of power between the two kingdoms; it did not lead to any fundamental change of policy. It has been suggested that William saw in the northern kingdom a lesser kingdom than his own: 'he would not have considered [it] the equal of the royal dominions and authority he had won for himself in England'.[40] Such an interpretation suggests an ideology of royal dignity which there is no evidence that William articulated. The real source of conflict remained rival claims to lordship in the north. In 1068 the flight of the Northumbrian rebels to Malcolm, together with Edgar *aetheling* and his sister, Margaret, revealed to William the measure of the Scottish threat, which was reinforced by Margaret's marriage to Malcolm. With the fall of Northumbria to the Normans, Malcolm in turn feared their aggression in Cumbria and Lothian. This inspired his raids into Northumbria in 1070, which brought about William's combined sea and land expedition to Scotland, culminating in a treaty at Abernethy in 1072. According to the Anglo-Saxon Chronicle, Malcolm became William's man. But (as in 973) the king of England may have required the king of Scots's support as much as his submission. If William recognised the futility of an attempt to conquer Scotland – and that may lie behind the Chronicle's cryptic comment 'he found nothing that they were any the better for' – he needed to break up the Scottish – English alliance. This he did achieve (temporarily), and Edgar and the other English rebels were expelled from their Scottish refuge. As for the alleged homage, at most Malcolm only intended by this a personal pledge of allegiance. Certainly, twenty years later (according to John of Worcester), Malcolm was to claim equality with the English king, arguing that justice should be done between the kings on the border and by judgement of the magnates of both kingdom.

In 1074 Edgar was back in Scotland at Malcolm's invitation, and at about the same time Malcolm gave the former earl of Northumberland, Gospatric, the earldom of Dunbar. Clearly the king was not taking his vassalage too seriously. In 1079 Malcolm again invaded England, a venture which led to a new Norman invasion under Robert Curthose the following year. As in 1072, Malcolm avoided battle, and at Falkirk the agreement of Abernethy was renewed. On his return south Robert fortified Newcastle: it was to be the lynchpin of defence of the eastern route to and from Scotland for centuries. But once again Malcolm had secured his frontier by an easy acknowledgement of William's overlordship, and he remained secure till the latter's death. Malcolm, though he did not take advantage of the grave disturbances that followed the Conqueror's death, did invade in 1090, perhaps on the persuasion of Edgar. Certainly he was not prepared to recognise the lordship of Rufus. In this he made his last miscalculation. Rufus marched north in 1091, with results identical to the expeditions of 1072 and 1079. The next year Rufus again moved, this time to southern Cumbria. This was decisive. Carlisle was captured, a castle built, peasant settlers were brought from the south to colonise the region, and it was placed under Durham's ecclesiastical jurisdiction. From now on the Normans could advance and settle, on the west to the Solway, on the east to the Tweed. For the first time since 1058 Malcolm was in serious trouble. In 1093 he came south to meet the English king. Why he did so remains unclear. He was certainly concerned for the stability of the frontier, and it may be that in his illness a few months earlier Rufus had promised to cede Cumbria back to Malcolm. Now Rufus refused to see him. Malcolm returned to the north, angrily launched his last raid, and was ambushed and killed by a force led by Robert of Mowbray, earl of Northumberland. The death of Malcolm Canmore was indeed the end of an era. His reign spanned that of four kings of England. He had been brought to power by an English king, fighting a rival claimant who was himself using Norman mercenaries, and hoping to maintain the north with the agreement of a friendly and grateful neighbour. Throughout his life he had struggled to preserve the integrity of the kingdom by pushing north and westwards against the Vikings, but primarily by ensuring that the buffer zones of Cumbria and Northumberland remained debatable lands. In the end he failed, because William I and William II quickly learned that control of these regions was as essential to the security of *their* kingdom.

On Malcolm's death there was an anti-Norman and anti-English reaction, led by Malcolm's brother and successor, Donald Bán. Malcolm's son by his first marriage, Duncan, invaded with Norman troops placed at his disposal by Rufus. He was briefly successful but soon defeated and killed. Donald Bán was restored; Rufus recognised Malcolm's second son, Edgar (by Margaret), as legitimate heir, but not till 1097 did Edgar invade Scotland, again with an army recruited in England. He, and his two brothers, Alexander and David, were to rule over a kingdom increasingly influenced by its southern neighbour, settled (at least south of the Forth) by Anglo-Norman adventurers, and with a Church colonised both institutionally and in its personnel by Normans.[41]

On William I's death, in 1087, the Anglo-Saxon chronicler wrote how he ruled England, Wales was in his power, Scotland was subdued, he had inherited Normandy and ruled Maine; 'if he could have lived two years more, he would have conquered Ireland' – a threat also allegedly made by William Rufus. Years earlier it had even been suggested, perhaps not wholly seriously, that he had designs on the German Empire itself. His success was due to many factors, not least the lack of any coherent native opposition after the defeat and death of Harold Godwineson. Moreover, his acceptance as king by the native ecclesiastical establishment, combined with his claims to rule as the legitimate successor to Edward, removed much of the theoretical justification for resistance. The localised rebellions, particularly in the north, delayed conquest, and also changed its character as William came increasingly to rely on his compatriots for government and administration, and conversely removed all native leaders from their lands and offices.

But as important in securing William's hold on England as his ruthless suppression of unrest and the lack of coordinated opposition to his rule was the freedom William enjoyed from external interference, particularly from Scandinavia. Wales and Scotland had been neutralised and Ireland never posed a serious threat, though it did provide hospitality to William's enemies. Harold's sons had taken refuge there, as did the son of Rhys ap Tewdwr, and there was always the possibility of raids either along the Welsh coast or in south-west England. The northern kingdoms had influenced and sometimes controlled England for more than two centuries; from their bases in Ireland, Scotland and the Northern Isles Danes and Norwegians had more or less continually disrupted and determined royal government. But after 1066 and the defeat of Harold Hardraada the Scandinavian threat never came to fruition. Swegn Estrithson, for all he claimed the English throne, devoted most of his energies to the extension of royal power within, rather than outside, Denmark; a policy which was continued after his death by his successor, Harold Hen, and Cnut. The latter's intention to invade in 1085, in alliance with the king of Norway and count of Flanders, failed through internal unrest in Denmark, and his fleet never sailed; Cnut himself was killed the following year. The king of Norway concentrated his attention on the more northerly and westerly parts of the British Isles. Magnus Barelegs raided in Man, captured Dublin, and his unexpected arrival on Anglesey in 1098 resulted in the death of Hugh of Montgomery. Norwegian interests had long been strong in these regions. Extensive trade and kinship ties had been developed. Gruffudd ap Cynan had been born in Dublin to an Irish–Scandinavian mother; Magnus Barelegs died in

1103 on campaign in northern Ireland. By the late eleventh century, then, England was somewhat peripheral to the interests of the kings of Denmark and Norway. While they were prepared to intervene and to take advantage of William's difficulties, paticularly in 1069, 1075 and 1085, there is little evidence that these adventures were intended to seize the kingdom rather than more portable booty.

4

SETTLEMENT AND COLONISATION

According to Orderic Vitalis, Gilbert d'Auffay fought loyally with his vassals in all the major battles of the 'English war'. But when the country was pacified Gilbert returned to Normandy, though the king offered him great estates in England, for 'he declined to have any part in plunder. Content with his own, he rejected other men's goods.'[1] How far this story can be taken at face value is unclear; Orderic knew the family well, since they were generous benefactors of St Evroul, and Domesday indicates that in 1086 Gilbert indeed held nothing in England. The attitude portrayed here is paralleled by Orderic's account of his fellow-monk Guitmond's reluctance to take ecclesiastical spoils of office in England, and the two stories are probably included to indicate the chronicler's less than whole-hearted support for Norman seizure of English lands.[2] A similar story is told by William of Malmesbury of Roger of Beaumont, who allegedly refused lands that did not belong to him, in spite of King William's frequent urgings that he should avail himself of the opportunities that England offered.[3] Whatever the truth of these accounts, Gilbert and Roger are the only Normans who are anywhere said to have had scruples, and to have refused what the king and his followers regarded as legitimate spoils of conquest.

That conquest resulted in an unparalleled enrichment of an alien aristocracy – and to a lesser but still substantial extent, of their vassals. Their numbers were small. Corbett demonstrated that at the time of the Domesday survey over 50 per cent of the recorded landed wealth of England was in the hands of less than 190 lay tenants-in-chief, but nearly half of this wealth was held by just eleven men.[4] Moreover, these figures are to some extent misleading. Corbett made no distinction between lands held in demesne and those which had already been subinfeudated. In many cases the additional lands held by a tenant-in-chief of other lords more than compensated for subinfeudated lands from which he derived little direct economic benefit. When, to this calculation, is added the unknown, but in many cases considerable, profits derived from the farming of royal demesne, and whatever might be obtained from urban properties, it seems most likely that the greater tenants-in-chief towered even more over their lesser colleagues than appears from Domesday evidence alone.

At the apex of this steep pyramid were the king's half-brothers, Odo of Bayeux and Robert of Mortain; beneath them most of the greatest were linked by kinship or marriage to the ruling house. They had already profited from ducal patronage, which had brought them offices and lands commensurate with their dignity. As many recent historians, notably Hollister and Bates, have stressed, they constituted a close-knit group bound by ties of marriage and loyalty to their duke.[5] It was these men whose counsel and military support during 1066 would be so richly rewarded. Amongst them, only the Beaumonts and the counts of Evreux do not seem to have shared in the largesse, and it may be (as Hollister suggests) that the Conquest occurred at the wrong time for them, just when the senior member of the family was too old to fight, the junior too young to be given much responsibility.[6] At the same time, other families seemingly owed their prominence in Anglo-Norman England to services rendered or proffered in the conquered kingdom, as did Geoffrey de la Guèrche, who, in a charter of 1077, explicitly referred to the English lands he had earned by royal service.[7] Conversely, those who left the king's service might expect to lose their land. Orderic tells how, on his death-bed, William restored the lands of Baudri fitzNicholas 'which I (i.e. the king) confiscated as a punishment because he foolishly abandoned my service and went to Spain without my consent'.[8] Orderic also comments on how William raised the humblest of his Norman followers to the greatest wealth, so that their very vassals were wealthier than their fathers had been in Normandy, and Hollister has drawn attention to the relatively modest origins of such men as William de Warenne, Roger of Mowbray, Richard fitzGilbert and Geoffrey de Mandeville, all of whom established aristocratic dynasties of the first rank in late-eleventh and twelfth-century England.[9] To their number could be added men like William de Briouze, who emerged from nowhere to great power and authority after 1066, and whose descendants were to figure so largely in the history of twelfth and thirteenth-century England and Wales.

But William's generosity extended beyond the frontiers of Normandy to reward allies and neighbours who had supported him at home. Eustace of Boulogne was given some lands, though not perhaps as many as he might have wished, a fact that may have encouraged his rebellion in 1067, but by 1086 he was one of the wealthiest of the Anglo-Norman aristocracy.[10] However, he never seems to have been close to King William, and his son, Eustace III, a friend and supporter of Robert Curthose, was to join the rebellion against William Rufus, with the result that his honours were confiscated. A substantial Breton force had fought (not wholly successfully) at Hastings. Many were well rewarded.[11] Amongst them were Judhael, who gained the honour of Totnes (Devon), and Geoffrey de la Guèrche, a lord on the Breton–Anjou frontier, who received extensive estates in the midlands. These were lords of some standing, but they were accompanied by lesser men, who are found settled in England by 1086, particularly in Cornwall and on the Yorkshire estates of Alan de Penthièvre. No Breton was more richly endowed than he. Though his largest holding was the huge honour whose caput ('head' or 'centre') was at Richmond (Yorkshire), he held additional lands in many other shires.

Also in Yorkshire, the Fleming, Drogo de la Beuvrière, a kinsman by marriage of the king, was granted the strategically equally important honour of Holderness. He, however, returned home in late 1086 or early 1087.[12] Another Fleming, Gerbod, obtained the county of Chester; likewise he went back to Flanders before 1071, when his English lands passed to Hugh of Avranches. These were the most prominent Flemings, but there were many others, including Gilbert de Gand, lord of Folkingham (Lincolnshire), and Ernulf de Hesdin. Drogo's lands were given to another non-Norman, Odo, count of Champagne, who had established himself in Normandy in the late 1040s, and who then married Duke William's sister, Adelaide. Less well-documented are the Aquitanian colonists, particularly from the region of Poitou, who may have settled in England after following Aimeri of Thouars to Hastings. At least one Anglo-Norman, Roger, son of Roger of Montgomery, married into a Poitevin family, from which he derived his nickname, le Poitevin. By contrast with some of the Bretons and Flemings just mentioned, the men from Poitou were all of relatively lowly status. Though Aquitaine was on good terms with Normandy, England was too far away to attract more than a few settlers.[13] Maine was nearer. Yet, though men from Maine also fought at Hastings, the uneasy relations between the county and the duchy, and the related fact that Maine was more closely tied to Anjou than to Normandy ensured that Manceaux settlers in England would be few. The most significant of these were the brothers, Hamelin and Winebald de Ballon, who were established as lords of Abergavenny and Caerleon respectively by William Rufus, who also granted Winebald the lands of Thurstan fitzRolf, in England.[14] Other non-Normans who had fought at Hastings may not have been rewarded with lands or felt the need to retain them for any length of time. For example, Orderic mentions Geoffrey, son of Rotrou of Mortagne, amongst those who were richly endowed with English lands, but he does not figure as a tenant-in-chief in Domesday.[15]

The royal redistribution of lands was an ongoing process, begun in 1066 but incomplete even by 1100.[16] Land was continually coming into royal hands by death or forfeiture: it was continually leaving to reward supporters or to purchase salvation. Just occasionally Domesday reveals a little of the circumstances, as when we are told that Robert d'Oilly was given Ludwell (Oxon) by the king at the siege of Sainte Suzanne, in 1083.[17] There were certainly times when there was greater tenurial readjustment: for example, in the months immediately following Hastings, when, with understandable exaggeration, the 'E' version of the Chronicle recorded that William, on his return from Normandy, gave away every man's land –

certainly Eustace of Boulogne had received his lands before his rebellion in 1067, for he then forfeited them; or after the failure of the northern rebellions; or in 1075, as a result of the forfeiture or death of the Earls Ralph, Roger and Waltheof, and their vassals. 'New men' continued to appear during the reigns of both William Rufus and Henry I. The most successful of these during Rufus's reign was Robert fitzHaimo, son of the sheriff of Kent, who gained the honour of Gloucester and the lands of Queen Matilda. Others, however, did almost as well. Henry de Beaumont received the earldom of Warwick, William de Warenne that of Surrey, as well as large estates in Yorkshire. The creation of the Warenne honour should, moreover, be seen in the context of the establishment of several new baronies in the north, intended to consolidate military control and rule in Yorkshire and beyond, and concomitantly to expand settlement there.[18]

The balance between incoming and outgoing royal land fluctuated considerably. No other Anglo-Norman king enjoyed the territorial resources and advantages William I achieved in 1066. The size of the royal demesne doubled. Domesday clearly shows that, *T.R.E.* ('in the time of King Edward'), the lands of the Godwine clan far outstripped those of the king in both extent and value. Robin Fleming has shrewdly observed that the real shift in the political balance of power between the king and his magnates in the crown's favour came with the accession of Harold, when the Godwine lands were united with the *terra regis* ('royal lands').[19] This substantial increase in royal lands fell to his supplanter's benefit. But not only did the area of land under the king's direct control expand considerably, the king now held estates in shires where previously the crown had had no interest, thereby increasing the potential for royal control across the country. While land remained the paramount currency of power, William thus ensured his dominance. Moreover, new estates continued to accumulate, as more and more English magnates were disinherited, and through the forfeitures consequent upon the earls' rebellion in 1075 and the fall in 1082 of Odo of Bayeux, whose English lands were half as valuable again as those of the next largest tenants-in-chief, Robert of Mortain and Roger of Montgomery. During Rufus's reign there were other windfalls. The defeat of Robert of Mowbray's rebellion in 1095, for example, led to the forfeiture of his lands and those of many of his vassals. Nevertheless, in spite of these accretions the royal demesnes declined under William II and Henry I as the kings purchased, or rewarded, loyalty by alienations to their own followers. This reduction in royal lands seems to have been a catalyst, as Judith Green has argued, to the more efficient exploitation of the lands that did remain under royal control.[20]

Though recent research is now establishing a much fuller chronology of the process of settlement, and the framework of its strategic and political dimensions is now evident, the actual process of post-Conquest land transfer and acquisition still requires detailed elucidation. Nearly all seizures of power and property are accompanied by protestations of legality and claims that nothing fundamental has changed. That of William was no exception. One way to stress business as usual was to grant royal protection, particularly to religious communities that might have felt threatened by the change in government. In 1067 William issued confirmation charters, probably for a price, to a number of abbeys, including Westminster, Bury St Edmunds and Chertsey. In the same way, the king moved to gain the support of London by confirming all the burgesses' pre-Conquest privileges. Shortly afterwards William restored lands claimed by Ely as they were held on the day King Edward died, as testified on oath by English witnesses, 'except those lands which men claim that I gave them'.[21] According to William of Poitiers, nothing that had been unjustly taken from any Englishman was given to any Frenchman. There are fundamental ambiguities here: how far would Norman claims to the promised land override the rights of an English abbey? What constituted unjust seizure?

Undoubtedly the process of transfer was a mixture of royal grant and self-help. The latter might be licensed retrospectively, other *invasiones* ('seizures') were discussed and resolved in 1086. Domesday contains numerous references to the exchange of properties, sometimes to consolidate them for mutual benefit, but often to compensate an aggrieved party, frequently an ecclesiastical community, for earlier losses. The resolution of these cases was inevitably dependent upon political factors, the status of the litigants, and the wishes of the crown. Domesday, too, refers to formal transfer transactions. As before the Conquest, land was legitimately conveyed by royal writ or seal, and it may be, as Campbell has suggested, that writs were chiefly used to confirm minor native, rather than Norman, tenants, in their lands.[22] Some English tenants successfully established a right to lands in 1086 by producing King Edward's seal. At Tytherley (Hampshire) the hundred declared that they saw neither the seal nor the royal *legatus* ('representative') who put the tenant's *antecessor* ('predecessor') in possession: 'unless the king testify, he (i.e. the then tenant) has nothing there'. The *legatus* is identifiable with the *liberator* referred to in a number of entries, who, to use a term more associated with later centuries, delivered seisin. This royal official clearly had executive power. In Bedfordshire Domesday we read of Ernwin, who had succeeded his father, a man of King Edward, but 'he does not have a *liberator* or writ for this land'. In the same county a tenant 'had been seised by the king and his *liberator* but William de Warenne has disseised him without royal writ'. Another tenant had appropriated land 'for which he found neither *liberator* or *advocatus*'. In Surrey there are several references to the men of the hundred testifying that they saw neither writ, seal nor *liberator* putting the tenant in seisin, and entries in the same county relating to the lands of Richard fitzGilbert refer to land 'delivered' to him.[23] All this suggests a considerable degree of formal recognition and regulation of tenure in the immediate post-Conquest generation. Who might have been responsible for the general supervision of this process remains conjectural, but it is at least possible, as Bates has suggested, that Odo of Bayeux acted in this capacity, and probably used the opportunity to enrich himself thereby.[24] William fitzOsbern may have been similarly employed, particularly in regions where he himself had extensive lands, before his death in 1071.[25] Even less is known of the process of subinfeudation. What, for instance, are we to make of Domesday's reference to William fitzOsbern's grant of 50 carucates in the Welsh Marches to Ralph de Limesi, *sicut fit in Normannia* ('as it is done in Normandy')?[26] In a world where private charters of enfeoffment are almost unknown, the uncertainty is inpenetrable. Only when the king himself intervened in the process (which itself is atypical), as he famously did by appointing new

tenants to lands which the abbot of Bury St Edmunds had surrendered to him, and which had been held by those who had fought
against William in 1066, is there any indication of procedure.[27]

Native Winners, Native Losers

We know that the native lay aristocracy all but disappeared, but
how that dispossession operated remains unclear. How brutal were
the confiscations? What happened to the disinherited? Occasionally
Domesday sheds some dim light on the process. Azor, a *dispensator*
('steward') of Edward the Confessor, had a small estate which
William granted to him at Windsor by putting a writ into his hands,
but Robert d'Oilly seized it unjustly.[28] Here the realities of Conquest at local level superseded legitimacy. The experience of Ailric,
a free tenant in 1066 in Marsh Gibbon (Buckinghamshire), but who
held his land of a new Norman lord in 1086 for rent, 'harshly and
wretchedly', is well known. Domesday also tells how in Benfleet
(Essex) a free man who had held half a hide was 'now become one
of the villeins'.[29] The thegn, Cheping, held lands in Hampshire
valued at £127 in 1066, besides houses in Southampton and
Winchester. All of his estates had passed to Ralph de Mortimer by
1086, but it is probable that Cheping is to be identified with a
Domesday tenant of the same name, who held a ploughland of the
bishop of Winchester and a small manor of the crown as a king's
thegn.[30] How far their experiences are typical of the sufferings of
other thegns can only be surmised, but undoubtedly many lesser
English landowners did continue to hold their land but at a higher
cost and lower status. In general it would seem that the more
prosperous native landholders lost all or most of their lands, while
lesser men were more likely to be able to retain theirs – but at a
price.

The Anglo-Saxon Chronicle certainly draws attention to the
redemption of their estates by native survivors and, though the
evidence pertains almost entirely to the monasteries, it seems most
likely that lay tenants also bought back their lands in the months
following Hastings. Hampshire Domesday records how, after King

Edward's death, two of his tenants died. Their land was then redeemed by a close kinsman from William fitzOsbern, who seems to have had local responsibility for the reallocation of property.[31] Some native landholders survived after 1066, even flourished in a modest fashion. Domesday contains a number of references to grants of lands made by native lords after 1066, which were later either revoked or confirmed by incoming Normans. The English abbot of Tavistock (Devon), Sihtric, seems to have been active in the land market till his death in 1082; nevertheless he was unable to hang on to the large estate of Werrington granted to him by Gytha, Harold's mother, shortly after the Conquest, and it was left to a later, Norman, abbot to buy it back from William Rufus in 1096.[32] Some native lords, like Eadnoth the staller, even acquired new lands from the king, but Eadnoth died in 1068 defending the south-west against the sons of Harold, and most of these grants seem to have been made very soon after 1066, when the new king still hoped to work with native support. Eadnoth's son, Harding, was also a loyal supporter of the new dynasty, and, like his father, had his reward: he founded the Berkeley (Gloucestershire) dynasty.

While a number redeemed their lands, others perhaps gave up some of their properties to the new men in order to retain a substantial portion of their estates, possibly purchasing lands from less fortunate compatriots. Wigod of Wallingford hung on to the majority of his lands; his son, Toki, served the king and sacrificed his life for him at the battle of Gerberoi. The family lands then passed, via Toki's sister, into the hands of her husband, Robert d'Oilly. Mortimer has pointed to the examples of an Azor and Oswald in Surrey, both pre-Conquest thegns. Though they lost some lands to Richard fitzGilbert, they retained considerable estates and influence in the shire.[33] In Essex, the land of two other pre-Conquest lords, Wihtgar and Finn the Dane, also passed to Richard. Wihtgar ultimately forfeited his lands, though not before he had seized land in Bendish 'after the king came into this country'. Finn was luckier and seems to have held on to his estates till his death, after which his widow continued to hold two of them. Like Wihtgar, but to a greater extent and more successfully, Finn had increased his lands since 1066, and Domesday gives some indication of his authority by referring to the 'honour of Finn', which was apparently based in and near Ipswich, and also gives a hint as to how he had survived, for the sheriff admitted that he had some of his land 'by arrangement (or accommodation) with the sheriff'.[34] These men, and others like them, might have made themselves useful to the new rulers, perhaps in an administrative capacity, and thus reaped their modest reward. Others had a ministerial function – several continuing, for example, their father's job as royal foresters, falconers, or huntsmen – they might perhaps serve as interpreters, more necessary than ever in an increasingly multi-lingual society. It has been pointed out that many survivors had urban connections and toponymics, such as Odo of Winchester or, less certainly, Edward of Salisbury (whose grandson became earl of Salisbury), which supports the hypothesis that these men were local administrators.[35] Some certainly continued to serve as sheriffs early in the reign, as did Aethelwine, sheriff in Staffordshire, who was succeeded in this office by his son, Thorkil. The latter may have benefited from William's grants of lands confiscated from Mercian rebels between 1067 and 1071 – Freeman thought him a quisling – but he also held much land by inheritance from his father. Only on his death, c.1088, were Thorkil's lands granted to Henry de Beaumont.[36] Others undoubtedly served as reeves, and sometimes farmed one or more manors for themselves, like Aelfsige of Faringdon or Godric, a royal reeve in East Anglia, who prospered from his office, and also held lands as a minor tenant-in-chief. Rents might, however, be high, and on occasion so excessive that a loss was made. At Thaxted (Essex) the English lessee paid a rent of £60 per annum, but lost at least £10 each year on the deal.[37]

Notwithstanding these more or less fortunate individuals, there is considerable evidence to suggest that it was not only the lands of the great Anglo-Saxon lords which were granted away, but those of relatively minor thegns or clerics were also forfeit. This sometimes caused problems for their own lords. Thus Ramsey abbey had granted lands to a certain Aluric. He was killed at Hastings, and though the abbot did briefly recover his lands, shortly afterwards he was dispossessed by Aubrey de Vere.[38] Blacheman the priest held three manors at farm (i.e. for a money rent) of Abingdon. When he left England with Harold's mother, his lands were forfeit to the king, and were only redeemed with great difficulty (and, we might surmise, expense) by the abbey.[39]

The dynamic of colonisation and redistribution of lands seems to have varied partly according to whether estates were held by lay or ecclesiastical lords. While some individual clerics did die on campaign in 1066, and others, like the abbot of St Benet of Holme, were actively employed in the defence of the realm, their military role was naturally limited in comparison with lay lords, nor did they suffer such attrition.[40] Therefore we should expect a much greater degree of tenurial continuity on their estates, and though most religious communities did suffer from Norman greed (as we shall see below) there is little evidence of direct royal confiscation of their estates. It was unusual for an abbot to be removed, as was Godric of Winchcombe, for championing the native cause, and even here there is little evidence that his abbey suffered overmuch through its abbot's impetuousity.[41] On the ecclesiastical estates change occured at the level of the churches' tenants, who, like Eadric the steersman, leader of the bishop of Worcester's military forces, might be dispossessed with few repercussions on their ecclesiastical lords.[42]

Certainly the post-Conquest allocation of lands was determined by both political and military considerations. The events of 1066 had created a considerable tenurial vacuum. Royal lands and those of lords who had fallen or fled were immediately available for redistribution, but as long as William hoped to integrate the newcomers into pre-existing patterns of lordship, scope for a full-scale reconfiguration was limited. In the years immediately following Hastings, Edgar *aetheling* and the Earls Edwin and Morcar continued to exercise considerable regional authority and to hang on to their estates. It was only after they had forfeited their lands in the north and midlands that new men could be introduced. In this way, for example, Drogo de la Beuvrière obtained the greater part of his estates in Holderness and Lincolnshire. Queen Edith survived until 1075 and her lands remained inviolate till her death. She continued to make grants of property to tenants, as she did of Wix (Essex) to Walter the deacon 'after the coming of king William', seemingly without hindrance.[43] William's need to make careful calculations between 1066 and *c.* 1071 precluded wholesale and cataclysmic appropriation. Political expediency demanded continuity. But William's intentions were disappointed, on the one hand by the greed of his followers, and on the other by the rebellion of native magnates. Le Patourel (and several other commentators) have described the Conquest in terms of two stages, military and colonising.[44] This interpretation has much to recommend it, so long as we remember that the two phases overlapped, as le Patourel recognised, colonisation being well advanced in some regions, while elsewhere the military subjection had hardly begun. Orderic Vitalis's account of the first stage of the Norman settlement (usually regarded as running from Hastings to *c.* 1071) indicates that for the most part the incoming Normans were based in newly-built castles which the king placed in the charge of trusted vassals, who were responsible for garrisoning them. Orderic linked the granting of *beneficia* to the need to persuade men to guard these castles, and he writes how the 'petty lords who were guarding the castles oppressed all the native inhabitants'.[45] Though he rationalises the return of prominent Normans, like Hugh of Grandmesnil and Humphrey of Tilleuil, castellan of Hastings, to Normandy by reference to the lust of their deserted wives, it is clear that William was facing difficulties in keeping the support of his followers. Some undoubtedly found the pressures of controlling the new lands too much.[46] The return of both Drogo de la Beuvrière and Gerbod to Flanders has already been noted; Aubrey de Courcy briefly held control of Northumbria, but by the early 1080s he had returned home when 'things became difficult', as Symeon of Durham laconically puts it. Only 'the friendly offer of lands, revenues, and great powers' (Orderic Vitalis) could retain Norman interest.[47] This was the driving force behind the appropriation of estates, which was at once the cause and the consequence of native unrest.

During the first stage of settlement Norman lords were usually granted, or purchased, the lands of one (or more) *antecessor* whose lands had been confiscated.[48] According to the Anglo-Saxon Chronicle, the king sold his land on the hardest terms he could to the highest bidder – though this account may relate to the redemption of confiscated lands by native tenants, rather than the auction of royal demesne. These lands might well be scattered over several shires, and reveal a respect for existing tenurial patterns, which was perhaps inevitable given the piecemeal nature of redistribution. Yet even in this early period more radical changes occurred in sensitive areas such as the south-east, at once most strategically vulnerable and nearest to France. In Sussex, along the 'Channel march', as early as 1070, at least four large consolidated honours had been constructed. These 'rapes' were all in the hands of trusted magnates, all controlled a major route from the sea inland, and most strikingly they cut clean across old estate boundaries. The lords positioned their own *capita* close to the sea (as, for example, at Hastings and Lewes) and the bulk of their estates lay on the more prosperous coastal plain, while they enfeoffed knights on the inland manors. The count of Eu, lord of Hastings rape, had already enfeoffed his vassals with estates in his honour before the foundation of Battle abbey in the early 1070s.[49] Another large, consolidated holding, and even more militarily important, the Isle of Wight, was in the hands of William fitzOsbern by 1067, probably at the same time as he was placed in command of the king's new castle at Winchester. Before his untimely death in 1071 he had already built a castle at Carisbrooke. Richard fitzGilbert had probably gained his Kentish lands by *c.* 1070. A similar policy of consolidation is equally apparent in the north midlands, at Tutbury or the Peak, as well as in areas traditionally unstable, such as the Welsh Marches. Here Shropshire and Cheshire were under virtually the sole control of William fitzOsbern and Hugh of Avranches, while another vulnerable region, south Lancashire, was held in the early 1080s by Roger of Poitou.

Till *c.* 1071, therefore, redistribution was determined, according to circumstance, by both tenurial and territorial criteria, though it might be suggested that William preferred the former, except where persuaded by military considerations. Thereafter there seems to be a clear shift of policy. Orderic Vitalis certainly thought that the fundamental redistribution of property occurred after the defeat of Edwin and Morcar. Now lands that became available were granted away primarily according to territorial divisions, respecting administrative frontiers but ignoring old tenurial patterns. Perhaps there was a tendency for a new lord to take over the demesne manors of his *antecessor*, while lands of the latter's tenants passed to other hands, though this hypothesis requires further examination.[50] After 1071, therefore, there was major disruption to the old tenurial organisation: indeed, it has been suggested by Robin Fleming that this 'tenurial revolution' was on such a scale as to seriously affect the economic well-being of the country.[51]

By 1086 the revolution was irreversible, though it was far from complete, particularly in the north. But already the kaleidoscope had been shaken several times: Odo of Bayeux, greatest of all the magnates, had irretrievably lost his lands in 1082, and echoes of the upheaval were still felt in Domesday. Roger of Breteuil, heir to another of the most substantial immigrants, William fitzOsbern, had fallen in 1075, taking many lesser men with him; so had Earl Ralph of Norfolk. A generation later the Bellêmes and William, son of Robert of Mortain, would follow them into disgrace and disinheritance. One further illustration of this changing pattern of colonisation must suffice. Roger of Poitou was established in a lordship between the Mersey and the Ribble around 1080. He was removed about five years later. He may have joined Duke Robert of Normandy's rebellion against William II, but if he did so, on its collapse he quickly made his peace and was put back into authority in Lancashire. His role in Robert's next rebellion against his brother, in 1094, was ambiguous, but Roger retained his lands. In 1102 he joined his elder brother, Robert de Bellême, in yet another of Duke Robert's rebellions, this time against Henry I. It was his last indiscretion for he lost the Lancashire honour for good – though he seems to have later regained some of his Lincolnshire lands. The wheel of fortune kept on turning.

Thus no baronial honour was fixed for all time; its dimensions were in a constant state of flux, expanding through royal grant, marriage or inheritance, contracting as a result of forfeiture, death or failure of heirs, economic misfortune, or grants to vassals and religious houses. It follows that the overviews of baronial resources provided in Domesday, or in the *cartae baronum* of 1166, are somewhat misleading snapshots of this ever-changing development. Estates were frequently exchanged to enable the consolidation of holdings. Exchanges might be initiated by tenants. These had, it appears, to be licensed by the crown, though there were doubtless less formal agreements between neighbours that went unrecorded. Others might be imposed by the king: none were more far-ranging than the so-called 'exchange of Lewes'. William de Warenne had been established in the rape of Lewes by 1070. But soon afterwards he lost estates on the east to Robert of Mortain, lord of the rape of Pevensey, and more significantly on the west, when William of Briouze was set up in a newly constructed rape, that of Bramber. For compensation Warenne received lands in Suffolk and Norfolk, where he already had some property once held by his brother-in-law, Frederick.[52] Only a few miles away from Lewes the count of Eu also lost lands through royal intervention, when William I founded Battle abbey. Though the count's vassals remained as tenants of the abbey there is no indication that the count himself was compensated with other properties.

Typically, Anglo-Norman magnates aimed to hold their lands in concentrated blocks, though they frequently also had widely scattered estates in many different counties. The bulk of Eustace of Boulogne's estates lay in Essex, but he held estates in ten other shires. Robert of Mortain had land in twenty shires in 1086, but his chief powerbases were Cornwall, where his authority was unmatched by any other lord; the rape of Pevensey, and the honour of Berkhamsted (Hertfordshire). Richard fitzGilbert's estates were concentrated in Suffolk and Essex, centred on Clare (Suffolk) and Kent and Surrey, with a *caput* at Tonbridge (Kent). These lands made up 90 per cent of Richard's landed wealth.[53] Within these regions the density of their estates was determined by a number of factors, including the degree of manorialisation achieved, and the number and status of *antecessores*, since concentration of manors was more complicated and tenurial readjustment more difficult if the new lord acquired his lands from a number of small predecessors.

Settlement by the great lords was sooner or later followed, as the military situation stabilised, by enfeoffment of their vassals who had accompanied them to England. Establishing this process is, if anything, even more difficult than determining how and when the tenants-in-chief were rewarded, but again certain conclusions can be suggested. In general, tenants-in-chief retained their most valuable, or strategically useful, estates in demesne, though these manors might themselves be at farm, i.e. leased to a *firmarius* or farmer. Enfeoffment tended to be heaviest on lay honours, where typically perhaps 40 per cent by value of the land was tenanted, though ecclesiastical communities with heavy *servitium debitum* obligations might also be obliged to grant out considerable estates to maintain the knights they were required to furnish to the crown.[54] Typically vassals were recruited from those who already held lands of their lord in Normandy or elsewhere. Many of the count of Mortain's tenants can be identified as belonging to families around Mortain and in the Cotentin, where the count had large estates, and a similar pattern has been observed in the estates of Richard fitzGilbert. In Holderness the high proportion of Domesday tenants with Germanic names suggests that they had followed Drogo de la Beuvrière from Flanders, while a number of Eustace's vassals in Boulogne were established on his English lands.[55] Orderic describes how Roger of Montgomery gave his loyal followers land and power in Shropshire. One, Warin the Bald, was given Roger's niece in marriage and the sheriffdom of Shrewsbury.[56] The group solidarity of the conquerors was often further strengthened by ties of kinship and friendship. Thus, Robert of Rhuddlan was both a relative and vassal of Hugh, earl of Chester, and familial ties are sometimes reflected in local tenurial geography, where lords of the same family or related by marriage are found as neighbours. According to a late, but probably reliable, source, Robert d'Oilly and Roger d'Ivry followed Duke William to England 'as sworn brothers', a friendship that seems to be reflected in the close association of their landed holdings, particularly in Berkshire and Oxfordshire, and in their patronage of Abingdon abbey.[57] Such men might themselves thrive to the baronage. Sometimes they prospered through their own patron's fall. Hugh de Port came from Port-le- Bassin, only a few miles from Bayeux, and was a prominent vassal of Bishop Odo, becoming his leading tenant in Hampshire. But by 1086 he held his estates directly of the crown. At Trematon (Cornwall) Reginald I de Vautorte was a tenant of the count of Mortain, but the family had acquired baronial status by the early twelfth century, perhaps as a consequence of the fall of William, count of Mortain in 1106.

Beneath these settlers we find other, humbler newcomers, the *milites*, who are identified only by Christian name, if that, in Domesday. Though the status and definition of the Domesday *miles* remains a subject of lively debate, it is clear that in many instances these men had very modest estates and concomitant military duties.[58] This group shades into those of lowest status amongst the immigrants: the *francigenae*, who are recorded in far from negligible numbers in some of the Domesday counties. These anonymous settlers are usually grouped indiscriminately with the native villeins and bordars; like them they had little land or wealth. Their function in the manor cannot be determined – it is most unlikely that they were soldiers though it has been argued that they were armed household retainers – they may, like their Anglo-Saxon counterparts amongst the *servientes*, have had a managerial or ministerial function. According to the miracles of St Ive of Ramsey, there was a French-speaking gardener at Buckden in the early twelfth century; he was perhaps in the employ of the bishop of Lincoln, who had a palace there.[59] Such men are a valuable reminder that post-Conquest settlement was not exclusively confinded to a military aristocracy and to merchants eager to take economic and commercial advantage of the new order: they, perhaps more than their more high-profile superiors, made the Norman Conquest a success at the grassroots.

The Colonisation of the Towns

So far, this chapter has concentrated upon the Norman colonisation of the great English landed estates: a settlement which had both a military and an economic function. As important, though less dramatic, was the colonisation of English towns.[60] Many Anglo-Norman magnates owned urban property, as their Anglo-Saxon predecessors had done, which was presumably used to provide either a rental income or a base for the lord and his household when travelling. But more significant was the insertion of Norman merchants and traders in the urban economy. They looked to benefit from new commercial opportunities, and seemingly, more favourable trading and fiscal privileges than their native rivals enjoyed. Foreign merchants had long been a feature of the larger English towns, notably London, and there is some indication of pre-Conquest trading links with Flanders and Normandy. After 1066 these were not unnaturally reinforced. At Southampton, Domesday records that since 1066 96 French and English had been settled – and though it has recently been suggested that these may have been mercenaries, it remains most likely that these were merchants attracted to the town by the opportunities offered by this cross-Channel port.[61] Moreover, a number of Anglo-Norman magnates are recorded as having property in the town in 1086. In Winchester, it has been pointed out that the percentage of recorded citizens bearing native names had fallen from over 70 per cent *T.R.E.* to less than 40 per cent by *c.*1110, and though this may reflect changes in naming practice amongst the native population, particularly those who wanted to succeed in a changing world, it also probably indicates a growing number of foreign merchants and administrators attracted to the Anglo-Norman capital.[62] Elsewhere Domesday notices the presence of sizeable French contingents in a number of English towns and it is likely that many more went unrecorded. Even in recently-devastated York, Domesday records that they held 145 houses. Sometimes, as at Norwich and Nottingham, they were established on new sites outside the Anglo-Saxon settlement, and centred on a new castle. In Southampton they gravitated to an area within the town still known as French Street. But it was not only large provincial centres that appealed to Norman entrepreneurs. At Battle, where a town soon emerged at the gate of King William's penitential foundation, the abbey's chronicle records how 'a great number of men were recruited, many from the neighbouring districts and some from across the Channel', and a rental dating from early in Henry I's reign shows that about 40 per cent of the town's recorded population bore continental names.[63] If there was an influx of foreign merchants, was there conversely a decline in the number, or at least the status, of native traders? Though it has been noticed above that some of the most successful 'survivors' had urban connections, there is evidence that, like their country cousins, urban English dwellers were often seriously disadvantaged. Many towns had suffered physical destruction, either, like York, during the troubled times following 1066, or more often, as occurred in a large number of towns, such as Winchester, Wallingford or Exeter, by the construction of a castle, which resulted in the destruction of a large number of dwellings. All towns suffered through royal and baronial cupidity. Urban taxes bore heaviest on the native population: in towns there were excellent opportunities for shrieval peculation and extortion: a famous Domesday entry records how bordars in Norwich paid no custom because of their poverty.[64]

It was also during the reign of William I that the first Jewish settlers to appear in England since Roman times arrived.[65] They came from Rouen, one of the largest Jewish communities in western Europe, and there is a tradition that they were introduced through the good offices of the king himself. Though their paramount role for the next two hundred years was to facilitate the flow of capital both in the urban economy and to rural landholders, how far any colonies were firmly rooted, other than in London, before 1100 remains in doubt. Both Eadmer and William of Malmesbury report with disfavour William Rufus's alleged sympathy with Jews, but this may have been primarily to blacken further the king's reputation, and there is no indication that either William I or II had financial dealings with Anglo- Norman Jews.[66]

Norman Settlement in Scotland and Wales

Political conditions ensured that no Norman penetration north of the border was possible till after the death of Malcolm Canmore and the establishment of King Edgar, at the very end of the century, and it was not to be till the accession of David I, in 1107, that a very different set of circumstances brought about a rapid, if comparatively short-lived, colonisation of the Lowlands, in particular by the western Norman supporters of Henry I, who saw their opportunity to migrate into Scotland as they had not been able to do earlier in England.[67] Nevertheless, it is possible that some limited settlement in Scotland did take place during the reign of Malcolm. Queen Margaret was certainly instrumental in bringing Norman clerics to court, and in particular to Dunfermline abbey, while she is also said to have fostered commerce and to have encouraged foreign merchants to come to Scotland. Many Anglo-Saxon *émigrés* had found shelter at the Scottish court, and it is not unlikely that Normans too found refuge there. The short-lived Duncan II, successor to Malcolm, is said by John of Worcester to have been accepted as king on condition that he bring no more English or Normans into Scotland 'and bind them by military service', which certainly suggests a degree of colonisation from the south. But though some individuals might have sought refuge or fortune in Scotland there was no large-scale settlement, and when that did come it was to proceed on very different lines from the settlement of England.

The pattern of Norman settlement in Wales shares some similarities with that of England, but, as in Scotland, deep penetration of the country was not to be achieved till the twelfth century. As we have seen, infiltration of the Welsh border lands began under Earl Ralph and other military colonists during the Confessor's reign. Following 1066 the settlement proceeded, but much more fitfully than in England. Unlike England, the Welsh did not suffer a series of rapid, crushing defeats; military fortunes fluctuated, and by 1100 the Norman presence in Wales had been reduced to little more than the command of a few, well-fortified strongholds and their immediate hinterland, which provided a framework for future expansion. For the most part, it remained until the reign of Henry I, which saw a more concentrated immigration, a military occupation rather than colonisation. This is not to deny that in some parts of the country there was already more intensive settlement. Domesday Book shows the north-eastern litoral to have been quite densely settled by 1086. Smallholding anonymous *francigenae* held land, along with radknights and bordars; there was already a flourishing small borough at Rhuddlan.[68] Similarly in the south-cast, which had always been more open to English influence, settlement was well advanced and a mint had probably been established at Cardiff.

There are two fundamental differences between the Norman

settlements of England, and those of Wales and Scotland. In the Celtic lands neither William I nor II ever took any land for themselves or established any royal garrisons. Their influence across the borders was mediated through their vassals. It is not, of course, that they were not concerned with developments, and they were frequently ready to orchestrate them, but, here as in the frontier zones bordering Normandy (such as Maine and the Vexin), the Anglo-Norman kings wanted acknowledgement of overlordship from client princes rather than their absorption into the kingdom. Nor were the great Anglo-Norman magnates concerned to settle themselves across the frontier. In England, by contrast, many of them made their home, established castles in which they lived and monasteries where they were buried. Indeed, the roots put down in England were in many cases stronger than their ancestral ones across the Channel. The leaders of the Welsh campaigns were great lords with considerable English interests, like those of the earl of Chester, with huge estates throughout the midlands. But they were concerned to subdue Wales, not to settle it, and the colonisers here were lesser men, the castellans of royal and baronial castles, families like the de Barri, with few, if any, tenurial interests elsewhere. Indeed, the colonisation of Wales owed most to ambitious younger sons with few prospects.

As in England, too, the settlement was far from homogenous, and since colonisation proceeded much more fitfully than in England, assimilation probably took longer. Many immigrants to south Wales came from south-west England, and may have formed a more or less coherent tenurial and cultural group, but there were also settlers from Maine, Brittany, and above all Flanders (primarily during Henry I's reign), as well as native English, including peasant colonists. But, to a greater extent than in England, native elements survived in Wales, even in regions where settlement was heavy. Intermarriage served to cement the new order and to legitimise political change. Osbern fitzRichard, son of Edward the Confessor's Norman settler, Richard fitzScrob, married Nest, daughter of Gruffudd ap Llywelyn, while Gerald of Windsor married Nest, daughter of Rhys ap Tewdwr, c.1100, in order to strengthen his authority in south Wales. A hybrid culture emerged, partly dependent on the old order, be it administrative, as in the retention of *cantrefi* as units of government, or social, as demonstrated by the Anglo-Normans' integration into native kindred groups. In the same way, the incomers soon gave their spiritual allegiance to St David and his cathedral. Such necessary accommodations were the foundation for the appearance, already visible in Gerald of Wales, of a new cultural identity, neither wholly Welsh nor Anglo-Norman, but an amalgam of the two.

Conclusion

The Norman settlement concentrated the landed wealth of England as never before or since. Begun in Edward the Confessor's reign, it was not to be complete, though by then it had slowed down considerably, until well into the twelfth century, when Henry I augmented the ranks of the tenants-in-chief by patronage of supporters recruited primarily, though not exclusively, from western Normandy. These generations saw, of course, the almost total disinheritance of the native ruling class. But continuity amongst the colonisers was also by no means assured. Amongst the families of those who had been settled in Herefordshire by King Edward, only two, Alfred of Marlborough and Osbern fitzRichard, son of Richard fitzScrob, prospered under William I. Alfred, who had been expelled in 1052, returned in (or possibly before) 1066. However, though he flourished under the new regime, the greater part of his estates were other than in Herefordshire, and he was particularly prominent in Somerset. The same is true of Osbern, whose lands now lay chiefly outside Herefordshire. Corbett listed eleven magnates in his famous list of 'Class A' greater tenants-in-chief during William I's reign. Their fate, or that of their families, is worth considering. Odo of Bayeux fell from power in 1082 and never recovered his position. William fitzOsbern died in 1071: his son, Roger of Breteuil rebelled in 1075 and his lands were confiscated. Roger of Montgomery played a prominent role in the 1088 baronial rebellion, though he made his peace sufficiently quickly to retain his lands till his death, in 1094. His sons, at least three of whom joined their father in revolt in 1088, survived and one at any rate, Arnulf, prospered under Rufus, only to fall in 1102. Eustace of Boulogne supported Robert Curthose in 1088 and lost his lands, though his son recovered them by the Treaty of Alton. Geoffrey, bishop of Coutance's lands passed to his nephew, Robert of Mowbray, who was only to forfeit them as a consequence of his rebellion in 1095, a rebellion which dragged down many more great lords, such as the unfortunate William of Eu (though his son, Henry, ultimately succeeded to his lands). Of the other greater magnates, Richard fitzGilbert and Geoffrey de Mandeville survived into Henry I's reign, though their loyalty to William Rufus had not been absolute. Only William de Warenne, Alan of Brittany, and Hugh, earl of Chester, remained constantly faithful to the English king, and hence remained constantly secure.

If relatively few of the Conqueror's beneficiaries or their descendants retained their honours for more than one or two generations, were they replaced by others? Orderic famously, though with some exaggeration, wrote of the 'new men' whom Henry I raised from the dust, but he also told how when many of William I's magnates died, during Rufus's reign they were replaced by 'underlings, whom he exalted by granting them wide honors as a reward for their flattery'. Yet we should beware of taking Orderic wholly at face value. His statements should be seen as a variation on the common theme of the wheel of fortune, on which lesser men were constantly replacing their superiors.[69] Undoubtedly some men did profit in the reigns of both of William I's sons by their service, and in both reigns it was perhaps the clerical bureaucrats, most notably Ranulf Flambard and Roger of Salisbury, who most obviously benefited from royal patronage, and their rewards may have included cash payments as well as landed endowments. But lay magnates also prospered. Though Rufus kept some of the lands forfeited by rebels in his own hands, much had for political necessity to be re-granted, and the quickening pacification of the north during the reigns of Rufus and Henry I could only be achieved by substantial alienation.

When considering the impact of the Conquest on the tenurial structure of England we should always remember that, though the range and scale of change might have been extraordinary, similar transformations had occurred before. The establishment of Cnut's Anglo-Scandinavian empire had resulted in the disinheritance of many, and the advancement of a new aristocracy, of which God-wine was the most spectacular example. His house had proceeded to build its fortunes on a policy of acquisition quite as aggressive as that of the Normans. The impact of his aggrandisement continued to be felt after the Conquest, and many of the land pleas of Anglo-Norman England, at first sight occasioned by post-Conquest rivalries, turn out to be continuing disputes reflecting pre-Conquest situations. In Kent, for example, the great dispute between Arch-bishop Lanfranc and Bishop Odo and his supporters, such as Hugh de Montfort, that culminated in the trial of Penenden Heath, had its origins in the struggles for authority and land between pre-Con-quest archbishops and Earl Godwine.

Within a generation the Norman settlement had percolated throughout England, and was already spreading into Wales. There has sometimes been a tendency to understate the Norman impact upon English tenurial structure. It has been argued that the number of Norman barons was small, and so, if we take the fewer than 200 Domesday tenants-in-chief as the sole criterion, it was. Certainly the early years of settlement saw comparatively little disruption of the tenurial framework, and certainly, too, the Norman lords were concerned above all for the financial exploitation of their new lands, for how else could they maintain both their new status as colonial magnates and their position at home? It was in their interests to preserve the manorial status quo. Yet to suggest that it was merely the upper social strata which endured traumatic change is surely misleading, for it was not just the commanding heights of English landed society that had been occupied, but towns and small villages as well. Domesday shows both the wealth and authority of the great magnates, like Robert of Mortain and Hugh of Chester, and the nameless *milites, servientes* and *francigenae* of the countryside; the powerful ecclesiastical lords, such as Geoffrey of Coutances or the already-disgraced Odo, along with the French burgesses dwelling in so many English towns.

Writing in the 1170s, the author of the Battle Abbey Chronicle records the defence justiciar Richard de Luci made of the abbey's privileges in 1157. Speaking for his class, the 'gathering of Norman nobles', he declared: 'as for us, it is by virtue of gifts conferred by William, and by succeeding to our kin, that we possess great estates and riches'.[70] Richard, however, was himself a *parvenu*, not a descendant of the Anglo-Norman nobility but sprung from the ranks of the *milituli* ('little knights'), whom he so despised. Already we see the outlines of the myth of the 'companions of the Conqueror' and the belief, that was to remain potent for centuries, that conquest and colonisation legitimised the English aristocracy.

5

GOVERNING THE CONQUERED

England not only had to be conquered: it had to be governed. In administrative (as in so many other) terms England was already an 'old country': in some regions, particularly the north, but also observable elsewhere, as in Kent for instance, institutions of government and the exercise of lordship were now centuries old, perhaps predating the Saxon settlement in origin.[1] That the kingdom was the most 'organised' state in western Europe in the eleventh century is generally recognised. By 1066 the whole country, with the exception of the region north of the Tees to the east and the Mersey to the west, of the Pennines, along with the anomalous region of the latter-day shire of Rutland, was divided into shires, which were further subdivided into hundreds or wapentakes, which were the fundamental units of local administration. Though the shires were not of uniform creation, and though local customs continued to operate within the shire structure, the establishment and expansion of West-Saxon rule throughout most of the country during the tenth century gave a degree of organisational cohesion to the structure of local government.[2] Each shire usually contained a number of hides, on which taxation and military burdens were assessed. The hide itself, it has been argued, has its roots, or at the very least parallels, in early Irish society. Post-war research has increasingly demonstrated that the administrative history of England from the Roman to the Angevin centuries is, if not a seamless robe, at least woven from long lengths of cloth. This does not, of course, mean that adjustments were not constantly made. Shifting political frontiers, and in particular the division between those areas subject for long periods to Scandinavian control and influence, and those dominated by Wessex, and the extension of the authority of the Wessex kings into the midlands, inevitably affected administrative organisation.

This organisational structure allowed for the levying of a land tax, or geld, which was both efficient and flexible, controlled at the centre and administered at shire level by the king's official, the sheriff. Royal finances were generally well-regulated. Revenues came increasingly in cash, and old renders in kind such as the *firma unius diei* ('farm of one night') were commuted to money payments, while royal demesne lands were leased out (or farmed), often to the sheriff.[3] These developments could not have taken place without the keeping of written records.[4] Collection of geld was noted in accounts, and the surviving pre-Domesday geld rolls of the south-west and Northamptonshire testify to their sophistication. Additionally both the king and the ecclesiastical lords recorded details of their property and stock.[5]

But the use of the written word in government was not confined to the geld accounts, it was seen most powerfully in the writ. The origin and function of the writ remain controversial, but during the reign of the Confessor, and perhaps that of Cnut also, it was used essentially as a title deed.[6] In brief, the writ was simply a letter, written in the vernacular and authenticated with the royal seal, and addressed to local officials, most typically the sheriff'. It was a terse statement intended for the public notification, in the shire court, of royal grants of lands or privileges. It was related to the more elaborate diploma, which it gradually supplanted and to which it had originally been complementary, the former detailing the land given, the writ announcing the judicial and financial privileges that accompanied the grant. But the dividing line between a notification of privileges and the public expression of the royal will was a thin one, and by the time of the Conquest the writ was already being used for more 'executive' functions, such as the announcement of ecclesiastical appointments. Moreover, it is likely that the vast majority of pre-Conquest writs are lost. Those that remain are those preserved by the beneficiaries (and ecclesiastical records have survived to a far greater extent than non-royal lay archives) and which were valued as title deeds; those that conveyed more ephemeral judicial or administrative orders were far less likely to have been long retained. The few writs of an executive nature that do survive from before 1066 certainly suggest that they initiated a wide range of business. That they were not preserved or copied after the Conquest may be partly because they were in the vernacular, though the degree to which language determined preservation remains controversial.[7]

Kingship

By the mid-eleventh century the overriding authority of the crown had long been recognised – in theory at least, however much there might be practical political constraints to its exercise – and the king had long been established as the paramount lawmaker in the realm; his military supremacy was normally acknowledged, though it might be challenged, as it was in 1051–2; to a large extent he controlled economic and mercantile activity, and above all exercised a monopoly of coinage; the king in his court was the chief maker of foreign and diplomatic policy, and through royal officials such as the sheriff, and with the necessary cooperation of the great magnates, the royal will was transmitted to the regions. The king also exercised a quasi-sacerdotal function, symbolised in his anointing at coronation and in his thaumaturgic powers, which both Edward and Henry I (and perhaps William I as well) exercised. This was a rich inheritance for the new kings of Norman England.[8]

The Conquest made little, or no, difference to the theoretical powers of the king in England. William's claim to be Edward's legitimate successor could best be substantiated by continuing to operate within the parameters of royal authority. In any case, the ducal power that William enjoyed in Normandy was not so very different in scope; by conquering England William had extended the frontiers of his rule rather than its nature. This is not to argue, of course, that there were not changes in the way royal government was exercised, but these were due to practical needs, especially the problem of effective rule over both England and Normandy, and above all to the emergence of what is now generally styled 'administrative kingship', a phenomenon common to western Europe and characterised by rulers' much more *dirigiste* approach to government, an attitude that was itself only possible as the written word became increasingly dominant.[9]

The problems of royal control were exacerbated by the practical difficulties of cross-Channel government. So long as executive authority was vested solely in the person of the king, his absence in Normandy would require delegation of his powers, to be vested in regents or deputies, either on an ad hoc basis or with a function and authority akin to that of the justiciars of late twelfth-century England. The ducal family could certainly be used as royal representatives. During the invasion of England, Orderic says that Roger of Montgomery acted as *tutor* ('regent') of Normandy in association with Matilda. Thereafter both Orderic and William of Jumièges refer to Normandy being left in the hands of the queen and her eldest son, Robert, sometimes in association with the greater Norman magnates, notably William fitzOsbern, whose ill-fated expedition to Flanders in 1071 was a response to King Philip of France's summons to him for aid as 'regent of Normandy'. Matilda continued to act as regent in Normandy until her death, in 1083, when it is likely that her role was transferred to William Rufus. She also on occasions acted for her husband in England. Thus Ealdred, brother of Odo of Winchester, proved his claim, before the queen, to a virgate in Compton (Hampshire) of which he had been deprived 'after King William had crossed the sea', and the Abingdon chronicle refers to the queen staying at Windsor and hearing judicial matters *in vice regis* ('in the king's place') while he was absent in Normandy.[10]

Central to the debate concerning the nature of delegated royal authority at this time is the absence of a formal or official title.[11] The term *justiciarius* is occasionally used, but in the more general sense of 'minister' or 'justice', though we must wonder whether Orderic had something more in mind when he styled William de Warenne and Richard fitzGilbert *praecipui justiciarii* ('chief justices') appointed during the king's absence in Normandy in 1075. However, William of Malmesbury describes Odo of Bayeux as *vicedominus* of all England under the king which at least suggests viceregal power, and it has been convincingly argued that, until his fall in 1082, Odo performed many of the duties of the later justiciars. By contrast, it is suggested, other leading administrators, like the prelates, Lanfranc and Geoffrey of Coutances, had no formal viceregal status. Lanfranc's role has (I think rather unfairly) been described by David Bates as 'a postman and a counsellor', while Geoffrey was only a (well-used) justice. The problem with this interpretation is that it does not address the situation after 1082. If arrangements for delegation were 'much more systematic and well-organised than is normally acknowledged', then why was Odo not replaced during William's last visits to Normandy? Lanfranc seems a likely candidate – and certainly Canterbury tradition ascribed him a gubernatorial role. The *Vita Lanfranci* styled him *princeps et custos* ('prince and protector') of England during William's absences, with all things pertaining to the defence and peace of the realm being subject to him.

Following Rufus's accession there was less need for a regent, since the king made no extended visits to Normandy till 1096. Moreover, there were no obvious members of his immediate family on whom the king could rely. Ranulf Flambard is the most likely candidate to have exercised viceregal powers, but contemporary and near-contemporary chroniclers stress his judicial and financial powers under the king, rather than his activities in the king's absence.[12] In 1097 the Winchester annalist states that the king 'committed the kingdom' to Bishop Walkelin of Winchester and Ranulf. Walkelin died the following year, and thereafter, till the end of the reign, Ranulf seems to have supervised royal administration in England. But in the search for a justiciar we may distort the structure of Anglo-Norman government. Its strength lay not in the abilities of one powerful viceroy but in the pool of highly talented and experienced administrators and counsellors, mostly but not exclusively high-ranking clerics, on whom the kings could rely during their frequent cross-Channel absences.

It has been argued that the Conquest led to the development in

England of a 'feudal' kingship that was fundamentally different from its Anglo-Saxon predecessor, and which was defined by the king's status as supreme lord; it is customary to distinguish between the pre-and post-Conquest royal court as non-feudal and feudal: 'the Norman *curia regis* was under William the Conqueror a feudal court'.[13] Now while it is true that in hearing cases that involved his tenants-in-chief in the royal court the king might be perceived to be acting just as any other lord in an honorial court, what little is known of the exercise of justice at Edward the Confessor's court suggests that he also consented to land transactions and heard disputes between his magnates, as he did between Tostig and Harold in 1065. Moreover, as Bates has pointed out, there is little evidence that the pre-Conquest Norman *curia* was perceived as specifically judicial in function, though it did adjudicate cases and ratify compromises.[14] At the same time, private immunities and franchisal privileges were no post-Conquest 'feudal' innovations. Anglo-Norman kings, though they might accept that their vassals had jurisdictional rights, were not tramelled by any 'feudal' sensibilities when it came to asserting their authority, as the Salisbury oath or the enforced exchanges of land during the Norman settlement made clear. Any challenge to royal authority came from ecclesiastical, especially papal, ideologies, not from such baronial opposition as was to typify high politics in thirteenth-century England.

To be effective, medieval kingship had to be displayed through visual as well as written propaganda, and nowhere was kingship more visible than at coronation or crown-wearings. The anointing and coronation of the new king legitimised his rule, and was perhaps the more symbolically necessary for one like William I, whose claim to reign was ultimately predicated on victory in battle. From the reign of William II onwards, coronation was accompanied by a charter or oath, a royal manifesto containing promises (usually unkept) of good government. Coronation demanded loyalty, the oath signified the king's acceptance of the responsibilities of rule; the obverse and reverse of a contract between ruler and people. It is highly probable that both William I and William II were crowned according to a coronation order which can be attributed to Archbishop Ealdred and was heavily reliant on a German model. This *ordo* would have been that used at Harold's coronation, as would the coronation regalia, both would have emphasised continuity.[15] But there were also changes. The most significant was the introduction to England of the *laudes regiae* in praise of the king. These were imperial in origin and served to emphasise the new king's authority. Though their first recorded use is at the coronation of Matilda in 1068, it is likely that they were also sung at William's own coronation. Certainly the *laudes* were not confined to coronations and soon became an integral part of the crown-wearing ceremonies.[16]

Royal coronations were public occasions and seemingly attended by large crowds, if William of Poitiers's and Orderic's accounts of William I's coronation, with their references to the 'joyful crowd' in Westminster abbey church and the 'throngs of men and women of every rank and condition', are to be believed. Crown-wearings were more private, though hardly less solemn. Periodic and regular crown-wearings were innovative – evidence for the ritual before the reign of the Confessor is unconvincing – and designed to reinforce the king's majesty.[17] That this ceremony did indeed impress contemporaries is suggested by the Anglo-Saxon Chronicle's special mention of it in the obituary of William I, and by the attention William of Malmesbury gives to the practice. Nowhere perhaps do we get closer to the political ritual of the crown-wearing than in the accounts of William II's Whitsun court in 1099. This was held, as customary, at Westminster. Edgar, king of Scots, carried the sword before the English king at the ceremony, symbolising the accord between the two rulers, and the former's subordination. Then the procession crossed the road and entered the king's new hall, where the court was held for the first time. Westminster Hall had been begun several years earlier (perhaps in 1095) and was intended to rival – or surpass – imperial palaces like Goslar in its scale and lavish decoration. Here, surrounded by his magnates and courtiers, the king feasted with elaborate ceremonial: here his power, wealth, and, above all, his generosity were displayed.

But this living icon of monarchy was seen by comparatively few. The less fortunate had to make to do with visual representations on the king's seal and his coins. The seals of both William I and William II, by which their executive orders were authenticated, both showed on the obverse the king in majesty, just as had Edward the Confessor's, though Rufus's, for the first time, proclaims the king as 'by the grace of God'. Their coins are likewise closely modelled on Edward's and Harold's. The iconography of kingship, like its ideology, remained unchanged by conquest.[18]

The Royal Household

The crown-wearings displayed kingly power, the household was both its audience and the place where royal policy was articulated. In the opening chapter of his *De Nugis Curialium* ('Courtiers' Trifles'), Walter Map wrote of Henry II's court: 'what the court is, God knows, I know not. I do know, however, that the court is ... changeable and various. When I leave it, I know it perfectly: when I come back to it I find nothing or but little of what I left there. The court is the same, its members are changed.'[19] Map's characterisation of the centrality of the royal court in government and of its ever-changing composition as it expanded or contracted in size could be equally well applied to that of the Anglo-Norman kings. Like its predecessors it remained peripatetic, though certain centres were especially utilised. Both William I and William II continued the practice begun by the Confessor, when in England, of holding courts with strong ceremonial and ritual elements, at Gloucester during Christmas, Winchester at Easter, and at Westminster at Whitsun, when the king wore his crown and the *laudes* were sung. Gloucester was seemingly chosen because of its strategic importance; Winchester remained a central place of ritual and the headquarters of the treasury; Westminster, raised to new eminence by the Confessor, was assuming its position as the *Eigenkloster* ('private monastery or church') of the English monarchy, a role it still fulfils.[20] The ceremonies here were only the great set-pieces of royal government, theatrical events where a jester before the king might exclaim with mock solemnity, 'Behold, I see God'; but courts were held elsewhere, when a great church was dedicated or on a hunting expedition or on campaign.[21] For William was always on the move on both sides of the Channel, travelling much more widely in his enlarged territories than Edward the Confessor ever had. This was both a measure and consequence of his increased authority, yet there was no change in the *modus operandi* of central government, no fixed capital had yet emerged, the king journeyed from region to region not from economic but from political necessity, to show his face, to exercise authority, and to dispense justice.

The household changed little in composition after 1066 but continued to be an amalgam of the king's family; domestic administrators; priests who served the king's spiritual needs, looked after his relics and other treasures of the royal chapel, and increasingly functioned as a secretariat; senior officers controlling royal expenditure; and commanders of the household's military wing. The whole was constantly joined by great magnates of the district in which the peripatetic court found itself. Yet these distinctions are arbitrary and misleading. Categories overlapped; many magnates were themselves royal officials, sometimes present at court, sometimes absent on royal or their own business. There was no quorum or fixed size of the court. Witnesses to royal charters rarely contain more than ten names, though we should be wary of assuming from this that only these individuals were present. How far their activities were normally confined to either England or Normandy remains contentious.[22] Certainly many leading household officials, such as William fitzOsbern or the constable, Hugh de Montfort, were already in post in the ducal household in 1066 and continued in the king's service thereafter, but this does not necessarily indicate that they now served on both sides of the Channel. Though William had only one household, this need not argue for administrative unity, the composition of the court varied from place to place, and in any case, so long as royal government remained essentially personal, we should not expect the king to maintain two distinct groups of courtiers. Only in its racial make-up was there any radical change in the household after 1066. Though in the years immediately following his coronation the king did retain some English members, including the surviving earls and leading churchmen, as they died or were dismissed the court became exclusively Norman.

The prime reason why the court is so difficult to define is because its role, like its composition, was constantly changing. At once a private community and a public body, the household was omnifunctional. Judith Green, whose study of Henry I's household contains many insights into the household of Henry's father and brother, distinguishes between its judicial role as *curia*, its military role as *familia*, and its domestic role as *domus*, and such a distinction is valuable so long as the considerable overlap between the functions is constantly remembered.[23] As a private, domestic body its life remained private. The royal family was seldom found together, both because of political necessity, which required that Queen Matilda, to whom William was seemingly attached, be often in Normandy while the king was in England, and because of the frequent antipathy between William and Robert, his eldest surviving son. The court housed the family's domestic servants, including the princes' tutors, and those responsible for their military training, which they probably undertook with the sons of some of the great magnates, who were in some instances perhaps royal wards, thus forging early ties of loyalty. The now-lost epitaph of William d'Aincurt told how he had died while being brought up in the *curia regis* of William Rufus.[24] He cannot have been alone.

Since the 'public' household had its origin in the military entourage of the warlords of early medieval Europe, it is appropriate to consider its military role first.[25] Though the bulk of the evidence relating to the military *familia* of the Anglo-Norman kings derives from Henry I's reign there are strong indications that it was already central to military organisation by 1100. Prestwich has documented its use by both William I and William II in their campaigns in Maine during the 1080s and 1090s, and by William II in his invasion of Normandy in 1089 and 1090. Clearly the rank and file of the *familia* was made up of lowly stipendiary knights who, though on the royal payroll, enjoyed no special status; but their commanders, sometimes styled *magistri militum* by Orderic, were men of authority and wealth. Some, like Alan, lord of Richmond or William de Warenne, were amongst the greatest magnates of the realm; most functioned as royal counsellors and were as prominent in peacetime government as in war. Constables also served as sheriffs; stewards as military commanders. Commands in the *familia* for magnates like William fitzOsbern or Robert de Beaumont were perhaps the result, not the cause, of promotion, but lesser men found service in the military household a means to further their status. By it they might perhaps regain royal favour or be elevated to shrieval or other high administrative office. Like Napoleon's army, the Anglo-Norman *familia* was a career open to talents. Its members were in a uniquely advantageous position to gain advancement; in return the Anglo-Norman kings had the service of a highly-trained élite which was conspicuously loyal, for it was they who gave their support and friendship and allowed the survival of both Rufus and Henry I at times of political crisis. The king's *familia* reflected his prestige and confirmed his power, and just as the presence of distinguished foreign guests at crown-wearings lent lustre to the Anglo-Norman kings, so too did their ability to attract military followers from outside their dominions.

'The whole history of the development of Anglo-Norman administration is intelligible only in terms of the scale and the pressing needs of war finance.'[26] To a large extent government was not about governing *per se* but about exploiting the sources of royal revenue to maintain the new regime. The *familia* needed to be lodged and paid, though its income was frequently supplemented by loot, to the dismay of contemporary commentators. In a seminal article, 'War and Finance in the Anglo-Norman State', Prestwich demonstrated the close relationship between military (and therefore, political) power and financial prosperity in post-Conquest England.[27] But the connection between treasure and military success had been recognised for generations before 1066. It is explicit in Bede and Beowulf. The currency of reward may have changed, cash and lands may have been more favoured acquisitions than rings and swords, but the basic equation remained.

So, too, were the most essential sources of royal revenue unchanged. The authority of the Anglo-Norman kings was founded on their wealth, and it was on the greed of both William I and Rufus that critical contemporaries most frequently focused. Orderic wrote that William I derived £1061 10s 1½d daily 'from the just rents of England'. For all its exaggeration, this statement is indication of the impression that royal revenues made upon observers.[28] As we have already seen, the Conquest vastly increased the landed resources of the crown, and income from the royal demesne remained a substantial element of total revenues, though it was steadily declining as these lands were increasingly alienated. Sheriffs farmed their shires, paying a fixed sum to the crown for the right to most royal revenues and impositions in the county, including profits of justice. For all its anomalies and exemptions, geld was levied by the Anglo-Norman kings at rates that were sometimes punitive, and brought in considerable sums, to which could be added various payments by the towns, and aids from both secular and ecclesiastical magnates.[29] Cash was also derived from taxes on commercial activities and through tight royal control on the coinage. Rufus was particularly notorious for his exploitation of Church revenues by keeping bishoprics and abbacies vacant while he enjoyed their income, but this practice was also known, even if it was less prevalent, in his father's reign. Both father and son also exacted payments from their secular tenants-in-chief through reliefs, escheats and wardships, the whole range of impositions whose severity Henry I promised to reduce in his coronation charter in 1101.[30] How all this income was administered and collected between 1066 and 1100 is not easy to ascertain.[31] Norman ducal government certainly knew a chamber which controlled central revenues under chamberlains, who were already hereditary office-holders. In England fiscal organisation was perhaps slightly more sophisticated, but in both countries treasure, including cash and plate, was kept at a number of strategically important centres, in England principally at Winchester, in Normandy most probably at Rouen or Fécamp. We do not know how local collectors of revenue accounted for their monies, or how disbursements were recorded and audited, or the other essential minutiae of financial administration, and it would be dangerous to extrapolate back from known twelfth-century practices, just as it is misleading (if tempting) to turn to the 1130 Pipe Roll for guidance concerning royal income and expenditure before 1100. We should certainly not see in the *thesaurarii* ('treasurers') of the reigns of William I and II the great officer of state, the treasurer, as typified a century later by Richard fitzNigel. These treasurers, like those chamberlains recorded during Edward's reign, were of modest standing, based in Winchester, and with estates confined to that city and the nearby region. One of them, Henry, had property in Winchester prior to 1066, which suggests that he may have been a native administrator. Slightly later, one of the treasury chamberlain- ships was held by William Mauduit, lord of Portchester, and though he was of higher status the post remained ministerial till well into Henry I's reign, and financial policy was almost certainly overseen by someone of higher rank and authority, like Ranulf Flambard in Rufus's reign.[32]

Yet though the bureaucracy of royal finance was seemingly rudimentary it is unlikely (as already noted) that no written records were kept. Certainly the Domesday inquest would not have been conceivable without hidage lists and analogous documents, and two geld accounts, one for Northamptonshire, known only from a twelfth-century copy and written in the vernacular, and the other for the south-western shires, preserved in the Exeter Domesday and written in Latin, give some slight indication of the documentary wealth that is no more. Where were such records produced? The most likely answer is in the royal writing-office. No matter of Anglo-Saxon governmental history has occasioned so much recent controversy as the existence, or otherwise, of a central chancery. Some, notably Chaplais, have argued that royal charters and many royal writs were written by their beneficiaries or in monastic *scriptoria* ('writing offices') working for the king, while more recently Keynes has presented cogent arguments for a pre-Conquest chancery headed by a chancellor, Regenbald.[33] In William's Normandy there was certainly no ducal chancery, though there is some indication that one had existed during the reign of Duke Richard II, and even after the Conquest it was not until Henry I's reign that the use of the writ became widespread in the duchy.[34] The presence of chaplains of considerable learning and ability in the ducal chapel, however, should warn us against too hasty a dismissal of the administrative potential of Duke William's household.

The Anglo-Norman chancellor was head of the king's chapel. This oratory had for generations housed the royal relic collection and other treasures (including, perhaps, administrative archives) and was staffed by royal chaplains. Some of these at least were clerks: what is debated is the extent to which they were *formally* organised as a chancery. Clerks at Edward's court were often well rewarded for their service, Spirites and Regenbald in particular receiving substantial estates and ecclesiastical benefices, while others (like their post-Conquest counterparts, such as Gerard, royal chancellor and, later, bishop of Hereford and archbishop of York) were raised to the episcopacy.

By the time the *Constitutio Domus Regis* ('The Establishment of the King's Household') was compiled at the beginning of Stephen's reign (though it apparently reflects conditions current during Henry I's rule), the chapel had emerged as a full government department.[35] The problem here, as with the origin of the treasury, is to determine the chapel's status prior to 1100. There were certainly chancellors, but was there a chancery? – and, in any case, what is meant by this term? If we accept that a chancery was an organised royal secretariat that gave written expression to the king's will, then there seems little doubt that early Anglo-Norman kings had one. That it was small is immaterial – the Carolingian chancery, the usual benchmark against which other emerging medieval bureaucracies are measured, was no larger – nor is the fact that royal scribes also performed other duties. That the bureaucracy of the early Norman kings was rudimentary by comparison with that of the Angevins is clear enough; the number of surviving documents (and the number of scribes) is meagre in the extreme when set aside those from Henry II's reign, let alone the chancery rolls of the beginning of the thirteenth century. At the same time, the chancellor was already the highest royal office in the land, and chancellors were routinely rewarded with bishoprics. The chancellor's deputy, the master of the *scriptorium* ('writing office') and keeper of the royal seal, could also expect lavish emoluments. Chancellor Maurice's deputy, Ranulf Flambard, rose to dizzy heights of temporal and ecclesiastical power. But, as Barlow has pointed out, contemporaries seldom styled Ranulf by his office. His role was difficult to categorise; sometimes a judge, sometimes a steward, sometimes master of the writing office, but always the king's chaplain.[36] This very lack of precision indicates that the chancery was as yet inchoate, while

Ranulf's career shows how, while the writing – office remained literally in-house, there were unprecedented opportunities for advancement. Lesser men might also find service in the chapel profitable. Scribes were rewarded with modest estates; some were English, perhaps mostly retained from Edward's administration, and in this way, like Bernard (and his brother, Nicholas) in Henry I's reign, recouped their family's fortunes.[37]

There remains the household's judicial function, the household as *curia regis*, where laws and policies were promulgated and the most important legal cases heard. Some of this business was largely formal, and took place at the crown-wearing ceremonies, but a great deal of practical business was also discussed. This included the granting of honours and the nomination of bishops. Here, too, royal grants might be made, or those of leading magnates confirmed. Thus, William Rufus confirmed Robert, count of Meulan's gift to Préaux abbey 'when he first held his court in his new hall at Westminster'. It was here that the decision to make the Domesday inquest was taken, and here too, the Chronicle implies, that Rufus discussed with his magnates the invasion of Normandy.[38] The royal court would also hear pleas involving the great magnates, and though many of these were deputed to be heard, like those of Penenden Heath or the series of Ely land pleas, before royal justices, rather than the king himself, who would merely confirm their verdicts, some did come before the king. In 1086 William I heard a case at Laycock between Fécamp abbey and William de Briouze before over forty witnesses, including two of his sons, both archbishops, eight bishops, and the cream of the Anglo-Norman nobility. Such a gathering must have been awe-inspiring to the three monks sent to plead their abbey's cause – nevertheless they won.[39]

What must remain unknown is how far the *curia* was more than a ratifying body, and actually made and implemented policy. Did it merely act as a sounding-board for the king's will and function as a consultative body merely ritually? Occasionally records of legal cases emphasise the deliberative nature of the decision. William I settled the dispute between Abbot Baldwin of Bury St Edmunds and Bishop Herfast of Thetford 'with the advice of his archbishops,

bishops, earls, and other barons', while at Easter 1080 the king heard a case between Holy Trinity, Rouen, and the bishop of Evreux before 'churchmen and high-ranking laity assembled at the king's court for the festival'. Witnesses included the queen, Robert and William, the king's sons, Robert of Mortain and 'all the greater nobles of the king's court'.[40] Undoubtedly William I and William II took advice from close associates, like William fitzOsbern or Ranulf Flambard, but such consultation is likely to have been informal and private: we need to distinguish between the king's councillors, who attended the formal meetings of the *curia regis*, and his counsellors, men like Robert fitzHaimo, who is described by William of Malmesbury as one of Rufus's *secreti* ('confidants'), and who are the Anglo-Norman equivalents of the king's familiars in Angevin England, whom Jolliffe long ago identified.[41] Yet even if the consultation was no more than window-dressing, it fulfilled a valuable function, for it at once emphasised the solidarity of the governing class and the majesty of the king.

The Normans and the Law

But the law the *curia regis* and (as we shall see below) the local courts administered was seldom new law. The Norman kings promulgated no new law codes, and such innovations as there were were issued primarily as ad hoc responses, like the *murdrum* arrangements, to practical problems of government, or were merely, as in the introduction of trial by battle, extensions to existing procedures, in this case in the administration and use of the ordeal. Late Anglo-Saxon law employed the ordeal of fire or water in the investigation of serious crimes but it was not employed in property disputes.[42] After the Conquest, however, though ordeal was very occasionally so used (or at least proof by ordeal was offered), judicial combat became the usual method of proof in both criminal and land cases. Nevertheless, William I allowed an Englishman charged by a Frenchman the choice of battle or ordeal, while a Frenchman accused by an Englishman had the additional choice of compurgation, whereby 'oath-helpers' swore to the accused's innocence.[43]

Trial by battle, though found almost throughout western Europe, and though the judgment of God in battle (as at Hastings) was accepted by Anglo-Saxons, was unknown in pre-Conquest England. How often it was employed before 1100 cannot be determined: the most famous example is in the case of William of Eu, accused of treason before William Rufus in 1095.

However, one innovation was much more far-reaching in its scope and implications for the future. No oppression by the Normans was seemingly so resented as the development of the forests as distinct juridical and administrative units.[44] The Anglo-Saxon Chronicle commented wryly on William I's love of hunting, and William of Malmesbury condemned him for his creation of the hunting preserve, still known (as it has been since at least 1087) as the New Forest, and attributed the death of the king's sons, Richard and William Rufus, both killed in hunting accidents there, to divine retribution. In his love of the chase William was not extraordinary: pre-Conquest kings, including Edward the Confessor, had been enthusiastic huntsmen, they had their own hunting reserves, they employed foresters, several of whom are recorded in Domesday as continuing to hold estates by virtue of office.[45] Hunting had for long been considered useful training for a military aristocracy, an enjoyable recreation, and a valuable source of food to maintain the royal, and baronial, household. The laws of Cnut protected the king's monopoly over his own hunting lands and Anglo-Saxon kings expected their subjects to maintain these grounds in good order, but where post-Conquest conditions were innovatory was in extending royal hunting rights over non-royal lands. Though this had been the practice in Carolingian France, there is no direct evidence that Anglo-Saxon kings followed suit. But in addition to royal forests, many of the leading magnates also possessed considerable preserves of their own, with privileges that sometimes matched those of the crown.[46]

Attempts have been made to endorse the introduction of forest law, seeing it (rather as modern apologists for hunting) as a valuable conservation measure preserving the natural resources of timber and game from the excessive demands of agriculture.[47] It has also been pointed out that criticism of the laws came primarily from clerics, who objected to the creation of the forest jurisdiction and who condemned excessive hunting as a waste of time. Yet there is little doubt that the forest law was deeply resented. Writing in the reign of Henry II, the author of the 'Dialogue of the Exchequer' emphasised, not without implicit criticism, that forest law was based not on the common law but on the arbitrary will of the king. Certainly the forests did not reach their full range, nor was the full apparatus of law in place, till the twelfth century, but the extension of the royal prerogative in the reigns of Williams I and II was resented, so too were both the dislocation that accompanied a forest's creation (though the degree of disruption in Hampshire when the New Forest was made has been questioned), and the draconian punishments imposed on forest offenders.[48] In 1088 William II is reported to have sought English support against his brother's rebellion by promising the restoration of free hunting. Like so many of his promises this was soon forgotten, and at least one chronicler comments on his stern enforcement of the forest law. Anglo-Norman forest law both impeded agriculture, and, more importantly, came to symbolise for centuries the 'Norman yoke'.

From the Centre to the Regions

The most pressing problem of administration faced by medieval English kings was how to transmit central government directives to the localities. On their ability to surmount this difficulty depended their survival. If the geld, a national tax collected locally, could not be delivered to the treasury, the stipendiary army could not be paid. If the loyalty of the regions was not assured, the centre could not hold. Here, then, financial, political and military imperatives coalesced.

Crucial in this process of communication was the writ. As we have seen, by the middle of the eleventh century the writ had developed as a highly efficient instrument conveying the royal will to all corners of the kingdom. It was the writ's versatility that appealed to the new rulers. In essential form the writ survived the Conquest, retaining much of the diplomatic (i.e. the formal style) of the earlier vernacular version. It continued to be authenticated by the royal seal, though this was now reinforced with the testimony of named witnesses, and the document was now dated, and soon afterwards further identified by place of issue. One more significant change was linguistic. After 1070 almost all were written in Latin. The last vernacular writ can be dated to 1075, and though a very few bilingual writs are known from the early years of Henry I's reign, these had also largely disappeared by Rufus's reign.[49]

Writs fulfilled the same function as before in publicly announcing royal grants. Many surviving writs, or copies preserved in later cartularies, are notifications of land transfers, while Domesday contains many entries referring to the livery of seisin of lands *per brevem regis* ('by the king's writ'), which in itself testifies to the orderly transfer of property in the shire court. To this were added other new, or greatly expanded, roles, for the writ was increasingly an executive order, sometimes addressed to the sheriff, and in some instances to other royal officials, to do right or enforce judicial decisions. Sometimes it was even used against local royal officials, as it was when a writ was issued ordering the judges to free the men of the abbey of Bury St Edmunds whom the sheriff, Peter de Valognes, was keeping in captivity, and then to do justice between them.[50] Van Caenegem has seen in these the precursors of the judicial writs, and indeed, though these were a development of the twelfth not the eleventh century, it was only a short step from using the writ like the Anglo-Norman kings did, to ensure justice in the shire, to its use in initiating cases, particularly those concerning seisin.[51] Until the end of Rufus's reign the writ remained almost exclusively an instrument of *English* government. In Normandy it continued to be unfamiliar and only gained wide currency during Henry I's reign, perhaps consequent upon growing integration between the two lands.[52] Its usefulness lay in its multi-functional adaptability; its origins in pre-Conquest England testify to that kingdom's administrative sophistication, its development under the Anglo-Norman kings to their expertise in using old forms to new ends.

The Sheriff and Local Government

The writ conveyed the royal will: the sheriff was expected to put it into effect. At a time when there were few earls, and while administrative and, particularly, judicial institutions remained relatively undeveloped, his services were indispensable.[53] The office had its origins in the tenth century and was clearly linked with the gradual extension of the shire system across England, a process that had not yet reached the north by the time of the Conquest, and whose progress is a useful indicator of the expansion of the authority of the Wessex-based kings. The sheriffs had various responsibilities: supervision of the collection of taxes and fines; hearing of cases in the shire courts; administration of royal estates; the raising and occasional leading of military forces. Yet locally they were subordinate to the much more powerful earls, even though they might not have been formally commended to them. After the Conquest, as the number of earls declined, the authority of the sheriffs grew: indeed, their power was never greater than between 1066 and 1100.[54] Where the earls retained considerable authority, as most notably along the Welsh marches, they continued to control local sheriffs, and William I's attempt to curb Roger de Breteuil's power in Herefordshire by the introduction of royal sheriffs largely contributed to Roger's rebellion in 1075. The functions of the sheriff remained essentially unaltered, though it may be that his military responsibilities declined towards the end of the eleventh century. As before, he was responsible for the management of royal demesnes (which he increasingly farmed himself) in his shire, for the collection of royal dues, and for the overseeing of royal justice in the public courts.

After the Conquest several English sheriffs remained. Some, like Maerleswegn of Lincoln, soon forfeited office for rebellion; others, such as Aiulf, sheriff of Dorset and Wiltshire, profited from the new regime. It is hard to generalise about the sheriffs' economic and social standing. Several were extremely wealthy, as was Geoffrey de Mandeville, but it is not always easy to tell whether they were wealthy as a result of elevation to the shrievalty, or were appointed to office because they were already leading magnates. In some instances, on appointment they seem to have been given blocs of lands for defensive purposes, as well as on occasion being granted custody of royal castles. Clearly the office did offer opportunities for peculation on a grand scale, particularly (but not exclusively) from the Church, as William I's writ of 1077, ordering sheriffs to give up lands taken from the Church, makes clear.[55] Some of the new administrators of Anglo-Norman England were certainly of modest status. Urse d'Abitot was one of the lynchpins of government. Appointed sheriff of Worcestershire shortly after 1066, and in office till 1108, as well as serving at the centre, particularly during William Rufus's reign, Urse had no Norman patrimony to speak of. The same is true of Picot of Cambridgeshire. His reputation as an arch-predator, recorded in the *Liber Eliensis*, is unparalleled, and it may well be that these men with names and fortunes to make were particularly unscrupulous.

The appointment of sheriffs called for considerable political skill. A too powerful local magnate might be difficult to control and have resources for rebellion; a too modest candidate might himself fall under the dominance of a great lord, with equally disruptive consequences. One solution, increasingly adopted, was to appoint a curialist, a policy which combined the advantages of knowledge of the candidate's loyalty and of his administrative ability. Even during the Conqueror's reign it clearly helped to have been in royal service, or in that of the king's closest colleagues, especially Odo of Bayeux. Once in office, the sheriff had estates, both of his own and royal demesnes at farm; he had local influence and authority; he had the possibility of further advancement and patronage. It is hardly surprising that these men were so hated by churchmen or that kings increasingly found it necessary to curb their abuses, and gradually to develop institutions that would restrain their power.

For post-Conquest kings, as for their predecessors, the overriding problem was to ensure the loyalty of the provinces. The possibility that justice might be distorted by the sheriff's personal interest, not least through his right to a third of all fines levied in the courts, was a serious threat to government stability. There is evidence from early in Henry I's reign that sheriffs were holding court at times and places convenient to themselves rather than the king.[56] How far this practice can be taken back to the reign of Henry's predecessors is impossible to say. One way to side-line the sheriffs, which seems to have been used for cases of more than regional concern, was to send out justices from the centre to hear specific pleas. This happened for example, at the trial at Penenden Heath and during the Ely land pleas, at both of which Geoffrey of Coutances presided, where although the local sheriffs were present – and Penenden Heath was an augmented meeting of the shire court – they were subordinate to the royal commissioners. William Rufus made similar use of leading magnates to hear cases of moment in the shires.

What is less clear is whether the first Norman kings, like Henry I, also employed local justiciars to hear a wider range of cases in the shires, and thereby more fundamentally supplanted the sheriff's authority, though there is some evidence that these justices were in place by the end of William Rufus's reign.[57] There is also increasing evidence that late-Anglo-Saxon kings also sent out prominent agents to the provinces to hear legal cases. This practice was later to develop into the system of justices in eyre. In this way central and local courts became an integrated and fully-articulated whole. Ultimately, and perhaps inevitably, the use of itinerant royal justices was to lead to a decline in the role of the shire and hundred courts, but the *Leges Henrici Primi* ('Laws of Henry I') make it clear that the king still perceived them to be important elements of royal justice, especially so perhaps as great lords tried to increase the competence of their own, honorial courts. Royal authority was even more constrained in regions, notably Chester and Durham, where the sheriff was responsible to the lord rather than to the king, as well as in the great honour of Lancashire, and perhaps also Shropshire and Herefordshire (until 1075). Another way of circumventing, or at least counter-balancing, the sheriffs' power, was by use of the diocesan bishops who co-presided at the shire court, and who were as, if not more, frequently at meetings of the royal court as their shrieval colleagues. Sitting next to each other on the court bench, close neighbours in the county town, there was always potential for hostility built on rival interests. At Worcester this was symbolically focussed by the sheriff, Urse d'Abitot, building a castle immediately adjacent to Bishop Wulfstan's cathedral.

The shire court was the forum for royal justice in the localities. Here land disputes were heard and royal rights were proclaimed and enforced. It is not surprising, therefore, that the post-Conquest reallocation of estates was primarily channelled through shire courts, nor that the court was central to the Domesday inquiry. At the same time, however, the court allowed local lords an opportunity to exercise a fair degree of control, and a concomitant share in the proceeds of justice. Such courts were unknown in pre-Conquest Normandy: their potential for the efficient delegation of central authority was obvious, and their continuation by the Conqueror was to be expected. Here most of the great land pleas of the reign were heard, though sometimes (as at Kentford) a number of shire courts were combined to hear cases that crossed shire boundaries.[58]

Like the shire courts, those of the hundred also survived. These, too, had no equivalent in pre-Conquest Normandy, though the English hundred itself, whose judicial function seems to have been a tenth-century innovation, probably owed something to Carolingian influence.[59] Already by 1066, a number of these were in private, particularly ecclesiastical, hands, like those of Worcester or Bury St Edmunds. Meeting more frequently than the shire court, the hundred was the lowest public court in the land and dealt primarily with the resolution of lesser land and other neighbourhood disputes, but it also had a valuable policing function, which the Normans extended as a useful means of controlling the native population. It was the hundred court, then, which was responsible for administering *murdrum* arrangements, and for ensuring that all free men who did not have a lord to vouch for them were in tithing groups, the self-policing units within the hundred responsible for the good behaviour of their members.

Much less is known about the local government officials below the sheriff.[60] While the sheriff was theoretically presiding judge over the hundred courts in his shire, there were too many sessions meeting too frequently for him to attend more than a fraction. Of his deputies, the *minuti homines* (literally, 'the tiny men'), who delivered verdicts of the hundred court, we know next to nothing. Englishmen were certainly used in unofficial or official legal capacities after the Conquest. English legal advisers were prominent at Penenden

Heath, and it was the English lawmen (*causadici*) seemingly retained by Abingdon abbey who were largely responsible for the monks' successful defence of their tenants against the depredations of royal officials.[61] Yet for how long their employment continued is uncertain, and Professor Warren has argued forcefully that it was as they retired, along with other native administrators on whom the government of England had so depended, that legal treatises such as the *Leges Henrici Primi* were compiled to explain customary law for the benefit of the new, Norman middle managers.[62]

Then there were the hundred and village reeves. The terms of the Domesday inquiry imply that there was a reeve in every village, though it is particularly where a royal estate still lay at the core of the hundred that its reeve had a supervisory role. Domesday entries, though exiguous in this respect, indicate that such men were amongst the wealthier of their community, that they farmed small estates, sometimes from the sheriff, and that like their superiors in royal administration they were not averse to peculation if opportunity arose. To survive, they did not have to be over-scrupulous. Some cash certainly stuck, legally or illegally, to their hands. They could also behave in a high-handed way. Abbot Aethelhelm of Abingdon complained of the reeve of the king's manor of Sutton Courtenay (Berkshire), who harassed both the abbot's men and beasts. Eventually the abbot took the law into his own hands, personally assaulted the reeve and confiscated his supply of wood that he had obliged the abbot's men to carry. The reeve complained to the queen, who was acting for the king in his absence. The abbot quickly paid money to atone for his action, but he gained much more, for the assembly agreed that Abingdon should always be exempt from similar exactions in the future.[63] Throughout the Middle Ages reeves had almost as bad a press as archdeacons, and for much the same reason. Their office mediated between the centre and the periphery, and at this frontier there were lucrative pickings. Estates could be acquired, capital accumulated. Campbell has recently convincingly developed suggestions that these officials must be seen in the context of a wide-ranging network of *ministri* ('servants'), whose functions can still be detected in later serjeanties. Writ, treasure and herring-pie carriers for the crown, these were the

English survivors of the Conquest. They held as *taini* ('thegns') or *servientes* ('servants') of the king; they kept the lines of communication open between the crown and the localities; without them royal government could not have proceeded.[64] In an age when the exercise of government was no faster than the speed of a horse they were indispensable; ultimately, perhaps, it was their loyalty and expertise that ensured the survival of the new regime in spite of the odds.

Above all, native officials were employed as revenue collectors. Since so much of the royal demesne was farmed out, primarily to the sheriffs, who then 'sub-farmed' some estates, rents (and food renders) had to be forwarded to the centre. Particularly at a time when the crown was raising rents, and increasing the exploitation of its demesne to compensate for the extensive alienation of royal lands, there was need for local efficiency.[65] Geld was still collected in the hundred, and geld collectors were vital first links in transmitting revenue from the localities to the treasury at Winchester. Though there was much that was antiquated in geld assessments by 1066, this national tax did have the advantage that it was easily adjustable to correlate with changing economic circumstances in the regions, or to reward individuals by reducing their assessment, or even cancelling their obligation altogether. Though ecclesiastical demesnes seem to have been exempt until 1096, and though at least on occasions tenants-in-chief did not have to pay on their own demesne lands, the king could still raise considerable sums by levying the geld at abnormal rates, as it was levied in 1083 when the rate was six shillings per hide.

Money and Mints

This brings us finally to the question of coinage and the money supply.[66] Though across the Channel the Norman duke also possessed a lucrative monopoly of coinage, and in Normandy as in England there was already 'une aristocratie d'argent', which included the minters, technically the Norman coinage was far inferior to the English, and newly minted coin still bore the name of the long-dead Duke Richard.[67] In England there was, by 1066, a well-established system, whereby silver pennies of standard weight and design were produced in some sixty mints located across southern and central England (York being the only town north of the Humber to possess one), from dies made in London. Normally, every three years a new coinage was issued, at which time their weight and design might be adjusted. Though coin to replenish the royal treasury may seldom have been assayed (or blanched) – rather, a compensatory increment would be added to the coin, rendered by weight or number – coins did have to be weighed. They also had to be transported, and we should not underestimate the logistic (and security) problems in carrying very considerable amounts of silver pennies across England and the Channel. After 1066 a few new mints were opened, including Durham, reflecting the intensification of royal authority in the north, or reopened. Mints could be used as instruments of colonisation. A mint was established at Rhuddlan and, most probably, Cardiff, which was perhaps organised from Bristol. The moneyers were English. After 1081 another mint was almost certainly established at St David's – coins were struck at 'Devitun', which can probably be identified with 'Dewi's *tun*'. These mints of South Wales seemingly reflect the political accord between William I and Rhys ap Tewdwr whereby the latter agreed to furnish an annual farm of £40 for his principality. During William Rufus's reign the Norman expansion further into Wales was marked by the opening of a mint at the isolated outpost of Rhyd-y-gors (near Carmarthen).[68] Otherwise the only innovations were to standardise the penny's weight and the levying of a new tax, the *monetagium*, on town moneyers collectively rather than as individuals.[69] In most cases the crown continued to control mints, though a few were operated for the profit of leading clerics, such as the bishops of Norwich and Hereford. In some towns, the burgesses farmed the mint, as at Colchester, where many of the minters can be identified with leading Domesday burgesses; elsewhere the moneyers farmed the mint directly; while it has been suggested that in some cases, including large mints like Winchester, Canterbury or York, the moneyers were directly responsible to the king, sometimes travelling from mint to mint in his service. In other words there may be a distinction between moneyers who held a minting franchise and those who were more specifically royal servants.

Certainly administrative continuity is nowhere better evidenced than in the coinage. The moneyers remained overwhelmingly English, and in many instances Harold's moneyers continued to work for William I and William II.[70] There is every indication that these men were generally of high status, possessing both urban and rural property, often holding their office by inheritance. Deorman, who was probably descended from early eleventh-century London moneyers, established an urban dynasty which survived until well into the twelfth century. Closely associated with the archbishop of Canterbury, he is listed as one of the latter's knights, but he is also described as a king's thegn, and held land in Hertfordshire and Essex.[71] Men like Deorman, as well as the goldsmiths Theodoric, Otto and Alward who are all listed as royal *ministri* in Domesday and who, it has been plausibly suggested, were responsible for supervising the mints, were officials necessary for the fiscal stability of the realm. No king could afford to dispense lightly with their services, especially a ruler like William, so notorious for his exactions in England. These men were influential royal servants: they were also wealthy men of affairs, who probably also engaged in money-lending and exchange as well as investing in foreign trade. By the mid-twelfth century many held high office in towns, at least one (Deorman's great-grandson) had married into the aristocracy: they were a force to be reckoned with. Both literally and symbolically they provided for exchange between natives and immigrants. Indeed, it is the English townspeople, rather than their rural counterparts, who generally seem to have survived the Conquest best.[72] Joining the talents of administrators with those of merchants they were invaluable to the newcomers. Like so many more recent businessmen, they demonstrate that a change of government seldom has serious repercussions in the finance houses.

Conclusion

'If it ain't broke, don't fix it': how far did Anglo-Norman government merely travel along pre-established lines, simply inserting new managers in existing administrative structures? Of one thing we can be sure. Those native administrators who survived are normally to be found below the shrieval level, though English sheriffs can be identified into Rufus's reign. For the most part we should look for survivors amongst the king's domestic servants and huntsmen, occasionally also among the scribes and royal priests at court, and in the regions, bailiffs and reeves, the geld collectors and the hundred-men, all petty officials on whom the functioning of the king's government depended. We should also remember that not all survivors from pre-Conquest days were themselves English. The prominent and wealthy goldsmith, Theodoric, was perhaps German. The same is true of Regenbald.[73] No one individual has been more cited to symbolise continuity in pre- and post-Conquest central administration than Regenbald, royal priest and perhaps chancellor of Edward the Confessor. Yet, it is important to keep a sense of proportion in all this. Regenbald was not, judging by his name, a native Anglo-Saxon – rather, he was German or French by origin, and hence is more representative of Edward's continental proto-colonists, found in many ranks of society and administration, than of an indigenous governmental tradition. Secondly, though Regenbald did continue in office briefly under William I, who confirmed his existing lands and privileges and added further estates to his already extensive holdings, by December 1067 Herfast was chancellor. Regenbald had presumably retired or been removed from office. Thereafter he was associated with the ecclesiastical establishment at Cirencester. He was seemingly buried in the church, and his lands later formed the nucleus of Henry I's Augustinian foundation there. Thus, though there is now, I believe, compelling argument for the existence of a royal chancery in Edward's reign and hence continuity of office, Regenbald's own post-Conquest influence was limited. Paradoxically, his contribution to continuity comes as a pre-Conquest continental administrator. As chancellor and *sigillarius* ('keeper of the seal') he was uniquely placed to influence bureaucratic practice; whether by introducing change before 1066 or by maintaining continuity thereafter.

But did the changes in personnel themselves contribute to governmental problems in post-Conquest England? This is the contention of Professor Warren, who has argued that the retirement or death

113

of native administrators by the end of the eleventh century meant that 'the whole system was in danger of foundering'.[74] The alleged decline in standards of coinage, ignorance of legal procedures, and problems in controlling local courts from the centre are attributed to a break in administrative continuity. Secondly, Warren argues, pre-Conquest local government was by no means standardised. Though shire organisation was still evolving, the Normans made no attempt to continue old procedures, so that the new, northern shires (like Cumberland) that emerged owed little to southern prototypes. Moreover, the failure to make a general reassessment for the geld, and the high level of exemptions, reduced the crown's income so that it had to look to other sources of revenue, in particular the exploitation of 'feudal dues' from tenants-in-chief, and in this way the relationship between the king and his barons was redefined.

Warren's hypothesis that old structures of government were collapsing under the weight of Norman incompetence and that the ad hoc solutions of the Anglo-Norman kings had no future, being replaced by Angevin new brooms, is stimulating, but ultimately unconvincing. The Normans inherited a well-ordered, wealthy and sophisticated government, containing as do all governments some anomalies, some structural weaknesses. But though there can be no strong government without a coherent organisation, the presence of the latter does not always guarantee the former. Moreover, it can be argued that the very reliance of the late Anglo-Saxon kingdom on the earls, who functioned, it has been suggested, almost as regional viceroys, and whose local power and economic resources were very considerable, were primarily responsible for the instabilities of Edward's reign. There was a real danger that the country would fragment in the same fashion as had France with the emergence of principalities that were, in practice, autonomous. Already the earldom of Northumbria had shown dangerous separatist tendencies, which Edward had unsuccessfully tried to curb with the appointment of the southern outsider, Tostig, as earl in 1055. It was the realisation of the dangers inherent in the provincial earldoms – after all, an earl had succeeded Edward as king – that led to their reduction by William, though there are indications that until 1071 he had been prepared to retain them.[75] Their removal from a position of authority within the shire courts, combined with the gradual withdrawal of ecclesiastical interests there, undoubtedly produced a shift in the balance of local administrative power, but to the crown's advantage. So long as the sheriffs, whose authority was commensurately increased, were kept firmly under royal control, the centre's supervision of the localities – bolstered by the use of royal justices – was strengthened.

Potentially more far-reaching in impact was the emergence of the honorial courts. Though most of what is known of these courts derives from the twelfth century, there seems little doubt that they were already in existence during the reigns of William I and William II, and it is clear that a lord's court had a judicial function long before the Conquest and that this was continued, and probably expanded, afterwards.[76] Moreover, courts for their vassals were held by the lords of pre-Conquest Normandy, though their autonomy was constrained by ducal authority, and this arrangement was seemingly transferred across the Channel to be integrated with pre-existing private jurisdictions. Even though some business was inevitably transferred from shire and hundred courts to the new honorial courts it is necessary to keep some perspective here. These courts only dealt with land pleas involving vassals of the same honour, and even in these instances it was possible for a plaintiff to obtain a writ for such a case to be heard in the royal courts. But not only was its competence limited. As Lennard long ago suggested, although in theory these courts were very important bodies, for those who owed them suit were themselves often of baronial status, it was difficult for the lord to enforce attendance given that estates were often so widely separated.[77] For all their potential for the distortion of jurisdiction, in the event they never seriously threatened royal authority.

Nevertheless, the operation of the baronial household, so central to the administration, military standing and judicial competence of the baronial honour in the localities, should not be ignored.[78] In these households business of all kinds would be transacted and counsel would be proffered by the lord's substantial tenants and servants. The venue for the household's deliberations was normally one of the lord's chief residences or castles, and it is hardly surprising to find honorial servants frequently holding small estates in their vicinity. Yet, of the household's activities we know little in detail. Occasional glimpses are found in charters, such as that issued by Ernulf de Hesdin at his manor house of Chipping Norton in the presence of his wife, children and many of his household knights.[79] Like the royal court, then, the baronial court comprised a mixture of family members and vassals.

Certainly all lords would have employed menials, though their presence is seldom noted in Domesday and elsewhere; they would have required reeves and other ministerial servants, including foresters and huntsmen; most would have had at least one chaplain. It is now evident that many of the great tenants-in-chief, and some lesser lords, had more prestigious officials as well, who often bore the same name and function as their royal equivalents. These men, unlike the humbler members of the household, were Normans, sometimes tenants or even relatives of their employers. Such a strategy must have helped to consolidate the settlement at a very local level, while the continued use of English reeves served to maintain efficient estate management. The officials named are a mixed bag. Often they were rewarded with estates, sometimes quite large, and often conveniently located near the *capita* of their employers. Baronial constables were sometimes responsible, like their royal counterparts, for castles, and like them oversaw the household's military operations. Other household officials, like butlers and dispensers, are also recorded, though it is uncertain how far their duties were honorific. Barons also had their chaplains: Orderic tells us the names of three (including his father) in the household of Roger of Montgomery, while Ralph the priest, chaplain to Robert of Mortain, who held a small property close to the count's *caput* of Montacute, is occasionally described as *cancellarius* ('chancellor').[80] Such an appellation of a baronial officer is unique: but Robert was the wealthiest lay magnate in the country and may have modelled his household on that of his brother, the king. Generally, however, lords would have used as scribes their own chaplains or monks, housed in a community conveniently sited close to their castle, as was the small priory at Tutbury (Staffordshire).

Occasionally we find baronial sheriffs, as in Cornwall or the rape of Pevensey under Robert of Mortain, or (until 1075) in Hereford-shire, though these officers are normally recorded only on large honours of the greatest tenants-in-chief. More frequent are stewards, who were often the senior officials, who seem to have fulfilled the same supervisory role over estates as they were to do in later centuries. The greater magnates may already have had several stewards, with responsibility for different regions. Did they present accounts? In a famous passage Orderic refers to the unthinking liberality of Hugh of Chester, who 'kept no account of what he gave or received', and it has several times been suggested that this indicates that it was expected that magnates of his standing would and should keep financial records, though we must remember that Orderic may be reflecting attitudes more current in his own age than in the immediate post-Conquest generation.[81] The question of accounts raises wider issues concerning the prevalence of demesne farming and the nature of baronial incomes.

The recent work of Dr Sally Harvey has suggested that lords, hardly surprisingly, often had large demesnes near their main residential and administrative centres, the *capita*, and that these centres may themselves have been consciously sited in places where *antecessores* already had substantial demesnes.[82] Some lords were active in personally supervising their estates. The example of Ernulf de Hesdin, recorded by William of Malmesbury, is well-known.[83] Ernulf carefully monitored agricultural production, and, as Domesday shows, the results paid off, as most of his estates showed a significant increase in value by 1086. But while a few other lords, like Roger of Montgomery, can be demonstrated to have developed demesne agriculture, the majority were more concerned to increase dues and their rental income. Money was necessary to finance the huge building works, that were not confined to magnificent new cathedrals or abbey churches, but included castles and manor houses; money was more convenient for non-resident lords; money could be used to hire troops when required. Conversely, demesne agriculture was labour-intensive and subject to disruption from many quarters, acts of God, such as bad harvests, acts of men, such as military campaigns, while the very act of tenurial reallocation could seriously affect production.[84] Undoubtedly, as always, management policy was determined by many factors. What united the new lords was aggressive exploitation, either by increased rents and/or agricultural production. Either required supervisors and record-keeping to be efficient. Exploitation was not, of course, confined to rents, labour and agricultural produce. Profits of private jurisdiction were especially lucrative and many lords probably gained more by control of assets such as mills, assorted dues, and urban revenues than from demesne agriculture. Robert of Mortain, in particular, appears to have been particularly aggressive in the exploitation of urban resources.[85] Not only did he, like most contemporary magnates, develop boroughs in close proximity to his castles, as at Pevensey, Launceston and Berkhamsted, creating centres that were at once defensive and commercial at the *capita* of his honours, but he unscrupulously removed neighbouring markets or put them out of business, as he did at St Germans (Cornwall) by holding a rival market in his neighbouring castle of Trematon on the same day. Such administrative and economic activity mirrored, and was probably adopted from, crown practice, but it did not constitute a serious rival to royal authority.

The opening clause of the so-called 'Laws of William the Conqueror' reads: 'First that above all things he wishes one God to be revered throughout his whole realm, one faith in Christ to be kept ever inviolate, and peace and security to be preserved between English and Normans.'[86] It was this desire for stability that underlies the government of the early Norman kings. That stability could only be achieved through a high degree of continuity in administrative practice. In other words, the traditional interpretation that the English ship of state sailed on, but after 1066 under a new, more vigorous crew remains valid.

6

MILITARY ORGANISATION

Post-Conquest Anglo-Norman society was a society organised for war. In this it was, of course, typical of its age. Though we cannot talk of a 'war economy' in the eleventh century, the Anglo-Norman kings spent at least as much of the country's resources on war and preparation for war as any modern totalitarian regime.[1] The bulk of royal taxation was employed for military purposes; the agents of royal government were first and foremost military men; land tenure was determined by royal and aristocratic need for armed forces. Yet *how* this society was organised remains the most vexed matter of all. How far did the Norman colonists depend on Anglo-Saxon practice? How far were they innovatory? How much did the mounted knights contribute to the armed strength of Anglo-Norman England, and when and how was knight service introduced? These are weighty questions. Their hypothetical solutions owe much to the prejudices – including those of race and politics – of contemporary historians; just as they have since the seventeenth century.

The military élites of both eleventh-century Normandy and England shared a common ethos, and on both sides of the Channel they held all the commanding heights of lay society and economy. In both countries rulers and great lords had their vassals, warriors bound to their superiors by commendation .by which they gained resources, usually, though not exclusively, land, in return for service, usually, though not exclusively, military. However much the details may have varied (sometimes quite considerably) between states, the fundamental structure of this relationship, for which most historians have used that misleading term of convenience, 'feudal', was well-established in both England and Normandy before the Conquest. But in all discussions of the military arrangements of post-Conquest England we should do well to remember the telling words of Prestwich: 'the feudal system is as inconspicuous in the pages of William of Poitiers, Orderic Vitalis and William of Malmesbury as in those of Geoffrey of Monmouth'.[2]

With his victory at Hastings, William's military strategies and needs changed at a stroke. The frontiers of his lands, which were previously drawn at the Channel, now extended to the Anglo-Scottish border and the Welsh marches, frontiers which were themselves, as we have seen, fluctuating and imprecise. Not only did the king–duke have a continuing need to retain the loyalty of his Norman magnates, and that of his family; to protect the integrity of the duchy against the threats of both Anjou and the king of France; to curb unrest in the border regions such as the Vexin and Bellême; he also needed to consolidate and extend his authority and control in England, to prevent or destroy rebellions, and at the same time, as far as possible, to work in association with Anglo-Saxon survivors whom he could trust. In such circumstances the king required military forces that could easily be mobilised on either side of the Channel, and he had to use all resources available to him. The resultant Anglo-Norman military machine was, in these circumstances, almost inevitably an amalgam of the old and the new, of Anglo-Saxon and Norman practice. But before turning to the solutions William employed we must examine arrangements then current on both sides of the Channel.

Pre-Conquest Normandy

In Normandy the duke possessed authority to call out a general levy of all freemen, but this right, similar to that of the Anglo-Saxon kings and derived from Carolingian models, was only employed in times of crisis and can only be documented after 1066. More usually, the duke relied upon his *milites* ('soldiers'). Earlier orthodoxy, following the influential work of Haskins, maintained that already by 1066 vassals of the duke were obliged to perform military service for a specified period of time with a fixed quota of armed retainers. This view has now been comprehensively challenged, and it is apparent that arrangements for military service were a great deal more fluid and less formalised.[3] Men – and women – held *beneficia* (or *feoda*, which they were increasingly being called as they became heritable) for service. These might comprise landed estates, or castles, or even churches. Though they could be given for services already rendered, they were primarily granted for services to be performed. These included not only military duties but a variety of other activities, or a money rent. Such arrangements are reminiscent of those found in Anglo-Saxon England, in the Oswaldslaw for example. On both sides of the Channel military obligations were not yet divorced from other forms of service, and ties of personal dependence could be expressed in many ways.

The dynamics of the extension of ducal authority under Duke William are hard to determine, but its results are apparent in every aspect of the duchy's administration. One expression of ducal power was the control of military service. Though it now seems most unlikely that fixed quotas and terms of service had been imposed on vassals by 1066, it is clear that they did have a responsibility to serve when required. The duke also received military service from the abbeys under his patronage, though here, too, quotas had probably not been formalised by 1066. Indeed, it may have been the bargaining to provide ships and armed forces for the invasion of England in 1066 that laid the foundation for the later imposition of fixed quotas.[4] In any event, William's military strength was located in the ducal household and extended outwards through a kinship network that bound together many of the greatest magnates of the duchy, such as William fitzOsbern and Roger of Montgomery. These men had been enriched with lands and offices; in return they were expected to provide military aid when required.

Pre-Conquest England

In the early Anglo-Saxon period land had customarily been 'loaned' by a lord to a follower in return for his faithful service.[5] But the loss of military services through the increasing tendency to grant (or 'book') land by charter rather than loan it, a practice that was initially confined to ecclesiastical grants but which soon spread to the laity, and the fact that such grants (unlike loaned land) were in perpetuity, led kings in the eighth century to impose general military obligations, the so-called 'common burdens' of bridge and fortress-work and service in the fyrd. The disadvantages of alienation by book were heightened by the Viking threat; this was the catalyst to the refinement of military organisation under Alfred and his successors. By the mid-tenth century all those who held by book-right had an obligation to serve in the fyrd, which, far from being the democratic army of a free peasantry, 'the nation in arms', was a well-trained force recruited from the thegnly class. Obligations were based upon the hidage assessment of each estate and were apparently calculated on the latter's value, and (at least in central southern England) it was understood that one soldier would serve for every five hides. Elsewhere there were variants (just as the size of the post- Conquest knight's fee varied) according to region, while individual bargains might be made between lord and vassal. Holders of large estates would be expected to bring a quota of followers similarly calculated, either according to x hides (or other notional land units, such as carucate or sulung) per man equation, or by individual negotiation.

Thegns were armed by their lords. The giving of arms by a lord to his vassal was common to both sides of the Channel, and on both sides it carried the same implication of service. On a vassal's death these arms would be yielded up as heriot (translated in Domesday as *relevamentum*, the relief, the term usually applied in post-Conquest England), which was only very gradually being commuted to a cash payment. That of an ordinary thegn was a saddled horse, armour, a sword, spear and shield, but a king's thegn was expected to have two saddled and two unsaddled horses, marking his superiority above the lesser thegns.[6] Indeed, in armour and weapons, the late-Anglo-Saxon thegn was a match for his continental counter-part, from whom he differed little, if at all, in appearance, as contemporary manuscript illustrations, as well as surviving artefacts, and above all, the Bayeux Tapestry, make clear.[7]

Anglo-Saxon lords were expected to own and use horses in war.[8] Before, as after, the Conquest a magnate might well maintain a stud farm, for horses were costly status symbols, whose gift or bequest was highly valued. Horses had been employed by the fyrd since Alfred's time to pursue a defeated enemy, and (given their expense) this provides a further indication that the fyrd was rather more than a peasant militia. Nevertheless, thegns were not alone in using horses in war: lawmen at Cambridge were expected to yield, as their heriot to the sheriff, a palfrey and the 'arms of a *miles*', (which should be translated neutrally as 'soldier'), and some burgesses at Hereford served the king 'with a horse', which was similarly surrendered at death.[9]

Where there was a difference between the Anglo-Saxon and Norman armies was in the function of the horse. Documentary and pictorial evidence suggest that the Anglo-Saxons rode to battle, fought on foot, and then pursued, or fled, on horseback, and the Anglo-Saxon Chronicle records a famous episode in 1055, when Earl Ralph led a mounted English force against the Welsh but the English were routed 'because they were on horseback', while John of Worcester adds that Ralph ordered them to ride, 'contrary to their custom'. We can conclude, therefore, that the English was essentially an infantry army while the Normans made their cavalry an integral and important element in their strategy and tactics, though not to the exclusion of other forces, such as archers (as Hastings reveals), nor did they disdain to fight effectively on foot when necessary. The Norman cavalry was highly trained and capable of skilful manoeuvres – and the evidence for the feigned retreat at Hastings is convincing, though not overwhelming; such training required time and money, it was above all a lordly pursuit. But whether we can go further than this and argue that therefore the post-Conquest Norman 'feudal host' was substantively different from its Anglo-Saxon predecessor is much more debatable.[10]

Possession of land was crucial to a thegn's status. A famous early eleventh-century legal compilation on status stipulated that thegn-right depended on possession of five hides and a defensible house, as well as on royal service; but the 'law of the north people' adds a rider that even if a *ceorl* (free peasant landholder) prospered to possess the arms of a thegn, 'if he has not the land he is a ceorl all the same'.[11] Land, then, was the defining currency of status. Moreover, in pre-Conquest England both lay magnates and monastic houses held some of their lands in return for obligations, including that of furnishing military service, while thegns were settled on the estates of a number of monasteries in return for the performance of military duties. By 1135 this obligation had been transformed into the provision of a fixed quota of soldiers for the royal army. How, and when, this change was effected is the crux of the question of continuity.

How these men were recruited and rewarded was not the king's responsibility: they might receive land for their service; they might be retained in the lord's household as 'housecarls'. The function of the latter, who are found both in the royal household and in those of leading magnates, has occasioned much debate.[12] For long they were regarded as a specialised élite fighting force or 'standing army', organised as a guild with its own draconian law code, storm troopers bound by a fiercely militaristic ethos, and certainly set apart from the national militia, the fyrd. But just as the fyrd's role has been reconsidered and made a more specialised and aristocratic force, the housecarls have been demoted. Hooper has presented a persuasive argument that housecarls were merely household retainers. In other words, he suggests, they had an identical status and function to that of the thegns, and the different nomenclature indicates their Scandinavian (or even, in the case of Richard fitzScrob, who is once styled King Edward's housecarl, Norman) origin. More often, however, the terms thegn, *miles*, *minister* ('official'), and housecarl are used interchangeably. Their origin is probably to be found in Cnut's household, and he and his successors used them both as a military force but also for the keeping of domestic order and the performance of dangerous administrative duties such as tax collecting, as well as for peacetime service

in the royal court, where they are found, for example, witnessing royal charters. They, like all contemporary household troops,
were paid and provided with food, lodging and wages, perhaps
with a geld specifically raised for the purpose from certain towns,
as Domesday evidence from boroughs like Wareham and Malmesbury would suggest. Later, the term 'housecarl' would be translated as *solidarius*, and Tostig's housecarls (amongst whom were
found men of high social status) are styled 'hiredmann', that is 'men
of the household', not mercenaries, who, though customarily receiving cash payments, were also frequently rewarded with grants of
land.

Nevertheless, something can perhaps be salvaged of the old
interpretation of the housecarls. By virtue of their life in the
household they probably had an informal group solidarity, they may
even have been organised in a guild, for guilds are frequently found
in other contexts in late Anglo-Saxon England. There is also the
possibility that they were used as garrisons, if the unique Domesday
reference to the fifteen acres at Wallingford 'where the housecarls
used to dwell' is so interpreted, and the fact that part of the geld
seems to have been set aside for their payment suggests some
demarcation from other military forces.[13] Perhaps they served both
as the king's bodyguard and as a 'regiment' in the army, providing
a 'rapid response' force in emergencies, or as the core of major
expeditions. Though there is every indication that the housecarls
did not survive the Conquest, that, in Professor Hollister's words,
they 'were shattered beyond recovery', there was little in the
organisation of the post-Conquest royal military household that a
survivor would not have recognised.[14]

Solution

As we have seen, the Anglo-Norman kings had three interlock-
ing strategic concerns: to defend the sea and land frontiers of their
enlarged territory; to prevent, or at least neutralise, rebellions;
and to maintain and consolidate their hold on newly-conquered
lands.

(a) NAVAL FORCES

It was always necessary to guard the seaways, most particularly to keep the lines of communication open between Normandy and England, but also to maintain security against threatened and actual raids from Scandinavia, which menaced not only the eastern seaboard but also the Welsh coast – Hugh of Montgomery was killed in Anglesey by King Magnus Barelegs of Norway in 1098. A fleet was also required for some military offensives, such as the Scottish expedition of 1072. But much less is known of the king's naval than of his land forces.[15] The pre-Conquest navy was, like the army, partly mercenary in composition. The *lithsmen* who served in the fleet were well paid and trained. London was their headquarters and they were frequently commanded by leading figures such as Tostig or Harold. They always represented a potential threat to political stability, which may be the chief reason why they were disbanded in 1050. In their place the king increasingly relied upon the *butsecarls*. These were based along the east Sussex and Kent coast, in towns that would later constitute the Cinque Ports, with their headquarters perhaps at Sandwich. These towns had obligations to provide naval forces, and Domesday makes it plain that this responsibility was maintained after the Conquest. The burgesses of Dover, for which the fullest evidence survives, had to give 20 ships of 21 men for 15 days a year and provide a steersman and assistant. In return, the townspeople received substantial autonomy. These forces probably provided the core of royal naval defences. They might be deployed against rebels, as at Ely in 1071, but their function, above all, lay in guarding the south coast from invasion.

The *butsecarls* could be reinforced by the national ship-levy. Much of the country was organised in ship-sokes, typically made up of three hundreds, with the obligation to provide a certain number of ships and sailors, captained by a steersman. However, there is no clear evidence that the ship-levy ever saw action after 1066, and it has been plausibly suggested that these obligations were generally commuted to a payment of ship-scot.[16] This revenue could be used to hire ships and crews within England or from overseas (perhaps Flanders) when necessary. The Anglo-Saxon Chronicle tells of naval forces used against Ely in 1071, and the following year in the Scottish expedition (as again they were employed against King Malcolm by William Rufus in 1091), and they must also have been used to carry William's army on the frequent expeditions to Normandy. Of their composition we are left ignorant, though John of Worcester refers to disloyal English *butsecarls* in Henry I's service in 1101. So, too, we know little of the rewards of naval service, though they were perhaps commensurate with service on land, and steersmen (or captains) received substantial lands. The captain of William's *Mora* acquired both urban and landed property, including, appropriately, houses in Southampton; and Domesday records that Ketel, the steersman, held a carucate in Sussex and houses in Chichester, also close to the cross-Channel ports. The fleet defended the sea frontiers, internal defence and security were provided by the castle.

(b) THE CASTLE

Contemporaries and modern historians alike have seen the castle as fundamental to the conquest of England, at once the most potent symbol and instrument of domination and oppression.[17] Orderic Vitalis showed how William used castles for both defence and offence, and suggested that the English, though brave and warlike, *were severely* disadvantaged in their resistance because there were so few castles in the English provinces.[18] Both Orderic and the Anglo-Saxon Chronicle record the tyranny of royal castellans, particularly Bishop Odo and William fitzOsbern, while the Chronicle's verse epitaph for the Conqueror commences: 'He had castles built and poor men hard oppressed.' In similar fashion the Chronicle's account of William Rufus's military campaigns reveals the castle to have been all-important. More recently, Allen Brown has regarded the castle as a *sine qua non* of feudalism, and the keep, or donjon, the outward and visible sign of Norman dominion, while John le Patourel has demonstrated how the castle was the paramount agency of settlement, being used as a forward base for further advance, and combined with the monastery and/or borough to form 'one of the chief instruments of Norman colonization in Britain'.[19]

How many castles were established in England before 1100 remains unknowable: Domesday Book records just under 50, but this figure is almost certainly only a small fraction of the total, and the two unusual and further references to *domus defensabiles* ('fortified houses') suggests that only the more substantial fortifications were identified as *castella*.[20] Virtually all were held by the king or his leading tenants, and many were associated with towns, which they were intended to control and overawe. Only a few were stone-built and most of these were royal in origin, though there are exceptions. Chepstow, perhaps the earliest surviving example, was built by William fitzOsbern; Richmond (Yorkshire) belonged to the great Alan the Red; Ludlow to Richard de Lacy. The two most impressive early keeps to survive, Colchester and the White Tower, London, were both urban and royal, and the latter was perhaps consciously intended to stress the replacement of a Roman by a Norman *imperium*.

No-one would deny the impact of the castle in post-Conquest Britain, or question Cathcart King's basic definition of a castle as a 'fortified habitation', owned, and periodically lived in, by an individual, whether the king or a minor lord, but sometimes having more public, communal functions, especially in an urban context, where a castle was typically the seat of the sheriff and local administration.[21] Much more controversial is the question of the origin of the castle in England. For a century a lively debate has raged as to whether there were truly castles in pre-Conquest England. Unfortunately, here as elsewhere, the issue has been overlain by assumptions of Norman military superiority. Certainly, 'private' fortifications in pre-Conquest Normandy could be more sophisticated than their English counterparts; motte and bailey castles (i.e. castles comprising a mound and adjacent enclosure) are already evident across the Channel by 1066. However, recent documentary and archaeological investigations suggest that fortified residences at this period in Normandy were largely confined to the wealthier aristocracy, that ring works (i.e. roughly circular fortifications surrounded with bank and ditch) were more prevalent than mottes, and that, where fortifications were built, they were usually additions to pre-existing dwellings rather than completely new structures.[22]

In England only the motte at Ewyas Harold is certainly pre-Conquest, another may survive at Richard's Castle, and there was certainly one, now destroyed, at Hereford. All but one (Clavering in Essex) were in Herefordshire, in a region of extreme military and political sensitivity; all were built by Normans during the Confessor's reign. By contrast, such thegns' residences as have been examined show little in the way of fortifications. Sulgrave may have had a stone tower; Goltho was surrounded by substantial banks and ditches; Portchester had the advantage of Roman walls; at Barton-on-Humber and Earl's Barton, earthworks seem associated with church towers. Of these, the first three were all re-fashioned after the Conquest with stronger defences. But how far were these changes consequent upon 1066, how much were they those sorts of additions to existing residences already encountered in Normandy? Such transformations and improvements continued after the Conquest, as when the early-Norman unfortified hall at Castle Acre was subsequently converted into a stronghold. What we may be seeing, therefore, is a gradual process of increasing fortification on both sides of the Channel, percolating down from the higher aristocracy.

Primarily there may be a change in the morphology, but not the functions, of the fortified residence. For the problem of origins is compounded by the multifarious nature of the castle, which took many forms and could fulfil many roles; indeed, the multi-functional adaptability of the castle was its greatest strength. The distinction between thegn's hall and knight's castle has perhaps been too sharply made because of a stress on the *fortification* at the expense of the *residence*. True, in the disturbed years after 1066 the need for defensive as well as offensive positions may have been paramount, but the castle also fulfilled other civilian and peacetime roles, which were not so very different, if at all, from those of its predecessors.[23] Many castles served as the *capita* (i.e. administrative and military headquarters) of their owners. As such they were administrative, judicial, social and economic centres of authority, controlling most activities of the lord's vassals and tenants. Peacetime roles are much more difficult to identify than military operations. There is a little archaeological evidence to suggest that castles were sometimes linked with mills, while Chepstow castle seems to have been the collecting point for dues from the region and for tolls for boats crossing the Wye. Certainly, castles were often associated with markets. Domesday records how Robert of Mortain held a market in his castle of Trematon, while at Launceston he moved a market from the control of the canons of St Stephen's 'and put it in his castle'.[24] Castles could be instruments of commercial as well as military oppression.

In one vital respect the post-Conquest castle was innovatory. Undeniably the castles were the building blocks of occupation and later consolidation. Castles were used initially as defences against native incursion, as Orderic Vitalis observed in his account of William's first northern campaign and elsewhere. Not surprisingly, they were particularly in evidence along the frontiers and other places of strategic sensitivity, and were normally royal creations, in which William would place a trusted lord as castellan. Soon, however, they took on a more aggressive function. Often they were established at the centre of castleries. Though the term, in Domesday, is nearly always confined to the Welsh Marches and Sussex, this arrangement, whereby local estates were militarily and economically dependent upon the castle and its lords, is found across early-Norman England; the examples of Montacute, Hastings and Beauvoir may be cited. Above all, castleries were created in the north. Pacification and colonisation here depended on the compact honours, based on a castle controlling strategic points, such as Holderness or the Pennine crossings. These were the nerve centres from which the Norman expansion proceeded: sometimes this operation is clear enough, as it is in North Wales or, later, Cumbria; more often it can only be conjectured.

Royal castellans were usually recruited from powerful baronial families. They commanded a permanent garrison and such additional forces as might from time to time be brought in, either from vassals owing castle guard or for particular emergencies or campaigns. At York William Malet succeeded the unfortunate Robert fitzRichard, who was killed in the northern rising; when William I built a second castle at York William fitzOsbern became its castellan. Sometimes royal castellans were sheriffs, as was Walter of

Gloucester at Gloucester and Urse d'Abitot at Worcester. Whether or not the keeper of a royal castle was also the local sheriff (and, of course, the latter's authority and power were considerably increased if he was) there was a tendency for the office to become hereditary, a development which the Norman kings did not wish to encourage, but which had sometimes to be tolerated. Ivo de Grandmesnil succeeded his father as castellan of Leicester, William followed his father, Walter fitzOther, at Windsor, and the Beauchamps of Bedford were hereditary castellans of Bedford.

While little is known of the operations of castle guard (the obligation incumbent upon a vassal to garrison his lord's castle for a stated term) before 1100, there are enough references to exemptions from this burden during Henry I's reign to indicate that it was already well established.[25] Service might be required either at the king's castles or at those of the tenant's immediate lord, but perhaps rarely at both. We know that the military tenants of Abingdon had to perform their castle guard at the royal castle of Windsor; by the twelfth century, service at Windsor, as at other royal castles like Dover and Rockingham, was organised on a rotational basis, with a number of honours, normally but not always local, responsible for providing a quota of men for a specified period. Similar arrangements also prevailed at large baronial castles, such as Richmond (Yorkshire). All this suggests that the garrison of a large castle could be substantial, and there are indeed indications to suggest that in the larger, strategically important castles there might be a military garrison of up to fifty at any one time, though this figure may well have been augmented at times of emergency.

In theory, castle-guard service was incumbent upon all vassals, however mighty, but lesser vassals might serve more or less permanently within the castle, and be rewarded with small estates close by, as appears to be the case, for example, at Robert of Mortain's castle of Montacute (Somerset). But there was also a civilian household. Recent work has shown that many leading barons employed a number of officials in the late eleventh century: clerics who provided spiritual and administrative services, and were based either within the castle chapel (though they might hold a small manor or two themselves) or at a neighbouring religious house;

sheriffs, stewards, chamberlains, butlers, as well as cooks, porters and other menials worked, if they did not live, within the castle. Senior estate managers and others were sometimes recruited from the lord's vassals in Normandy, or from cadet branches of his family.[26] Together they formed the teams responsible for the military subjection and the economic exploitation of the conquered land. But here, in another way, the wheel comes full circle. For we should remember that Anglo-Saxon lords had their stewards and chamberlains too: some of these may have continued as reeves of new masters. The castle as 'great house' was little distinguishable, if at all, from what had gone before.

(c) LAND FORCES

In the light of the castles' importance in the military life of Anglo-Norman England it is not surprising that they were frequently under attack. By contrast, the period between Hastings and Tinchebrai saw no major pitched battles in either England or Normandy, though they were occasionally threatened, as in the stand-off at Alton between Henry I and Robert Curthose.[27] There are several reasons for this seeming reluctance to engage in battle, though the most pressing was undoubtedly the fear of defeat and ensuing destruction. When battles did occur they were almost invariably associated with sieges of castles, such as those of Dol, Gerberoi or Tinchebrai. Sieges were essential elements in late eleventh-century warfare; the earls' rebellion of 1075 collapsed after the fall of Norwich castle; William Rufus crushed the baronial rebellion of 1088 by the systematic reduction of rebel castles. The centrality of siege warfare has long been recognised, but some of the implications of this for military organisation have not been developed. In sieges, cavalry forces are relatively unimportant, even useless, when compared with engineers and infantry troops. Moreover, when cavalry were deployed it was seldom in large numbers. The logistics of mobilisation, the demands of a considerable back-up force and of supplies for long campaigns, particularly those that involved a Channel crossing, were very substantial, as the difficulties encountered by Duke William in 1066 illustrate. The battle of

Hastings, in which the Norman forces numbered about 7000, was on an altogether exceptional scale, and even here the cavalry element probably only amounted to a third of the total force. When Robert Curthose invaded England in 1101 he is said to have crossed the Channel with 260 knights. Even allowing for the fact that Robert expected more forces to come in on arrival in England, it seems that he considered this force adequate for a claim to the throne that stood a realistic chance of success. The *cartae baronum* suggest that there were, by 1166, somewhere around 6000 knight's fees in England. In the light of what has just been said, only a very small proportion of these would be used on any one campaign, and even in times of national crisis it is difficult to imagine the whole number being mobilised. It might be argued therefore that the *servicia debita*, the military quotas imposed upon all tenants-in-chief, and which allegedly lay at the heart of the English 'feudal system', represented the maximum obligation that could be demanded, and that their burden was, from the beginning, more fiscal than military. It may also be the case that not all the *milites* demanded were cavalrymen, a point to which I will return.

(i) The Household

The royal (and baronial) household lay at the heart of Anglo-Norman military organisation.[28] It was at once both a social and a military phenomenon and, since *milites* were required to perform a wide range of peacetime administrative services as well as their military functions, it made much sense to have at least some of them in close proximity to their lord's *caput*. The royal household was the nucleus of the Anglo-Norman king's army. Just as royal chaplains often found service at court a 'fast track' for promotion, the king's household *milites* found ready advancement. True, not all were poor; their leaders were recruited from the highest aristocracy and included such magnates as William de Warenne and Alan, lord of Richmond, but the majority were indeed professional soldiers. Great magnates all maintained households at their administrative and military centres, even if they were not all of the dimensions of that of the earl of Chester, who is castigated by Orderic as surrounded 'by an army instead of a household'.[29] Monasteries had their own military establishments, from which they provided their quota of soldiers for the king's armies. In 1086 there were twenty-five houses close to Westminster abbey for its *milites*, and it is likely that it was through them that the abbey fulfilled most, if not all, of its obligation to provide fifteen men. Household troops were also found at Ely, Bury St Edmunds and Evesham, and were probably also used at Tavistock, which had a large burden of fifteen *milites*, before knights' fees were created by Abbot Geoffrey in the 1080s. At Ely the abbey was expected to feed, house and pay its household troops. Such warriors had few, if any, landed resources; they were generally young, and unmarried. These *iuvenes* ('young men') could be unruly and disruptive, particularly within the confines of a monastery – at Worcester, Wulfstan was obliged to place a ban on the consumption of alcohol within the monastic precincts by the stipendiaries temporarily quartered in the priory during the Danish invasion scare of 1085.

Though household troops continued to be a significant element amongst a lord's vassals for many years, they are especially associated with the first generations after the Conquest. For they had particular advantages during the period of political unrest and consolidation of Norman power, being easy to mobilise and garrison within strongholds. But, as the country was pacified, the need for a permanently maintained force grew less and many of those who had been retained were now granted their own estates. The Abingdon chronicle details the process on the abbey's estates. During the period of general unrest and the early rebellions against William, Abbot Aethelhelm was obliged to travel with an armed force, and he used stipendiary soldiers to perform the services he owed the king. 'But after the disturbances had died down', estates previously held by thegns who had died at Hastings were allocated to the abbot's military followers.[30] Yet the chronicle also makes clear that stipendiaries continued to be of paramount importance in the defence of the kingdom, for when the Danes threatened invasion it was these *solidarii* who were assembled and maintained, not the enfeoffed men.

(ii) Military Service: the Question of Quotas

The debate on military continuity and change in Anglo-Norman England has always centred around William's alleged imposition of military or knight service by quotas levied on his vassals. The title of the most influential, and controversial, study of the issue is entitled simply 'The Introduction of Knight Service into England'.[31] Using twelfth-century evidence extrapolated back to the reign of the Conqueror, Round argued that the imposition of knight quotas, normally allocated in multiples of ten, was an arbitrary act of an all-powerful king, that owed little or nothing to earlier structures of military organisation, notably the 'five-hide unit'. Though Round's thesis has been vigorously opposed, and as stoutly defended, ever since, the framework of the debate has remained virtually unchallenged, few daring to question the implied centrality of the knights' role in the military organisation of post-Conquest England.

Before turning to examine the nature of the required service we should examine the chronology of its introduction. Round and his disciples have always claimed that this occurred during the reign of William I. Professor Holt, who has provided the most sensitive recent restatement of this hypothesis, has argued that a demand for a fixed number of soldiers, based approximately on the economic capabilities of the lordship and the defensive requirements of the region, was 'a simple, rough-and-ready practical response to the hazards of conquest'.[32] Quotas are most likely to have been established when an honour was formed, and could then be adjusted as the dimensions of the barony fluctuated. They might also be arbitrarily raised, as William Rufus tried to do in the case of Ramsey abbey, whose burden was temporarily increased from four to ten knights. While there is little hard evidence that quotas were founded directly on old obligations, as has been argued in the case of Worcester, it is arguable that they were used as the basis for the calculation of the new quotas.[33] However, most of the early evidence relates to monastic quotas, which in itself distorts the picture, since in their case tenurial continuity across the Conquest 'divide' was much greater than in the case of the lay aristocracy.

However, these sources are, as recently suggested by John Gillingham, late and ambiguous, and it is striking that no contemporary chronicler lists the charging of an arbitrary quota among the evils of the Conquest. Conversely, the best-known source, the writ (conventionally dated to c.1072) summoning the abbot of Evesham, with 'those five knights which you owe me from your abbey', may be earlier than 1072, and reflect a quota imposed even before the Conquest.[34] If Gillingham would argue that some quotas at any rate are of Anglo-Saxon origin, as controversially, others suggest that they represent a twelfth-century rationalisation of existing ad hoc arrangements. This argument partly depends on the observation that the quotas were seemingly not a direct importation from Normandy. Though ducal vassals held their land in return for service in the field and for castle guard, the amount of such service is virtually never defined. By 1133, at almost exactly the same time as we have incontrovertible evidence for quotas in England, they are found in the Bayeux Inquest (which records the obligations of his knights to the bishop of Bayeux): these are, it has been plausibly suggested by Professor Tabuteau, an imposition of Henry I, and it is certainly arguable that in England, too, Henry, not William I, was responsible.[35]

Is it possible to reconcile these conflicting hypotheses? By the mid-eleventh century, on both sides of the Channel, it was understood that landholders, who had sufficient resources, had military obligations to the king or duke. In Normandy there were occasional individual contracts specifying precise duties, but these were rare. Perhaps in England, too, if Gillingham is correct, contracts were made. Certainly those abbeys which had settled thegns on estates in return for service must surely have known how much service would be required from them, in other words it is likely, to put it no more strongly, that they knew a quota. However, such quotas were normally reassessed and, we should assume, increased consequent upon the Conquest. In Normandy it may be that bargains made between individual magnates and the duke formed the basis of later demands, and that quotas were negotiated immediately prior to the invasion of England.[36] Hence they preceded the granting of lands to the tenants-in-chief.

So, the following scenario can be suggested. On assuming the

English crown, William had to defend his prize. He had been supported in conquest by his Norman magnates, who had been promised land in return for their aid, which included their bringing of vassals, the forces they had pledged to the duke. William was also aware that his English royal predecessors had raised their armies tenurially as well as territorially, and when the great abbeys came to make their peace and have their estates confirmed they were made responsible for the provision of similar quotas, assessed by various criteria that could be based on custom, specific local military needs, or which could be punitive. What is unknown is whether similar demands were made of the surviving English lay lords with whom William originally intended to work in amity, though it can be surmised that men like the Earls Edwin and Morcar were expected to serve with forces similar to those they had deployed prior to 1066.

Yet what was the reality behind the *servicia debita*? The fact that in 1166 many tenants-in-chief affected not to know precisely what their quota was, and needed to consult 'ancient men' to discover the answer, suggests that the quotas no longer reflected actual military arrangements – if they ever had. As already suggested, the theoretical number of troops provided by the *servicia* was far in excess of what would be required in the normal circumstances of warfare. If there was already a superabundance of warriors, why did the Anglo-Norman kings so frequently employ mercenaries? It might be argued that from the first post-Conquest generation military service was being commuted for a money payment – scutage. Though first certainly recorded in 1100, it is generally agreed that the practice pre-dates the reign of Henry I.[37] The introduction of military quotas allowed the mobilisation of extraordinarily large forces in a time of crisis, but it also gave the king the option of raising substantial cash revenues to hire alternative, and potentially more useful, forces. The *servitium debitum* established maxima for military service from the king's tenants, and increasingly proved a powerful taxation tool, but it no more implied a coherent 'feudal host' than the fyrd represented the nation in arms.

Nor is there any evidence that the entire *servitium debitum* was ever summoned for service in Normandy or England. Even when we know, or can infer, that a large force was assembled, as it was before the Scottish campaign of 1072, or in 1088 when Rufus defended himself against baronial insurrection, we cannot argue for a general mobilisation; indeed the fact that so many of his vassals rebelled in 1088 necessarily meant that Rufus could not utilise the quotas they owed. Moreover, the problems in mustering, provisioning, and transportation of such a substantial force as the entire *servitium debitum* precluded its use. In their use of inexact terms like *exercitus* or *expeditio*, often wrongly taken as synonymous with the feudal host, but best translated loosely as 'army' and 'expedition', chroniclers reveal little of the composition of the Anglo-Norman army, though their frequent reference to the presence of both English and Norman forces, as well as suggesting the diversity within it, witnesses to the degree of integration between the two, and to William and his commanders' skill in holding together a multi-national army composed of household, stipendiary, and enfeoffed soldiers alike.

(iii) The Obligations and Rewards of Service

Other questions remain. Above all, what was the nature of the military service demanded by the king? This is never precisely spelt out. The vagueness is capable of two interpretations. Either contemporaries were fully aware of what was required and no explanation was necessary, or, and I consider this the more likely, it was never defined because it was so seldom exacted. Moreover, early charters of enfeoffment are rare, and notoriously unspecific.[38] They are rare, both because written records of land transactions at this time were only slowly replacing oral ceremony, and because as long as most military forces continued to be raised from the household there was much less need for documentary evidence of a contractual relationship that was explicit in the charter of enfeoffment. The lack of precision in the charters that do survive is also significant. They mention neither length of service nor obligation to perform castle guard; the grant is for life and not heritable. It is only in the twelfth century that light is shed upon the nature of military service in more or less standard formulae, and how far it is possible to extrapolate back from twelfth-century obligations is difficult to determine.

During the twelfth century stress was laid upon the performance of castle guard, and since, as we have seen, the castle was so integral a component of military organisation during the post-Conquest years, it is likely that this obligation soon became central. By contrast, service in the field was limited, the full quota was seldom if ever summoned for overseas service, and Anglo-Norman kings relied much more on the more flexible opportunities that the hiring of mercenaries afforded.

Once quotas had been established, a tenant-in-chief had to decide how his obligations should best be met. We should remember, as Stenton insisted, that the late eleventh century was a time 'when men were still free to make experiments in forms of military tenure'; 'it was for a lord to decide how they [i.e. military duties] should be apportioned among his men'.[39] However, there is general agreement that a distinction should be drawn between the imposition of a quota and the creation of knights' fees. A lord might retain his followers in his household – a response that seems to have been particularly prevalent and long-lasting in the north; he might grant them landed estates, or he might hire soldiers for specific campaigns.[40] Often he would employ several options, but it is only seldom that the working arrangements can be observed. As noted above, charters of enfeoffment are very rare before 1100, and all relate to ecclesiastical lords. As scanty are observations in Domesday, such as that recording Bishop Wulfstan of Worcester's grant of an estate at Croome (Worcestershire), on the death of its English tenant, with the latter's daughter, to one of his *milites* so that he might maintain the tenant's widow and perform service for the bishop.[41] Ranulf Peverel held land in Tollesbury (Essex) from the abbess of Barking. He wanted to perform the same service for this land as his predecessor had given.[42] His case is not unique and Domesday furnishes a number of other examples where the new Norman tenant held land by the same service as his predecessor. In neither instance is the nature of the service specified but its continuity is clearly implied. Neither are early charters much more specific. Domesday shows Eudo, the king's steward, holding five hides in Barford (Bedfordshire) of Ramsey; the relevant charter (preserved in the abbey's cartulary) reveals this to be a life-grant for a half-knight's service.[43] It has been plausibly suggested that the monks of Westminster required money rents from their knightly tenants rather than personal service, and Domesday suggests that this practice was already current by 1086 – perhaps the monks had moved directly from a reliance upon household knights to scutage. However, the early charter recording the enfeoffment of William Baynard, with land conveniently close to the abbey, for one knight's fee, again indicates that lords raised their quota by a range of methods.[44]

Usually a *miles* received some land for military service. But that fee might comprise a great landed honour, an estate of some five hides (approximately 600 acres) held either as a compact manor or, perhaps more often, in several discrete parcels, or it might be merely a small-holding of about a hide, listed along with the lands of the villeins in a Domesday entry. Land, moreover, was not the only fee. Sometimes *milites* were enfeoffed with small estates near their lord's castle, and it is likely that in these cases they were employed as the castle's permanent garrison. Some may have been essentially household knights who derived most of their income from non-landed sources, and whose modest lands were used to provide a 'top-up' rental income.

Nor should we assume that every grant of land was made either to fulfil the quota or for military service. As the archbishop of York wrote to the king in 1166, his predecessors had made enfeoffments not because royal service demanded this but because they wished to provide for their kin and servants.[45] Abbeys might make grants to curry favour or through fear of powerful neighbours, and land might be farmed out for a money rent, which was then used to retain mercenaries. Enfeoffment was not necessarily to the king's advantage, for it enabled a tenant-in-chief to establish his own clientage. There are some indications to suggest that to counter this tendency the king attempted to control such grants. William Rufus ordered Ailwin, the English abbot of Ramsey, not to grant any of his or the monks' lands to any man without the king's licence. Occasionally, too, we see the hand of the king reconfiguring old military arrangements to new needs. One of the earliest (and best-known) surviving enfeoffment documents shows Peter, King

William's *miles*, becoming the vassal of the abbey of Bury St Edmunds 'by permission of the king'; much further west, at Potterne (Wiltshire), an English thegn, the nephew of Bishop Herman, is said in Domesday to hold land as a *miles* 'by command of the king'.[46] Another well-known account tells how the king obliged the abbot of Abingdon to provide an estate for one of his knights, who had been captured and mutilated by pirates and who was hence incapable of military service.[47] Domesday entries, such as that recording Ferron's holding of an estate in Northamptonshire, belonging to Peterborough abbey, 'by order of the king against the abbot's will', are further demonstrations of unwanted royal interference in tenurial arrangements.[48]

(iv) The Soldiers of Early-Norman England

No figure is more central in the Norman conquest and settlement of England, or more controversial, than the *miles*.[49] The problem is at root a semantic one. Can the ubiquitous *miles* be equated with the *chivaler*, can either be synonymous with *cniht*? By the twelfth century the Anglo-Norman term, *chivaler*, was being used to denote the heavily-armed mounted warrior or 'knight' of common parlance. The Anglo-Saxon *cniht* referred to an armed retainer of uncertain status and is, of course, the source of the later word, 'knight'. When the Anglo-Saxon Chronicle refers to the military entourage of Abbot Thurstan of Glastonbury, in 1083, it uses the word *cnihtan*: are these cavalry or infantry? The term *miles* is not of course static, its meaning and usage evolved throughout this period. Certainly, by the twelfth century, it was becoming increasingly confined to the cavalry warrior or *chivaler*. In the late eleventh century, however, it is by no means certain that the term was so exclusive. Unfortunately historians have often tended to assume this exclusivity, which has led them to adopt untenable positions. Some, like the late Allen Brown, have cogently argued that the *milites* of the eleventh century were of noble status.[50] Their rank was reflected in their life-style; they were clearly demarcated from even the wealthiest peasants; they were members of a military aristocracy that was highly trained to use expensive equipment, notably the horse. But problems immediately occur with this interpretation. Not only is there little evidence that *miles* was an honorific title by this stage, Domesday has numerous references to pre-Conquest *milites*, while contemporary sources similarly abound in references to English *milites*, and the term 'thegn' is frequently translated *miles*.

Also equating *miles* with the mounted knight, other historians, notably Sally Harvey, have come to a totally different, but equally extreme, conclusion.[51] Arguing primarily from Domesday, with its frequent references to *milites* with seemingly few resources, she divided the knightly class into two distinct elements; the high-ranking knights, typically important vassals of tenants-in-chief, and their own military vassals, who were the professionals, anonymous *milites* of little income and status. This influential analysis is useful at least in as much as it demonstrates that the term *miles* was an elastic one, covering a wide social and military spectrum. Most historians would now agree that in eleventh-century England and Normandy the term reflects function – whatever form that might take, not status. But on occasion it also seems synonymous with 'vassal', reflecting a tenurial relationship: the *Domesday Monachorum* of Canterbury lists Haimo the sheriff, Hugh de Montfort, William de Briouze, and Robert, count of Eu, as *milites* of the archbishop of Canterbury, along with many lesser Norman tenants and several Englishmen.[52] There is no suggestion that function (or status) is implied here, the great men are *milites* because they are the tenants of the archbishop. What is clear is that the term *miles* meant different things in different contexts. All those who fought in person, from the king down (and Don Fleming has reminded us that the royal seal showed the king as a cavalryman), were *milites* in function, even though they may not have fought on horseback.[53] *Milites* might be heavily armoured and trained cavalrymen, light cavalry, or infantry (who would later be distinguished as serjeants). They might be English or French. Just as a 'soldier' today can be used in different contexts to mean a general or a squaddie, a tank officer, engineer, or gunner, the term *miles* is no more specific in defining the function or status of the eleventh-century fighting man.

It is equally difficult to determine the role of the *vavassores*, a term which perhaps more than most seems to have shifted in meaning

across the medieval centuries and to have carried differing connotations in various regions.[54] In Domesday England they had few
resources and, moreover, seem to have been burdened with no
military service, certainly none are recorded. However, by the
beginning of the twelfth century the *Leis Willelme* equate the
vavasours with the pre-conquest thegns, and they are understood to
carry, and presumably serve, with full arms. In other words, by then
they are regarded as knights and mesne vassals. As such they more
or less correspond to the vavasours found in Normandy, who had
fewer military obligations than the *chivalers* and who had cor-
respondingly fewer lands. In late-eleventh-century England they are
perhaps best regarded as analogous to the *radcnihts*, men of indeter-
minate status occupying a position somewhere between the knight
and the non-military free man. The *radcnihts* were mounted retainers
who performed administrative duties for their lord, perhaps as
bailiffs, though they also on occasion were liable for agricultural
service and unspecified, and probably lowly, military obligations.[55]

Conclusion

By 1066 both England and Normandy were familiar with tenurial
arrangements whereby land was held in return for military service.
In both states this service was channelled through lord–vassal
relationships. In what sense, if at all, then, can we speak of a
post-Conquest 'military revolution'? Any such consideration needs
to be distinguished from the 'tenurial revolution' discussed above,
for though the two are closely linked they are not identical. New
men could be settled but perform the same services as those they
displaced; survivors might continue to hold their lands but on
different conditions. There is little doubt that during the Conqueror's
reign military obligations were defined more rigidly, and probably
increased. The new demands of defence and the need to control a
vastly-increased territory stimulated these arrangements, but they,
like the settlement itself, were imposed at varying rates across
the country. There were two chief reasons for this. First, some areas
were militarily more sensitive than others, and it was specific

regional military needs which seem to have been primarily responsible for determining the different levels of service demanded from
the religious houses.[56] Secondly, knight quotas can only have been
imposed piecemeal, for the king never had, *pace* many commentators, a *tabula rasa*. Only as land fell to him, by death or confiscation, could it be redistributed. The very fact that colonisation was a
multi-stage operation meant that there could be no once-for-all
imposition of quotas; rather, they were (as they always had been)
individual contracts. This process could take a long time. In much
of the north, in particular, territory was only fully settled and
baronies established during Henry I's reign.[57] Moreover, many
thegns continued to hold all, or part, of their estates. The extent of
territorial survival at the level of the lesser thegns is only now being
fully recovered, and Domesday notoriously only records subtenants,
amongst whom such men were most likely to be found, erratically.
Dr Roffe has recently calculated that up to 40 per cent of Domesday
subtenants in Nottinghamshire were of native origin, a figure
probably replicated elsewhere.[58] These men probably held under
the same obligations as before the Conquest, and their tenure was
only gradually transformed from precarious loanland to the hereditary fee. But even the newly-settled Normans do not appear to have
had the advantage of hereditary tenure. Surviving early charters
stress the personal nature of the contract and the lack of hereditary
security.

The transition from thegn to knight moved at differing rates and
took differing forms. At Canterbury, according to a twelfth-century
source, 'Lanfranc made his thegns, knights', a statement which
seems to be supported by the list of archiepiscopal *milites* of the
mid-1090s, which includes a significant number of Englishmen
holding one, or a fraction of a, fee. Did this mean, however, that
they were retrained? Was their function any different? In 1097
Rufus complained that the *milites* sent by Archbishop Anselm for the
Welsh campaign were substandard; they were poorly trained and
unsuitable. This has been taken to mean that they were English
tenants retrained unsuccessfully as cavalry, though it might just as
well mean that as cavalry they were unsuitable for the guerrilla
warfare practised by the Welsh.

The royal army was a very heterogeneous institution. It included cavalry forces, though we should remember that not every holder of a *feodum militis* was a cavalryman, nor did every cavalryman possess a *feodum*. It follows that though there were, by 1166, perhaps 6000 'knight's fees', there was nothing like this number of mounted soldiers. The army also included infantrymen and contained the engineers and arblasters mentioned in Domesday, and that other element of the Anglo-Norman army that has been largely ignored (though Jim Bradbury's work is an honourable exception): the archers.[59] This is partly due to the paucity of evidence, but there is enough to indicate that archers and crossbowmen were frequently employed, and, of course, Norman victory at Hastings owed at least as much to arrows as to lances. William's army was born of practical necessity: he used all means at his disposal to defend his territories. His Norman followers pledged to provide military forces, which could be raised through the grant of lands or money payments to their own vassals. Those English tenants who survived and were allowed to remain could also give military service, though what their military function was remains unclear. From many, though not all, English abbeys William also demanded forces, which could likewise be retained in the monastic household or granted estates. Where the abbeys' thegns had survived, they too might continue on their lands and perform due service, perhaps on old pre-Conquest terms.[60] Victory at Hastings had brought new problems for William, but it had also brought new resources of land and cash. Both these currencies were negotiable. Used together they enabled a multi-faceted 'system' to emerge. This was notionally, and to some extent actually, based on landed wealth, but it was the transformation of those assets into cash by scutage, the geld, and all the other exactions for which the Anglo-Norman kings were notorious, that gave them the revenues for the maintenance of a cash-based force, centred on the household that proved so effective on both sides of the Channel.

7

A COLONIAL CHURCH?

Writing at the beginning of the twelfth century, Eadmer of Canterbury thought that 'all things, spiritual and temporal, waited on the nod of the king [i.e. William I]'.[1] The king controlled all communication with the pope, approved all measures laid down in ecclesiastical synods, and only by his express leave could bishops impose canonical sanctions for grave moral offences on his barons and ministers. To Eadmer, William had brought from Normandy a heritage of tight secular control over the Church, which he then successfully imposed upon its English counterpart. There can be no doubt that William I took an active interest in the affairs of the Anglo-Norman Church, nor that William Rufus was equally forceful, if less diplomatic. Yet when we look at the post-Conquest Church it is hard to evaluate what developments were directly attributable to the Normans. Many changes were the result of new policies and ideologies affecting the western Church, and emanating primarily (but not exclusively) from Rome.[2] By introducing bishops and abbots from Normandy and beyond, William may have accelerated the pace of change, but he did not alter its direction. Continental bishops of integrity and learning had been chosen by the Confessor; an English bishop, Wulfstan of Worcester, represented all that was best in the secular Church. Reform was already in the air before 1066, but in many respects post-Conquest reform was archaic, in the light of new ideas current at the Roman *curia*. The reforms of the late-eleventh-century papacy irrevocably changed the face of the western Church; there is a deep faultline running here, but, as Margaret Gibson has convincingly demonstrated, Archbishop Lanfranc lay on the Carolingian side of the divide.[3]

Papacy and Primacy

(a) THE ANGLO-NORMAN CHURCH AND THE PAPACY

William I's relations with the papacy were governed on both sides by political expediency.[4] Alexander II, and more especially Gregory VII, praised William as a righteous king, at least partly in the hope that he would act in the manner expected of a secular ruler by the reformed papacy, that is to say that he should be the pope's executive arm in rectifying ecclesiastical abuses, and open up the Church to Roman influence through his prelates' attendance at synods and by the reception of papal legates. The English king would then, it was hoped, favour the papacy in its struggles with the rulers of Germany and France. William, in his turn, looked to Rome for support and further legitimisation for his claim to the English crown. Before the invasion, William had sent Gilbert of Lisieux to the *curia*, presumably to present a case against the perjured Harold and schismatic Stigand. Papal support for the expedition was granted, symbolised by the grant of the banner of St Peter. For this ideological underpinning of his claim, and the additional support given in 1070 when papal legates re-crowned William, deposed a number of English bishops, and approved the decrees of the councils of Winchester and Windsor, William was expected to be grateful. Yet Gregory VII did not call in his debts till 1080, when he firmly requested fealty and the payment of Peter's Pence, the traditional annual payment by a number of northern kingdoms to Rome, which had its origins in ninth-century England. These were contentious issues. Quite what Gregory had in mind by fealty is unclear: he 'used a single feudal vocabulary to describe the various different relationships of the papacy with secular princes'.[5] He may have considered that the grant of the banner in 1066 implied some

147

overlordship, rather as, two generations later, the king of France's reception of the banner of St Denis was seen to create a royal obligation to that abbey. Alternatively, he probably saw the payment of Peter's Pence as indicating some sort of subordination, an interpretation William rejected, viewing it instead as a payment of alms. Whatever he meant, William refused fealty, and the pope was in no position to pursue a hard line. William was prepared to be the pope's friend and, within limits, supporter; he would be vassal to no-one. But he did agree to resume payment of Peter's Pence, which had been interrupted, perhaps since Stigand's appointment as archbishop of Canterbury.

Relations between king and pope were correct, and on occasion cordial. It was different with Lanfranc.[6] The archbishop had been brought to Canterbury by the King *and* the pope's command, and his relations with the papacy remained ambivalent. On the one hand he needed papal support for his claim to primacy in Britain and supremacy over York, on the other he was determined, while showing respect to Gregory, in no way to accept an extension of papal over archiepiscopal authority. For Lanfranc, submission was symbolised by attendance at Rome. In 1071 he was obliged, against his wishes, to go in person to collect his *pallium* in order to receive papal recognition; thereafter he successfully resisted all attempts to get him there, in particular to attend Gregory's Lenten synods. Relations cooled even further on the issue of the primacy. Gregory was, in general, opposed to these claims, and was certainly not prepared to allow Lanfranc his way without his coming to Rome, and so the archbishop looked increasingly to William and the royal court to uphold his rights. Time and again, in the late 1070s and early 1080s, Gregory tried to get Lanfranc to Rome; his letters were refused or ignored. Gregory became increasingly forceful, ultimately threatening Lanfranc's episcopal suspension.[7] But both sides were fully aware of political realities. To alienate Lanfranc, and inevitably his royal patron as well, would have been disastrous just when Gregory's own struggle with Henry IV of Germany was reaching a critical stage.

Since the imperial election of the anti-pope, Clement III, in 1080, Gregory's and his successor's room for manoeuvre had been increasingly circumscribed. It was the uncertainty of papal politics consequent upon the schism that gave William I, and more especially, Rufus, the opportunity either to ignore papal directives or to use them to gain valuable concessions. Papal weakness in the 1080s probably accounts for Gregory VII's very muted reaction to the overthrow of Odo of Bayeux, though if the bishop had been hoping to become pope in 1082 Gregory may have been pleased to see the back of him. William and Lanfranc took care neither to recognise Clement III nor to condemn him, a policy of playing off the two claimants which was continued more explicitly by Rufus. Gregory died in 1085, his successor, Victor III, who ruled for little more than a year, had no contact with England. The next pope, Urban II, was not recognised by Rufus till 1095, in return for the acknowledgment that papal legates could only enter England by royal consent. The catalyst to recognition was the appointment of Anselm as archbishop of Canterbury. Anselm, who had already acknowledged Urban, wanted his *pallium*; the king would not allow this till he (Rufus) had duly recognised the pope. The impasse was solved by a compromise, heavily in favour of the crown, whereby the king accepted both Urban and Anselm in office in return for all the freedoms from papal intervention in English affairs that William I and Lanfranc had enjoyed. William Rufus triumphed in 1095, as he had in 1088 during the William de St Calais case, because his prelates supported royal, not ecclesiastical, authority.[8]

(b) THE PRIMACY

No issue so divided the early Anglo-Norman Church as the question of Canterbury's primacy within the realm. Apologists for the protagonists did not mince their words. To Eadmer, Archbishop Thomas of York had set out to humiliate the Church of Canterbury to glorify his own Church, while Hugh the Chanter, historian and member of the cathedral chapter of York, after admitting Lanfranc's learning and piety, could not disguise his feelings when he wrote of Canterbury's 'victory' in 1072: 'so ends the shocking story of the ambition of a proud prelate'.[9] Yet, writing half a century later, Orderic, normally so meticulous a chronicler of the English Church, scarcely mentions the primacy dispute. This may be because by his time the question was largely dead. For all of Canterbury's efforts, which included spirited attempts, and forgeries, to influence both king and pope, by the 1120s Canterbury can be seen to have failed.

The sequence of events is clear enough. On 29 August 1070 Lanfranc was consecrated archbishop of Canterbury in the stead of Stigand, deposed the previous April. Shortly afterwards Thomas of Bayeux was appointed to York. Both were the first Norman holders of the archdioceses and were undoubtedly concerned to discover and protect the privileges of their church. Here both parties were disadvantaged, since all archives had recently been destroyed by fires at the two cathedrals. When Thomas went to Canterbury for consecration, Lanfranc demanded a written profession of obedience. Thomas refused unless written evidence and witnesses to the claim were brought. Even when this was done, Thomas refused to submit. Initially he had royal support, but Lanfranc was able to persuade William of the merits of his case, and Thomas agreed to submit to Lanfranc's authority, though not to his successors without certain evidence of precedents for this. He was then duly consecrated. However, when both men went to Rome the following year to collect their *pallia* Thomas reopened the question and added a new ingredient, a claim by York to the obedience of the dioceses of Lincoln, Worcester and Lichfield. In the long run Thomas's appeal to Alexander II may have prejudiced his case, for the king was sensitive to papal authority in his dominions. In stating that precedence had, since Pope Gregory I's time, gone by seniority, Thomas was correct, and Lanfranc the innovator. Alexander did not, however, voice an opinion, but referred the matter back to England, where the Council of Winchester (Easter 1070) resulted in Thomas making an unconditional oath to Lanfranc and his successors and ceding his claim to the three dioceses, though he did gain theoretical authority over the dioceses of Scotland. Lanfranc's attempt to gain papal confirmation of the agreement failed, because he did not journey to Rome in person to claim it, but his hold on the primacy remained unchallenged till his death.

When Anselm became archbishop of Canterbury in 1093, however, Thomas refused to consecrate him as 'metropolitan of all

Britain', which would have further diluted York's authority, but he did agree to the phrase determined in 1072, 'primate of all Britain'. Here the matter rested till Thomas's death in 1100; when it re-emerged a few years later it was in the context of Henry I's own conflict with the English Church and the papacy.

What, then, was the debate about? Lanfranc and Thomas knew, and perhaps respected, each other well: indeed Thomas may have been a former student of Lanfranc. But Thomas was a protégé of Odo of Bayeux, Lanfranc's rival in the Anglo-Norman ecclesiastical polity. The trial at Penenden Heath would shortly restore to Canterbury lands that Odo, as earl of Kent, and others had seized, but ill-feeling between the two may have earlier roots. Lanfranc had been abbot of St Stephen's, Caen, in Odo's own diocese. The abbey enjoyed certain exemptions, and in particular, financial rights, at the expense of Bayeux. By creating a cleric from the Bayeux camp as archbishop of York, William may have hoped to balance two factions in the Anglo-Norman Church. To personal rivalries were added other considerations. Questions of primacy were certainly in the air in the late eleventh century. After all, the entire edifice of Gregorian reform was predicated on papal primacy, as much over archbishops as kings. Therefore, the papacy was generally hostile to primacies, as potential rival centres of authority, though in 1079 Gregory VII did create the primacy of Lyons, whose archbishop was a papal supporter, making Rouen subordinate to it, and thereby incurring William I's displeasure. But anti-papalists, like the Norman Anonymous, were also opposed to notions of primacy: Lanfranc's scheme could not be assured of uncritical support from any quarter outside Canterbury itself.

How, therefore, did Lanfranc persuade both pope and king of the validity of his assertions? One clue may lie in the related dispute over the three midland dioceses. In 1070, York had but one suffragan diocese, Durham, and both dioceses were in a parlous state. There was considerable imbalance between the size, prestige, and wealth of the two metropolitans: Thomas could bolster his own position if he gained authority over three more dioceses. Conversely, to Lanfranc the idea that the tiny archdiocese of York had parity with his own might have seemed absurd. The primacy was, above all, a matter of prestige: Lanfranc and the monks of Canterbury were trying to establish a theoretical underpinning of a primacy which, in practical matters, the southern archdiocese had long enjoyed – except, significantly, during Stigand's tenure.

According to Hugh the Chanter, Lanfranc persuaded the king to support his claim by arguing that the unity of the realm demanded a single primate, since in the North a Scandinavian or Scottish claimant might be crowned king by a rebellious archbishop of York. This was plausible: the threats in the north were real enough. Certainly questions of political unity were involved. It was felt by some that religious frontiers should march with their secular counterparts, and a belief in the unity of the English, if not British, Church was certainly prevalent at Canterbury and elsewhere. Yet there is a paradox here. Canterbury claimed primacy over the British Isles, but the agreement of 1072 granted to York primatial rights over the Church in Scotland, as well as the northern English dioceses. In 1072 William was preparing to invade and conquer Scotland. If he had been successful, the ecclesiastical power of the northern metropolitan would have been considerably increased, and his scope for future recalcitrance would have been commensurately enhanced, not diminished. Even worse, from Canterbury's perspective, was the possibility that if York gained control of the Scottish dioceses there would then be the three bishops necessary to consecrate a new (northern) archbishop without reference to Canterbury, whereas currently a new archbishop of York necessarily required the presence of two southern bishops at his consecration. The agreement at Winchester, on the one hand confirming Lanfranc as primate of all Britain, on the other giving Thomas authority in Scotland, can be seen as a compromise preserving the checks and balances of the Anglo-Norman Church.

In the long term, perhaps the most significant result of the primacy debate was to provide a structure for future claims to English ecclesiastical overlordship of Britain. The title was essentially honorific, reflecting prestige not power, but it gave a unity to the Church analogous to that secular imperialism which le Patourel identified amongst the Norman aristocracy. In spite of all the later efforts of nationalists, like Gerald of Wales or Owain Glyn Dŵr, to create an archbishopric of St Davids, Canterbury's control over the Welsh dioceses survived till Disestablishment in 1914.[10] Though Canterbury had long claimed authority over the Welsh dioceses, just as English kings had similarly asserted sovereignty in Wales, and in 1056 the bishop of Llandaff was consecrated in England, it was only after the Norman military advance into Wales that this claim had any real impact. In 1081 William I made his famous 'pilgrimage' to St David's, which was probably about ecclesiastical as much as secular supremacy, but for all that, the first Norman appointment did not come till 1092, when William II's chaplain, Hervé, went to Bangor. At about the same time Anselm used his primatial authority to suspend the bishops of Llandaff and St David's from office. Yet Hervé's flight three years later, following the Welsh revolt, is a reminder that episcopal appointments were ultimately dependent on political realities.

Ireland was more of a problem.[11] Unlike Wales, the English kings had never asserted even theoretical rights there, but both Lanfranc and Anselm corresponded with Irish kings and clerics, as well as consecrating Irish bishops. How far this constituted recognition of Canterbury's hegemony is doubtful. However, several of these bishops (who were consecrated, and made profession, at Canterbury) had earlier been monks in English houses. Patrick of Dublin was a former monk of Worcester, and another, Samuel, came from St Albans, while Malchus, later bishop of Waterford, was a monk at Winchester. These prelates could have transmitted notions of Canterbury's primacy across the Irish Sea; Bishop Patrick seems to have acted as intermediary between Lanfranc and King Guthric of Dublin, to whom the archbishop wrote urging reform of native marriage customs. Anselm was also in contact with Irish kings and clerics. Did such pastoral correspondence imply primacy? Certainly Eadmer wrote that the Irish had approached Anselm to ask him to institute a bishop of Waterford by right of his primacy over them, but this may have been wishful thinking, since the letter Eadmer reproduces makes no explicit mention of primacy.[12] Canterbury's influence on the Irish Church is hard to quantify. Undoubtedly Irish bishops consecrated in England were open to reforming ideas, but practical reforms would only come in the following century, through

153

the work of clerics such as Gilbert of Limerick, and would owe as much to Rome as to Canterbury. It was Gilbert's achievement, while papal legate, to celebrate the synod of Rath Breasil in 1111, which created two Irish provinces freed from Canterbury's authority.

While Canterbury had mixed fortunes in extending its influence in Wales and Ireland, York attempted to make a reality of its new authority in Scotland.[13] Though Scotland did not have an archbishopric till 1472, York had to take its chance with other interested parties north of the border. Ecclesiastical structures were complex; not only York, but St Andrews, Trondheim, and Hamburg/Bremen claimed rights, a situation which reflected the tangled nature of Scottish politics. It is not surprising, therefore, that the northern metropolitan's influence was patchy. *C.* 1073 Thomas consecrated Ralph as bishop of Orkney, after Ralph's death Archbishop Gerard consecrated Roger, who had been a monk at Whitby. Here, as in Ireland, the Church beyond the frontier was being infiltrated by English Benedictines. Hugh the Chanter records how, early in the 1090s, on the advice of King Malcolm III and Margaret of Scotland, Fothadh bishop of St Andrews, came to York to make his profession.[14] It is not clear why the bishop came south, or what the visit implied. Margaret's links were with Canterbury rather than York. She had asked Lanfranc to be her spiritual adviser, and Lanfranc had also sent monks from Canterbury, at her request, to establish a daughter-house at Dunfermline, which was to become the burial place of Malcolm and his successors. Thus personal links did not intermesh with institutional structures: the former were the stronger, and even in Scotland Canterbury's influence at this time was greater than that of York.

Bishops and Abbots of the New Order

In significant respects the bishops and greater abbots were the ecclesiastical equivalents of William's lay tenants-in-chief.[15] Like them, by the end of William I's reign, they were almost exclusively from continental Europe, and no Englishmen had been appointed to high ecclesiastical office since 1066. They met in synods that were firmly under royal eyes, just like the leading tenants at the *curia regis*, which they also often attended. The great church councils of the 1070s, of London, Winchester and Windsor, were as much occasions for proclaiming royal as ecclesiastical policy, and the fact that Windsor had no ecclesiastical significance, but was a royal hunting lodge, is revealing. At Gloucester the Christmas 1085 meeting of the bishops, at which a number of new appointments were made, slid, probably imperceptably, into the commissioning of Domesday, which was perhaps their greatest achievement. Above all, bishops articulated royal policy. They also witnessed royal charters; they frequently chaired meetings of the shire court. In their diocesan shires they were as powerful figures as the sheriffs, with incomes that often exceeded those of the latter, though bishops often stressed their poverty in appealing to the benevolence of potential benefactors.[16] The source of their income was primarily the episcopal estates, which could be extensive, but added to this were customary dues paid by lesser churches, and profits of justice, while a bishop might be involved in a local mint.[17] Bishops also had an important military role. In 1075 Bishop Wulfstan of Worcester (and his compatriot, Abbot Aethelwig of Evesham) orchestrated the defence of the western march during the earls' rebellion, while Bishop Geoffrey of Coutances was similarly occupied in the rebellion's eastern sector. Wulfstan was responsible for the defence of Worcester castle in 1088, and Gundulf of Rochester, who was known to his contemporaries as 'very competent and skilful in building in stone', constructed the royal castle at Rochester; he supervised the building of the greatest monument to Norman military might, the White Tower in London, and may also have been responsible for the even larger royal castle at Colchester.[18]

The replacement of English abbots and bishops was undertaken primarily for political motives. In the immediate aftermath of Hastings some abbeys made new English appointments, and it was only in 1070 that a real shift to Norman nominees was apparent. The political dimension to this shift was recognised by John of Worcester when he wrote that abbots were deposed in 1070, 'the king promoting the deprivation of the English, and filling up their places by persons of his own nation, in order to confirm his power in a kingdom which he had but newly acquired'. Some, like Archbishop Stigand, could be deposed on canonical grounds, others were expelled for seemingly pragmatic reasons, like Aethelric, bishop of Selsey, who is said by John to have been uncanonically deposed and imprisoned by the king at Marlborough, 'though he was innocent of any crime'. Indeed, his deposition was not finalised till 1076 because of papal reservations. Aethelric, the former bishop of Durham, was imprisoned at Westminster; his brother and successor, Aethelwine, joined the English rebels at Ely, where he was captured. His subsequent deposition, and imprisonment at Abingdon, is hardly surprising. Abbot Godric of Winchcombe was confined at Evesham, Aethelnoth of Glastonbury at Christ Church, Canterbury. Some English prelates fled, as did Aethelsige, abbot of St Augustine's, Canterbury, in 1070. According to the later chronicler, William Thorne, through fear of the king he granted out lands and possessions of his abbey without consulting his brethren, but eventually, seeing that the king was implacable in his hostility, he fled to Denmark. This is confirmed by William I's writ ordering the abbey to be reseised of lands, including the borough of Fordwich, which Aethelsige, *fugitivus meus* ('my fugitive') had given away or caused to be alienated, whether through catelessness, or fear, or cupidity.[19]

Yet, by comparison with changes on the episcopal bench, where by 1070 more than half of the English sees were vacant, the process of change in the monasteries was generally gradual and there was no wholesale deprivation. Abbots of the smaller houses were most often left alone, and even in the larger communities there are indications of a modest revival in native fortunes by the end of the century. Aldwin became abbot of Ramsey in 1091, and in 1098 the monks of Peterborough gave 300 marks to William Ruftis for the right to elect an English replacement as abbot, Godric, to Turold. Unfortunately Godric did not last long, being deposed for simony by Anselm in 1101. At the same time, some English prelates were clearly valued and used by the new regime. In the power vacuum following the collapse of the native secular aristocracy they provided expertise and continuity, and could perhaps have influence in persuading their flock to accept the new order, to which they could lend legitimacy. Above all, they could interpret the old law, perhaps to their own advantage, as Aethelwig of Evesham, who enjoyed substantial judicial powers throughout the west midlands, appears to have done. Aethelwig also oversaw the raising of the royal army in the west midlands, c. 1072. Even the discredited Aethelric, the deposed bishop of Selsey, was wheeled on at Penenden Heath to 'declare and expound the ancient practice of the laws'.[20]

Like the great secular magnates, Anglo-Norman bishops tended to be recruited from the king–duke's immediate circle. Nearly all were of high birth. In an exchange (reported by William of Malmesbury) between the king and Bishop Walkelin of Winchester, the bishop said, 'Lord, I know that you have many clerks and chaplains to promote.' Many had indeed been royal chaplains, with all the spiritual and bureaucratic experience that implied, or, like Thomas of York, they had served in the household of prelates such as Odo of Bayeux. Three, Osbern, who became bishop of Exeter in 1072, Peter, bishop of Lichfield (appointed in the same year) and Robert, bishop of Hereford in 1079, had been royal chaplains at Edward's court. Others had been monks and scholars in the great monasteries of Normandy, notably Bec but also Fécamp. Some, like Remigius of Dorchester, were lawyers. The new abbots, too, were royal nominees, and though William I might take advice in the appointment the responsibility remained primarily his. Lanfranc probably had some influence. His nephew, Paul, became abbot of St Albans, his chaplain, Walter, abbot of Evesham. Serlo, a monk of Mont-St-Michel, was sent in 1072 to rule Gloucester, which then contained a mere two monks and eight novices, at the suggestion of Osmund, bishop of Salisbury. Other abbots might be freely transferred. The English abbot of Malmesbury, Brihtric, was sent to Burton; his Norman replacement, Turold, was soon moved to Peterborough, where his warlike talents could be better employed in 'pacifying' the fenlands.

William Rufus continued the appointing policy of his father. Vacancies were left unfilled for longer, and there were a few more blatant examples of simony – Herbert Losinga made a notorious purchase of Thetford, and Ranulf Flambard of Durham – but paradoxically, William's worst appointment was to make a saint, Anselm, archbishop of Canterbury. For the most part nominees were drawn from the royal chapel and were of proven administrative ability. There was less necessity to fill abbacies than bishoprics, since abbots generally played a lesser role in secular government, and Rufus kept abbatial revenues in his own hands for as long as he could and then tried to get a good price for them, but the appointments when made were neither outstanding nor scandalous.[21]

William I's and Rufus's clerical appointments were, for the most part, successful. Above all they were conspicuously loyal. No prelate joined Odo of Bayeux in disgrace in 1082, and in the 1088 rebellion, the greatest threat to their authority that either king had to face, only one Anglo-Norman bishop, William of St Calais of Durham, joined his Norman episcopal colleagues, Odo and Geoffrey of Coutances, in support of Duke Robert. William had initially supported Rufus in the north but his unexpected defection led to his dispossession and trial in the royal court, as a lay baron who had broken his oath of fealty. In spite of all his skilful efforts to be tried by canon law, and his appeal to Rome, he was finally broken – and he was broken primarily because none of the bishops, and in particular Lanfranc, would support him. Episcopal loyalty to the crown overrode their collegial loyalty.

The Organisation and Structure of the Anglo-Norman Church

The organisational framework of the Church in England, as it was to remain into modern times, was largely a product of the second half of the eleventh century. These years saw the creation of the parish as the basic unit of spiritual administration, the emergence of the archdeacon as leading diocesan official and the establishment of territorial archdeaconries, and the reordering of many English dioceses. The implications of these changes for ecclesiastical government and discipline were considerable and far-reaching. How far they were a consequence of the Conquest or merely contemporaneous with it is harder to determine.

(a) CATHEDRALS AND THEIR ORGANISATION

For centuries before the Conquest the English Church had been structured by dioceses; bishops had played a crucial role in both ecclesiastical and secular affairs; law codes recognised their cathedrals as the highest rank of minsters. By contrast with their counterparts in northern France, in general they had suffered less at the hands of the Vikings. Their organisation reveals considerable variations.[22] Many followed an arrangement common in north-western Europe since the ninth century, whereby the cathedral clergy lived communally, as they did at London or York, and followed a canonical rule, typically that of Chrodegang of Metz. Others, however, were highly unusual in this European context in being monastic cathedrals, as at Winchester or Canterbury, where the bishop had a dual function as diocesan ruler and head of his monastery. Post-Conquest developments followed both these tracks, with no central policy being imposed; rather, change or continuity were determined by individual bishops.

The ecclesiastical revival in Normandy had led to the restructuring of cathedral chapters, most notably at Bayeux and Rouen. These chapters were to provide many of the personnel for cathedrals across the Channel, and it is hardly surprising to find customs current in Normandy transplanted to England. At Salisbury, York and Lincoln, new Norman bishops carried through reforms that borrowed both liturgical customs and an organisational framework from Norman models. The fullest account of these changes is found in Hugh the Chanter's account of Thomas of York's archiepiscopate.[23] Because of the post-Conquest devastation at York, Thomas had a free hand. He introduced cathedral officers, such as the precentor and dean, and canons functioned as the administrative staff of both cathedral and diocese. Other reforms included the rebuilding of the dormitory and refectory. These measures suggest a continuance of the old communal life-style, but shortly afterwards he provided prebends, on the pattern common in northern France in the late eleventh century, for the individual canons who now lived in houses in the close. Sometimes canons were married; as were as many as a third of the chapter of St Paul's, London.[24] Eilaf, the grandfather of Ailred of Rievaulx, and treasurer of Durham before it was transformed into a monastic cathedral, was one of a dynasty of high-ranking clerics in the north. Though Eilaf was of native birth, there is considerable evidence that a substantial proportion of these cathedral chapters were Normans; perhaps related, or otherwise connected, to the bishop; perhaps nominees of the king.

Of the four monastic cathedrals, three were unchanged. At Wulfstan's Worcester this is hardly surprising, but at Winchester the new Norman bishop, Walkelin, who was not a monk and was unused to this organisational phenonomen, attempted to reverse the century-old reform, which had imposed monks at the Old Minster and expelled the canons. He may have been prompted in this by a distrust of the English monks, he may have regarded the tenth-century customs as aberrant, in any event the scheme was abandoned and the monastery survived in amity with its new master. By contrast, Lanfranc *was* a monk, and though unused to the arrangements at Canterbury, soon, if not immediately, welcomed them. But at Sherborne there were changes. The transfer of the see to Salisbury enabled Bishop Osmund, a secular canon, to reshape the community as a secular chapter. But some new monastic chapters were also created after the Conquest, seemingly running against the pattern in western Europe as a whole. At Rochester, monks were installed by Lanfranc and their bishop, Gundulf, formerly a colleague of Lanfranc at Bec; at Durham, the monk, William of St Calais, introduced monks in 1083, though his predecessor, Walcher, a Lotharingian clerk, may also have contemplated this transition; both followed the customs of Lanfranc's Canterbury. At Norwich, the monk, Herbert Losinga, transformed the community in 1100. Elsewhere change took place as much for economic as spiritual reasons. John of Tours, bishop of Wells, where there had been a flourishing secular community under his predecessor, Giso, moved the community to the abbey at Bath, and in so doing caused considerable distress to the canons. A similar change occurred when the bishop of Lichfield moved to Coventry abbey, after an abortive attempt to settle at Chester. In these cases, then, as at Salisbury, a change of site was accompanied by a change in organisation. If any pattern to these arrangements does emerge it is that they generally reflect the background of the new bishops. Clerks from Rouen or Bayeux normally preferred secular chapters, monks (notably Lanfranc) saw advantages in the structure of the monastic cathedral. Even the ex-monk, Remigius, who ultimately modelled Lincoln on Rouen, seems initially to have planned for a monastic cathedral.

(b) New Dioceses for New Bishops

Remigius was in many ways an archetypical episcopal appointment. A monk of the ducal monastery of Fécamp, Remigius accompanied the Norman invasion in 1066, which he supported with knights and/or a ship; the following year he was rewarded with the first available bishopric, Dorchester, made vacant by the death of Wulfwig. There was more than a whiff of simony in the appointment, and his problems were compounded by his consecration by Stigand. Such behaviour troubled the pope, it could be overlooked by the more pragmatic king. Lanfranc spoke for Remigius at Rome and he was pardoned. Shortly afterwards, probably in late 1072 or early 1073, William issued a writ transferring the see of Dorchester to Lincoln.[25] This was the first of such moves by the Normans, but they were not quite unknown in England. There was good conciliar precedent, and in 1050 the see of Crediton had been moved to Exeter. It is possible that this policy had been discussed first at the Council at Winchester in 1070, and decided at the Winchester and Windsor Councils of 1072. Certainly the move made much sense. In addition to the disciplinary and organisational advantages of having the bishop's headquarters in a large administrative and commercial centre, there were political and military considerations. Dorchester, the headquarters of the second largest English diocese, lay at the diocese's southern edge; Lincoln was over a hundred miles to the north, though still in the diocese.[26] It had been a target of the Danes in 1068 and William had already built a castle there. Strategically it was vital to the security of the north and midlands, a loyal prelate like Remigius could be far more effective in the defence of the realm on a secure hilltop than in Thames-side Dorchester. The Lincoln transfer was a model for others. The Council of London (1075) gave authority for Bishops Herman to move from Sherborne to Salisbury, Stigand from Selsey to Chichester, and Peter from Lichfield to Chester. Bishop Herfast had already moved from Elmham to Thetford: in 1094 his successor, Herbert Losinga, moved again, to Norwich. These moves have features in common. The new sites were all flourishing urban communities, and above all they were defensible. The strategic significance of Chester, in particular, was as great as Lincoln's. This policy was a response to military needs as much as to contemporary ecclesiastical good practice. Such moves came expensive; new cathedral churches had to be built, urban property had to be acquired, and endowments augmented. This could not have been possible without active royal support, but·in the creation of the new sees the secular programme of William converged with the organisational needs of the English Church.

(c) THE ARCHDEACON

The refashioning of the dioceses was accompanied by changes within the diocesan structure. Within a century of the Conquest, the archdeacon was the lynchpin of diocesan discipline; throughout the Middle Ages and beyond, a frequent butt of criticism and satire. Though the post was known at ninth-century Canterbury, thereafter evidence for the Anglo-Saxon archdeacon is very thin, and most significantly, he was not attached to a territorial unit, the archdeaconry. In contrast, this official was already in place in Norman dioceses, and in at least one instance had a territorial responsibility.[27] By the early 1070s archdeacons were found in several English dioceses: by 1089 they were almost universal. Seven archdeacons served under Bishop Remigius of Lincoln (d. 1092): these had responsibility for territorial archdeaconries, which seem to have been largely defined by shire boundaries, and a similar division was probably instituted at York by Archbishop Thomas I.

The archdeacon's chief role was to apply discipline within the diocese and to supervise its temporal administration: to function, in other words, as the bishop's deputy. He is therefore one expression of the general tightening of ecclesiastical good order apparent throughout western Europe at this time, and his introduction parallels, and slightly precedes, the rationalisation of other administrative offices in cathedral chapters.

(d) CHURCH COURTS AND DIOCESAN SYNODS

The archdeacon soon came to preside over diocesan courts, a role which more than any other attracted obloquy. The origin of these courts is obscure and contentious, and in particular the role of the Conqueror in their creation is debated.[28] Sometime between 1072 and 1085, and perhaps around the time of the Council of Winchester in 1076, William issued an ordinance forbidding bishops and archdeacons from hearing episcopal pleas in hundredal courts, and legislating for episcopal courts free of all lay interference. These would hear all cases involving issues of canon law. But how radical was this legislation? Ecclesiastical cases were only forbidden in the hundred court; in the shire court such pleas continued to be heard into the twelfth century. William's prohibition may have been directed against longstanding lay interference in church affairs, and the consequent diversion of fines to secular hands, at a very local level. Synods (or episcopal courts), on the other hand, were nothing new in either the English or Norman Church, though their organisation was not to be fully articulated for several generations. William's ordinance, and the edicts of the 1080 Council of Lillebonne (Normandy) with which it has often been compared, indicate the shifting balance of power between ecclesiastical and secular jurisdictions. Partly a response to growing ecclesiastical demands for autonomy, partly a revision of existing Anglo-Saxon legal practice, while at the same time reflecting contemporary Norman views on the role of the bishop in his diocese, it was a typical compromise measure. On one specific issue the reformers won. Trial by ordeal was firmly taken from the sheriff's to the bishop's control. Generally, however, shire court and synod for long operated in parallel: relations between Church and secular authority were still predicated upon a close working relationship between sheriff and bishop. Wulfstan of Worcester continued to be present at the shire court, to listen carefully during discussion of ecclesiastical matters, and to fall asleep when secular affairs were considered.[29]

The ordinance did provide a judicial space in which the synods could expand their competence. Just as papal synods were intended as sounding boards for papal policy, to reflect back reformist ideas via the bishops to the dioceses, so episcopal synods were intended to provide an opportunity for the bishop to transmit his authority to his clergy. Lanfranc ordered regular synods to be held in each diocese. Symeon of Durham records how Earl Waltheof and Bishop Walcher of Durham jointly presided at such a meeting – a useful reminder that laymen still 'interfered' in ecclesiastical meetings – and though the earliest account of such a meeting to survive, in which Bishop Wulfstan allegedly recounted how he had held a synod for his diocese in the crypt of his newly-built cathedral in 1092, is probably a twelfth-century forgery it is not inconceivable that a diocesan assembly was held at this time.[30]

(e) THE PARISH CHURCH AND PARISH PRIEST

In its concern with the jurisdictional rights of local churches the synod of Worcester reflected an issue of fundamental importance in the Anglo-Norman Church. The Norman Conquest coincided with what was probably the most important change in the organisation of the English Church between the Conversion and the present century: the emergence of the parish.[31] The old ecclesiastical structure, based upon the mother church, or minster (sometimes aided by a number of subordinate chapels), serving a large *parrochia* (large units of local ecclesiastical organisation, often ten times as extensive as a modern parish), was breaking down, and a new order was emerging, of independent churches with smaller areas of jurisdiction, the parish, which was often, though far from always, coterminous with the village. This process of transition was prolonged, and was not to be complete till at least the end of the twelfth century, while vestiges of the old system would survive for centuries more. As in so many other areas, however, it is difficult to determine how far the change was directly hastened or influenced by the new regime. Some minsters lost heavily as a result of the Conquest. Their endowments were frequently appropriated – Robert of Mortain did particularly well out of the Cornish minsters; some were subsumed into new monastic foundations or cathedrals; others found the greater part of their tithes granted to Norman monasteries, while yet more suffered from new church foundations within their *parrochia*, as new lords disrupted old patterns by erecting manorial churches in which they installed priests, just as their thegnly predecessors had done. Wulfstan of Worcester is the most famous, but certainly not the only, bishop or abbot to have built new churches on his own demesne and to have encouraged their building, several of which he is said to have consecrated, by lords in his diocese. The fate of the old minsters varied from case to case. The rights of mother churches that did survive were frequently protected by Anglo-Norman kings. Others were patronised by Norman lords – though they were frequently later transformed into monasteries – as happened at Daventry, which became a Cluniac priory in 1108.[32] Some great magnates, like Roger, earl of Shrewsbury, might use some of the minsters on their lands to support household clerks.

Before the Conquest the often well-endowed mother churches had frequently been used to reward royal or episcopal clerks: this practice continued. The royal clerk, Regenbald, retained his office and his churches, such as Cirencester and Milborne Port, where he was responsible for a lavish rebuilding; otherwise nothing changed.[33] Some Norman clerks did enrich themselves significantly. Ranulf Flambard acquired the mother church of Christchurch (Hampshire) *c.*1087. He drastically reduced the number of canons at this collegiate church, appropriated its tithes and much other revenue, dispersed the remaining canons from their conventual buildings, and converted the church into a very wealthy living for his own advantage, leaving it served only by hired chaplains.[34]

Domesday Book records around 2000 churches, a figure which rises to about 2500 if places where a priest (but not a church) is mentioned are added.[35] These churches range in status from the largest minsters to the smallest manorial or even field chapel, but they represent only a fraction, and probably a small one, of the number of churches that are known to have existed at this time. By the end of the eleventh century there were nearly as many parishes in Kent as in the nineteenth century, their rapid increase after the Conquest a consequence of Lanfranc's reforms, as he replaced the old minster system.[36] The eleventh and twelfth centuries saw an unparalleled surge in church building in England; but did village church building quicken after the Conquest? Did manorial lords feel the need to build bigger and better churches than those of their predecessors, just as did the new Norman bishops and abbots? Any assessment is made more difficult by the fact that it is far from easy to date these minor churches on stylistic grounds. Pre- Conquest churches sometimes show Norman Romanesque influence, many so-called 'Anglo-Saxon' churches were built in the decades after 1066 by native masons.[37] There is certainly clear evidence of considerable church-building before the Conquest. In 1056 Bishop Ealdred of Worcester dedicated a church that Earl Odda had built on his estate in Deerhurst (Gloucestershire) in memory of his brother; the ruined church at Kirkdale (North Riding, Yorkshire) was bought and rebuilt by a local thegn, Orm, in the time of Earl Tostig (1055–65). Nor was this dynamic confined to England; in the diocese of Llandaff the (English) bishop, Herewald, was busy consecrating new 'estate' churches. Yet undoubtedly many village churches were built, or rebuilt, in the Conquest generation. Domesday mentions a number of 'new' churches, and one famous passage tells how the oxen of a group of Worcestershire manors were being used to 'carry stone to the church', while other sources refer to the rebuilding of wooden churches – of which only one example, that of Greensted in Essex, survives. There might be several incentives to build or rebuild. An expanding population might necessitate the enlargement of an existing church or the provision of a new one, as certainly happened at Thorney in Suffolk. Where a village comprised two or more manors, each lord might desire his 'own' church, though sometimes, as at Kingston Bagpuize (Oxfordshire), two lords might cooperate to build a church. Moreover, the momentum to build 'private' churches probably increased. While churches continued to be regarded as manorial appurtenances, tenurial readjustments consequent upon the Norman settlement may have led to the erection of new churches on newly created estates. Several post-Conquest church-builders are known to have been native, thegnly survivors: if this largely dispossessed class was still active, then it is most likely that Norman settlers, from the knights up, were also diligent, allowing William of Malmesbury to write, with pardonable exaggeration, 'with their arrival the Normans breathed new life into religious standards . . . so that now you may see in every village, town and city churches and monasteries rising in a new style of architecture'. The Conquest, then, may have acted as a catalyst to church-building at a parochial level, but the changes in local ecclesiastical organisation mentioned above, which were primarily responsible for this growth, owed little to the Normans. Nor did the newcomers interfere greatly with the personnel of most of these churches.

For several generations after 1066 the great majority of parish priests continued to be of English descent.[38] Their status varied according to many factors, though their role in the collecting of data for Domesday suggests that they were regarded with some respect in the village community. Typically a village priest might have had a villein's holding, though priests with a hide of land, or even more, were not uncommon. Equally, on some manors, they are listed with *servi* ('slaves'), and sometimes explicitly stated to be landless. They were often married, passing on their benefice to a son, and in spite of all attempts of Rome and the English episcopate to enforce celibacy, a married parish priest was probably the norm until well into the twelfth century.[39] Little is known of their educational attainments. It was usually fairly rudimentary; attempts had already been made early in the eleventh century, by Archbishop Wulfstan of York and Abbot Aelfric of Eynsham, to raise standards. Yet there were clearly conscientious and moderately learned priests. As a young boy, Orderic Vitalis was taught by his parish priest in Shropshire, before he was sent to St Evroul, and it was at this level that vernacular culture was most likely to have been transmitted in the late eleventh and twelfth centuries.

The Cloister and the Conquest

Though the Anglo-Saxon Chronicle praises King William's and Archbishop Lanfranc's support of monasticism in England, the monastic chroniclers are in general agreement that the Conquest was a devastating disaster.[40] In particular, they complain at the seizure of lands and treasure, extortionate taxes, and the alienation of their property to relatives or hangers-on of new abbots. That there were considerable depredations is clear from Domesday and other sources. Some lands passed to the hands of Norman abbeys but the majority was taken by secular lords, the new sheriffs, like Urse of Worcester or Picot of Cambridge, being the most notorious despoilers.[41] Chroniclers also indicate that treasures of all sorts were shipped to Normandy. How far these seizures were counterbalanced by later generosity is a moot point, certainly Anglo-Norman lords are soon discovered as modest patrons of English houses. Moreover, we should remember that the Normans were not uniquely greedy; Harold's own reputation at many abbeys was as an arch-predator, while many of the great land pleas of post-Conquest England, notably at Penenden Heath, related to on-going struggles initiated a generation or more before 1066.[42] Neither was disorder in the king's interest; loss of monastic lands, like the despoliation of native lords, created a climate for rebellion. So writs were issued not only to protect loyal abbeys, like Bury St Edmunds under its French abbot, Baldwin, but more solidly English houses like Chertsey.

Monks also complained at the granting of estates to the laity, particularly by abbots favouring their kin, as happened at St Albans, even though, at the same time, some native abbots preserved and increased their abbey's estates. The *Gesta Abbatum* ruefully recalls how St Albans lost a manor held by a 'lowly Englishman', whom Abbot Paul 'despised', to Aethelsige, abbot of Ramsey, 'a most dear friend to his house and race'. The maintenance of military households was costly and disruptive, as at Abingdon or Worcester; it could have tragic consequences, as it did at Glastonbury in 1083, when the Norman abbot used his soldiers to shoot down the abbey's English monks who were protesting at his imposition of new liturgical practices. How far the maintenance of soldiers, in the household or on landed estates, was a response to the formal and novel imposition of *servitia debita* remains controversial, and is an element in the wider issue of Anglo-Norman feudalism; it has recently been argued that there is no contemporary evidence for such imposition by the Conqueror, and that quotas such as that recorded for Evesham, perhaps in 1072 but conceivably earlier, were already in place before 1066.[43] Whether or not the *servitia* were a post-Conquest innovation, it is probable that the Norman kings at least modified quotas, if they did not impose them *ab initio*, and the level of knight service demanded was determined as much by political as economic or military factors: at some houses it may have been punitive, at others the quota may have been fixed according to the scale of the abbey's pre-existing military household, while elsewhere the specific defensive needs of the region were probably a prime consideration. What is clear is that there was no correlation between the service demanded and the wealth of the community, and some houses may well have escaped relatively lightly through the king's favour, just as, before the Conquest, some monasteries had profited from beneficial hidation. The ensuing degree of tenurial disruption doubtless varied, but the experience of Abingdon and Bury St Edmunds is perhaps typical. Here lands held by thegns killed in the Conquest were granted to the abbey's Norman knights. At Bury these lands had first to be surrendered to the king, an indication (confirmed by other Bury charters) of the crown's direct interference in the tenurial structure.[44]

These changes were external, affecting the monasteries' economy. Within the cloister changes, and reforms, were more modulated and did not progress at an even rate, much depending on the attitude of the abbot or monastic bishop. How much racial tension existed in the post-Conquest communities is uncertain. Though the numbers of monks in many houses increased, it is hard to ascertain if they were recruited from the native or Norman population. There does, however, in general seem to have been little colonisation below the level of abbot or prior, except in the instance of new foundations; Shrewsbury was colonised by monks from Sées, Chester from Bec. In Wales, Brecon priory was colonised from Battle, and Monmouth by Breton monks established by the house's Breton founder. At Christ Church, Canterbury, Lanfranc imported a few monks from Bec to aid his reform of the house. These he intended for promotion, either at Canterbury itself, where all the priors till 1128 were non-native, or elsewhere, Gilbert Crispin, for example, becoming abbot of Westminster. The *Gesta Abbatum* records that at St Albans Richard was elected abbot after a power struggle had been resolved in the house between the Normans, who now 'increasing in numbers grew stronger', and the English monks, who were 'now growing old and fewer'.

It was at the frontier where Norman abbot met English monk that hostility was most likely. Lanfranc himself wrote of his communication problems, which he alleged increased his reluctance to assume office at Canterbury, and there is clear evidence from Eadmer that incomers and the native community could neither literally nor metaphorically understand each other, a *modus vivendi* at Canterbury only being established by a miracle, in 1076, whereby a 'mad' English monk was cured, an event which brought about the conversion of his ill-disciplined compatriots.[45] That this miracle focuses on inability to communicate, either between English and Normans, or between the speechless monk and his fellows, is surely reflective of racial tensions within the community. More serious problems were encountered at St Augustine's abbey, just across the road from Christ Church, where Lanfranc appointed Wido, one of his own monks, to the abbacy on Abbot Scotland's death. Most of the community (led by the English prior) refused to accept the nominee. Resistance was protracted and only died down after the ringleaders had either been imprisoned or transferred to other abbeys, including Christ Church. However, this did not prevent further unrest and a plot to kill the new abbot. Even after this had been scotched and the plotter punished and expelled, trouble flared again following Lanfranc's death. The monks, in alliance with the townspeople, rose in rebellion, a violent riot ensued, the abbot fled to Christ Church, and ecclesiastical order was only restored by bishops Walkelin and Gundulf, while the burgesses were severely punished by royal justices. However, this episode involved more than racial disharmony. Wido's predecessor, Scotland, was himself a monk of Mont-St-Michel, brought over to reform the house. His arrival, even though it was accompanied by rapacious kin, occasioned no divisions; his rule was prosperous and trouble-free, he rebuilt the church, built up the library, and reorganised the estates.[46] To explain Wido's problems we should rather look to deep-seated rivalries between Christ Church and St Augustine's, and in particular at resentment towards an imposed abbot, and unrest within the city, which fused with some racial tension to create an explosion.

To a considerable extent the English monks were cushioned from the calamities affecting their kinsfolk in the world, but they still felt keenly their exclusion from power and their communities' corporate loss. Though resentment occasionally led to violence (as at Glastonbury), more positively, as Professor Southern has so clearly showed, this alienation provided the dynamic for the post-Conquest monks' greatest achievement, historical writing.[47] Monks lamented their abbeys' losses; they defended, wrote down, and sometimes forged, their customs; they transcribed charters, like Hemming at Worcester, who wrote, at Bishop Wulfstan's order, to preserve a record of what belonged to the church and what had been seized, by Danes, royal exactions, but above all by Normans. By preserving the past, continuity was maintained and the Norman ravages could be placed in a more universal, teleological context. At Peterborough, Canterbury and Worcester the Anglo-Saxon Chronicle was continued. This most famous text was preserved in the vernacular, while Latin versions were also transmitted, especially from Worcester. This community's contacts with Orderic Vitalis, Eadmer, and Symeon of Durham ensured the survival of a native historiography, an ideology of continuity to set against the triumphalism of the conquerors' own historians.

Above all, continuity was preserved by the saints.[48] For Norman abbots to denigrate native saints could be counter- productive. The saints still had power to protect their own and punish plunderers, and were perhaps needed more than ever in the political uncertainties of late-eleventh-century England. In Susan Ridyard's revealing phrase, Norman churchmen were ready to make 'the heroes of the past serve the politics of the present'. The miracles of Cuthbert and Edmund were used as propaganda at Durham and Bury to preserve the monks' patrimony. Moreover, if Norman abbots denied the sanctity of Anglo-Saxon predecessors, pilgrims, too, would be denied, along with the income they generated. This factor may have lain behind the rather unexpected enthusiasm of Abbot Turold in reclaiming for Peterborough the relics of St Oswald, from Ramsey, which had appropriated them, and may also account for the fierce dispute between St Augustine's and St Gregory's, Canterbury (the latter a foundation of Lanfranc's), over possession of the relics of St Mildrith. Abbot Walter of Evesham was aware of the revenue-raising potential of the relics of St Egwin, which he sent around the country when he was rebuilding his abbey church. In many instances, relics of English saints were translated with great honour into the new churches of Anglo-Norman England, as happened, for instance, at St Augustine's, Canterbury, Winchester and Durham. Not surprisingly, Anglo-Norman hagiographers were concerned to rewrite lives of Anglo-Saxon saints for a new audience. Though scribes now wrote in Latin, they frequently told of English saints. At Christ Church, Canterbury, Eadmer and Osbern, both native monks, kept their houses' hagiographic tradition alive. The Flemish monk, Goscelin of St Bertin, had come to England with Bishop Herman before the Conquest and continued till his death an indefatigable hagiographer of English saints. He produced a life of Edith, founder of Wilton, for the nuns there, shrewdly dedicated to Lanfranc; he dedicated a life of Wulfhilde of Barking to Bishop Maurice of London; while at St Augustine's, he and a Poitevin monk, Reginald, wrote a series of lives and poems on English, and particularly Kentish, saints. At Worcester, Coleman wrote an Anglo-Saxon life of Wulfstan shortly after the bishop's death. But knowledge of the vernacular was seemingly fading – soon afterwards the monks asked William of Malmesbury, himself the most learned of the preservers of native monastic tradition, for a Latin translation. Similarly at St Augustine's, Canterbury, the 'F' version of the Anglo-Saxon Chronicle was written bilingually in Latin and English, while even the 'E' version at Peterborough has Latin interpolations. The counterpoint of continuity and change grew ever more complex.

There is no clearer indication of the subtleties of change within the cloister than a comparison of post-Conquest liturgical practices at three English Benedictine abbeys.[49] At Glastonbury, Abbot Thurstan, insensitive to native traditions, introduced the liturgy of Fécamp. This novel practice sparked the monks' rebellion of 1083, which left three of the community dead and led to Thurstan's own removal from office. At Christ Church, Canterbury, Lanfranc provided a new liturgy, based on those of Bec, but also drawing heavily on Cluniac customs. Within a short time it had been adopted at a number of other leading houses, including St Albans, Durham and Westminister. The liturgy (and the 'Monastic Constitutions' in which it is contained) reflected Lanfranc's desire to bring the English Church (and particularly its monasteries) into line with Norman and Cluniac best practice. But at Winchester the old liturgy of the *Regularis Concordia,* compiled a hundred years earlier, survived unchanged. Winchester proclaimed continuity. Here William was to rebuild the old palace of the Wessex kings, here he continued to wear his crown. The rebuilt cathedral housed the bones of the Anglo-Saxon kings in honour, Swithun was given a new shrine, and the church was now rededicated to him, as well as to Peter and Paul.

Within the monasteries (and cathedrals) of post-Conquest England, then, things are never quite as they seem. In the *scriptoria,* while Latin increasingly replaced the vernacular and scripts took on a Norman tinge, some legal business continued to be recorded in English; the Anglo-Saxon annals were maintained at Canterbury (as well as at Peterborough), seemingly under the patronage of the French prior, Ernulf. As bishop of Rochester, Ernulf may also have sponsored the *Textus Roffensis,* with its substantial collection of Old English law.[50] Bishop Osbern of Exeter, for all that he was William fitzOsbern's brother, was said to favour English rather than Norman customs. One final example must suffice. At Durham, monks led by the Norman bishop, William de St Calais, replaced secular clerks in 1083. At first sight this appears a straightforward act of Norman-imposed reform. But the clerks' expulsion mirrored events at Winchester more than a century before; the monks who entered came from Jarrow and Wearmouth, the majority were from southern England, the same monastic colonists of the north who had left

Evesham in the late 1070s to re-found Whitby. Their saint was Cuthbert, their historical writings proclaimed his authority and miracles against the ravages not only of the Normans but of earlier rulers who did not respect the northern heritage.

Anglo-Norman lords, wishing to insure their souls and perhaps make restitution for the slaughter of conquest, as the Penitential of Erminfrid enjoined, had several options.[51] They could endow abbeys at home, and most, if not all, of the Norman monasteries, and a few houses outside the duchy, such as St Denis, outside Paris, or Charroux in Poitou, profited directly from conquest, by grants of lands and churches in England.[52] They might found small communities on their English estates, the 'alien priories', subject to, and usually staffed by, monks from the Norman mother-house, as at Wilmington (Sussex), where Grestain established a small community through the generosity of its patron, Robert of Mortain. Many more grants of English property to Norman houses remained mere cells, small estates administered by one or two monks from the Norman abbey. A few of the greatest magnates founded independent abbeys, such as at Shrewsbury or Chester, which, though they recruited monks from Norman houses, were autonomous Benedictine communities. The king's own foundation, at Battle, was obviously established with a dual message: as a thank-offering for God-given victory, and as a penitential gesture.[53] It is self-evidently 'an abbey of the conquerors' as none other is, though it is tempting to see Bernard de Neufmarché's foundation, in newly-conquered Wales, of Brecon priory, a dependency of Battle, as a similar statement of victory. Other lords founded Cluniac priories.[54] While there were no such priories in Normandy at this time, Cluniac customs had been of wide influence in the duchy since the beginning of the century. The first Cluniac house in England was that of Lewes (Sussex), founded by William de Warenne in 1077; other magnates, such as Roger of Shrewsbury and William de Mortain, followed. By 1100 there were eight Cluniac priories in England. Of these, one, Bermondsey, was established by a rich Londoner, Ailwin Cild, with the assistance of William Rufus; the remainder were founded by Norman settlers. Frequently Cluniac priories were sited close to the castles of their founders, and their monks may have been expected to provide spiritual, and perhaps administrative, services for their patrons. The foundation of a Cluniac house gave a Norman lord an opportunity to establish a community unassociated with native English monasticism, while it was, at the same time, also free of constitutional ties with Norman houses.

Yet some Norman lords *were* patrons of existing English houses. Recent work, for example, has shown how lesser Norman lords soon became benefactors of Shaftesbury nunnery and St Peter's, Gloucester.[55] Also a number of the greater English houses, like St Albans, were establishing their own daughter houses through the generosity of Anglo-Norman benefactors, suggesting that they, at least in part, were beginning to identify with native monastic tradition. Within two generations, moreover, most Anglo-Norman magnates were choosing to be buried in English monasteries.[56] Nor is this to be wondered at. Patronage of, and burial in, English monasteries not only argues for a growing cultural and spiritual assimilation of the colonists, but in so doing the patrons made a statement of both continuity and legitimacy. Nowhere is this assimilation better illustrated than in the so-called 'northern revival', started by a Norman knight, Reinfrid, who had observed the 'harrying of the north' and who had then become a monk at English Evesham, with an English fellow-monk, and the English prior of Winchcombe. This trio, influenced by the northern native tradition, that went back to Bede and beyond, were responsible for the re-foundation of Jarrow and Monkwearmouth and the establishment of the monastic community at Durham, while Reinfrid went on to re-found Whitby with the patronage of William de Perci. One of their recruits, Turgot, an Anglo-Saxon who had experienced mixed fortunes after the Conquest, being first imprisoned as a hostage in Lincoln before escaping to Norway, travelled to Durham, where he later became prior, and ended his career as bishop of St Andrews.

Most historians have stressed the 'Normanisation' of the English church, and in particular, English monasteries. The spoliation of native houses, the removal of native ecclesiastical leaders and their replacement by Normans, the introduction of new liturgical practices and the extensive rebuilding of cathedrals, churches and abbeys, the imposition of *servitia*, and the endowment of Norman monasteries with English lands, were real enough. Moreover, Professor le Patourel persuasively argued that monastic implantation was integral to Norman colonisation: 'it was the combination of castle, monastery, and borough, or of two of these elements, that formed one of the chief instruments of Norman colonisation in Britain': a combination that is nowhere better evidenced than at Brecon, occupied by Bernard de Neufmarché since 1093.[57] But at the same time there is, as argued above, considerable evidence to show that by 1100 the English church was truly an amalgamation of English and Norman culture. English saints still protected their churches, English monasteries attracted lands from the colonists for whom they frequently provided mausolea, English and Norman reformers collaborated in the monastic revival of northern England.

8

ANGLO-NORMAN ENGLAND

Finally, and most fundamentally, how far was Britain Normanised by 1100, and conversely, to what extent was Normandy anglicised? In what is probably the most ranging and influential analysis of the Normans in medieval western Europe, Professor le Patourel presented a 'Norman Empire'.[1] He argued that notwithstanding the fact that the Norman state was not akin to the Roman Empire of the past, or its eleventh-century reincarnations – though this did not prevent Norman chroniclers comparing Duke William favourably with Julius Caesar – it did possess imperial characteristics. This 'empire' had a fundamental though fragile unity, which was fractured, once between 1087 and 1106 and again, for ever, in 1135, to be replaced a generation later by the 'Angevin Empire'.[2] The indivisibility of Normandy and England after the Conquest is central to le Patourel's analysis; these states lay at the empire's core, but the Anglo-Norman kings also had territorial and perhaps 'imperial' ambitions elsewhere on both sides of the Channel, in Maine, Brittany, Wales, Scotland, and even Ireland. In a recent critique of this thesis, Bates has suggested that this model is too simplistic.[3] He argues that the Norman dynamic needs to be seen in the context of a wider expansionism, in which all French principalities needed to participate in order to survive. In the intense rivalries thus generated, unstable frontiers and uncertain supremacies were the norm. These impinged upon, and often determined, politics and policies this side of the Channel. Bates's hypothesis suggests that though there was a degree of assimilation during the reign of Henry I, somewhat paradoxically at a time when the Norman settlement of England (though not of Wales and Scotland) was slowing, even then there is little evidence of a convergence of governmental practice: in other words, the Anglo-Norman 'empire' was essentially the same as its Angevin successor, a congeries of states held together by the person of the king, not by administrative structure.

Yet, even if the le Patourel thesis is abandoned, can we still discern imperial characteristics in post-Conquest Normandy and interpret the conquest of England as a colonial venture? Neither le Patourel nor Bates really address problems of definition, except by inference. This reluctance is hardly surprising, since 'there are so many definitions of colonialism and imperialism as to make the terms almost useless'.[4] It is doubtful if any one definition can embrace the empires of Athens or Rome, Spain in the New World, Napoleon's Europe, Hitler's *Reich*, the Soviet Union and the 'New World Order' of the United States. Moreover, the terms 'imperialism' and 'colonialism', though closely interrelated and sometimes used more or less interchangeably, are not synonymous. Empires cannot exist without colonies, though the control exercised over them may be economic rather than political; colonies may have such autonomy as to make imperial rule little more than theoretical.

A minimal definition of empire would be the extended exercise of power by one state over another. As such, it carries connotations of oppression and exploitation, often economic. Such control would normally include the restriction, or prohibition, of the subject state's autonomy in foreign affairs; interference in its political and judicial processes at a local level; the demand for military service; the confiscation of land, often accompanied by the removal or slaughter of the indigenous population and the introduction of settlers from the imperial power; the levying of some form of tribute, and other expressions of economic exploitation, notably in the control or monopoly of trade. These criteria are themselves very broad, concealing a spectrum of differing practices: compare, for example, the local administrations of British colonial Canada, India and Africa.

These criteria should be tested against the English experience after 1066. There is, however, one fundamental difference between the Norman colonisation of England and many, though not all, imperial settlements. England and Normandy largely shared a common culture. Above all, they were both members of the western Church under the papacy, which was itself at this very time establishing itself as a spiritual empire with an overarching hegemony. Their aristocracy shared a common ethos, expressed, as has been argued above, in very similar military organisations. Moreover, on both sides of the Channel, for all that in England Anglo-Saxon was used extensively as the language of government, Latin stood at the head of the hierarchy of languages. These congruities meant that the cultural affiliation of the subject to the dominant power, often perceived as the fundamental consequence of colonialism, was much less aggressive than in most colonisations. They also meant that it was more difficult to justify the conquest in quite the same moral terms as most colonial ventures, where the subject nation was presented ·as pagan or heretical, as morally, intellectually, or racially 'backward'.

More difficult, but not impossible. Already, it has been argued by Dr Loud, the Normans had a clear conception of themselves as a *gens*, an all-conquering, expansionist race who lorded it over other peoples by their military prowess and cunning.[5] Against these positive virtues were ranged the negative vices of their opponents, the Bretons and English in particular. Yet, it is noteworthy that the Anglo-Norman chroniclers, like Orderic Vitalis and William of Malmesbury, were, if anything, more censorious towards the English than Norman authors, like William of Poitiers, for the former could only explain the English defeat by reference to their moral shortcomings, which brought down God's judgement in the form of the Normans. In this way they contributed as much to the 'Norman – and English – myth' as any, while at the same time they mediated notions of racial supremacy through an interpretation of the Conquest by divine intervention, which enabled them to condemn both the English, for their immorality, and the Normans, for exceeding their brief as agents of God's retribution.

Though the conquest of England was accompanied by substantial alien settlement and the appropriation of territory, there is little evidence (except perhaps in the north) that native tenants were evicted *en masse* to make room for the newcomers. This is not, of course, to deny that many English lords lost all or most of their lands, and that in some instances the peasantry were faced with heavier burdens than before. Moreover, the colonisation was geographically much more wide-ranging than was commonly the practice in imperial ventures, which frequently established enclaves of social, political and military control, while leaving substantial territory in the hands of natives, as happened in much of British India or Spanish America. Certainly the Normans, particularly in the first uncertain generation, established themselves in castles as nodal points of exploitation, and occasionally can be found canalising trade into their own markets, or, by establishing rival centres, causing the decline of older settlements, as happened on the Arun when Arundel took over from the Anglo-Saxon *burh* of Burpham (Sussex), two miles upstream. But burgess rights in towns in Anglo-Norman England were never racially restricted, as they were to be later in some Welsh towns, nor was there mass settlement of the countryside by colonising Norman peasants, as English peasants were to be encouraged to settle in Wales. The fact that Norman settlers could be found right across the country and in the majority of villages ensured their survival, while at the same time making assimilation the more likely.

It has often been pointed out that though economic exploitation of the conquered may have been the prime reason for imperial conquest, in the long run few empires have actually profited from their colonies. That the Norman Conquest was brutal and was accompanied by widespread appropriation of lands and cash cannot be denied. Norman magnates and churches were enriched at the expense of their English counterparts, and the Anglo-Norman kings' war efforts in northern France were largely sustained by English wealth.[6] Indeed, their control of these fiscal resources gave William Rufus and Henry I a decisive edge in their conflicts with Robert Curthose and Louis VI. The Norman kings profited from their new kingdom in three chief ways. First, there was the widespread spoliation of treasure, particularly from churches. This was substantial and deeply-felt by its victims, but it was short-lived and within a generation Norman lords were replacing, to some extent, what had been lost with treasures of their own. Secondly, and much more long-lasting, there was the exploitation of land. As we have seen, the landed wealth of William in particular, but also of his magnates, was increased very significantly. The majority of late-eleventh-century Norman lords built their fortunes on their English, not their Norman, lands: a fact that was crucially to affect their political attitudes until the loss of Normandy in 1204. Finally, there is taxation. Contemporaries stressed the greed of Williams I and II above all else, even if they justified it by reference to the crown's need to pay for military defence. Geld was levied at a very high level, though it has been trenchantly argued that the tributes extorted by Cnut, early in the eleventh century, were of a far higher order.[7] Thus the landed and cash resources of England were largely diverted to the advantage of Normandy, though whether the taxes extorted in geld are exactly analogous to imperial tributes, which symbolised subjection, such as those frequently demanded by Anglo-Saxon kings of the Welsh princes, is debatable.

At the same time, while trade remained largely in the hands of natives, many of whom survived and even prospered after 1066, sometimes by intermarriage with the colonists, local markets were often controlled by a local lord who exacted tolls: some English towns were settled by Norman merchants on a considerable scale, and traders from Caen and Rouen, like Thomas Becket's father, established themselves in London and elsewhere.[8] Trade between England and Normandy almost certainly increased in volume, but there is no evidence that it came close to supplanting the much older links between England and Flanders, and thence to the Rhineland. The Normans never established commercial dominance in England.

But not only was there continuity of trading patterns and to some extent of traders too; a model of colonisation which fails to take account of the continuance in office of a significant number of native administrators is too simplistic. Though some regions may have seen a greater concentration of 'survivors' than others, perhaps because these lands were less attractive to Norman settlers, throughout

England we find sheriffs and others of native stock who came to terms with the new regime and profited in a modest way from it. These men should not be confused with short-term survivors like Maerleswegn, sheriff of Lincoln in the immediate post-1066 period, who soon lost office because of disloyalty to the new order; these were astute trimmers, such as Regenbald, or Aiulf, the chamberlain, sheriff of Dorset and Wiltshire, men whose twelfth-century descendants would be numbered amongst the honorial barons and would found religious houses, as the fitzSweyns did at Monk Bretton (Yorkshire) or William, son of Hacon, at Sixhills (Lincolnshire). And, as we have seen, below the sheriffs a significant number of Englishmen continued as geld collectors and as reeves, as administrators of royal and baronial estates, sometimes themselves farming manors, often at seemingly excessive rents. It is significant, too, that within a few years Englishmen were taking part in the internal colonisation of Britain. Although much of the secondary phase of settlement, particularly in Wales, Scotland, and above all Ireland, was led by Norman families already established in England, it included sizable English (and Flemish) elements, like the English followers of Richard de Granville, a lord from south-west England, established in and around Neath by c.1130.[9]

Orderic Vitalis provides the best-known evidence for integration. English and Normans lived peaceably in the towns; they intermarried; French goods were available in the markets; the natives adopted French fashions. 'Everyone lived contentedly with his neighbour.' Even the king attempted (unsuccessfully) to learn English so that he could be an unbiased judge for all.[10] Yet how much credence should we give to this portrayal of a golden age? Orderic, himself a product of integration, is writing c.1125. By this time assimilation had certainly occurred, and the prevailing historiographical orthodoxy stressed continuity and harmony. But this passage explicitly relates to the period *before* the 1069 rebellions: it is hard to believe that such racial harmony prevailed at this early date; more probably Orderic is both projecting back conditions prevalent in his own day, and seeking to highlight the disorders of 1069–70.

Integration, like colonisation, certainly proceeded at an uneven pace. Recent work on linguistic and cultural changes in post-Conquest urban society suggests both substantial assimilation and the survival of English in the community.[11] But even in towns, where commercial interests perhaps stimulated racial fusion more rapidly than in the countryside, it is hard to generalise. At the new town of Battle, growing up at the foot of the monastery which, more than any other, proclaimed the new order, the majority of burgesses were English, and predominantly local; the Norman-French minority tended to belong to the abbey's administrative staff or to be scions of minor knightly families. There is some evidence to suggest that here, by c.1110, Normans and English were beginning to live side-by-side, perhaps as intermarriage became more widespread.[12] Yet elsewhere there may have been greater divisions. At Southampton there were 65 French immigrants concentrated in the road still called French Street, worshipping in churches dedicated to saints favoured in Normandy – Michael and John. In both Nottingham and Northampton there were new boroughs where property was almost, if not wholly, exclusively in Norman hands, including such great men as Robert of Mortain or Geoffrey of Coutances. Canterbury was a wealthy and populous city, an unparalleled ecclesiastical centre, as well as being within easy access of both London and Normandy, and hence highly attractive to cross-channel settlers. Yet, though there were many immigrants into both the city and, more markedly, its hinterland, onamastic and other evidence argues for a wealthy and self-confident native population gradually absorbing French influences, but never overwhelmed by them.[13]

It has already been suggested that acculturation in Anglo-Norman England was much more muted than in many colonial situations, since in vital respects Normans and English already shared common values. There was probably little distinction in dress; in fashion, particularly that of the English wearing their hair long while the Normans were short-shaven, there are some indications that by the reign of Rufus it was the latter who copied the former rather than *vice versa*.[14] Nor was there an 'imperial' architecture, as seen, for example, in the provincial towns of the Roman Empire or in the British Raj. The impact of the Conquest on the direction of architecture in England is complex, particularly when the larger, more prestigious churches are considered. While some Anglo-Norman churches undoubtedly borrowed features and motifs from Norman models, others used themes found in late Anglo-Saxon architecture.[15] In part this may have been due to the continuing use of native masons, but it may equally have been a conscious decision for continuity on the part of the patrons, the bishops and abbots. But, as we have already seen, not all these prelates were of Norman origin, and those who were Normans had frequently had experience of the culture of other nations. Lanfranc's cathedral at Canterbury, while based on a Norman plan, also has elements found in Italy and the Empire; the transeptual towers of Exeter and the west front of Salisbury (Old Sarum) both owe much to Rhenish models, as do aspects of Anselm's rebuilding at Canterbury.[16] Most interesting is Professor Fernie's suggestion that the York minster created by Archbishop Thomas is self-consciously built to a different design from that of its southern provincial rival.[17] In short, while most Anglo-Normans built big (though we should remember that Edward's Westminster was considerably larger than the two great contemporary ducal abbey churches at Jumièges and Fécamp), they drew their inspiration from many sources: their 'colonial' architecture was no mere restating of familiar models of the home country. The use of Caen building stone for more ambitious building projects has also been seen as an expression of Norman colonial attitudes. Certainly such stone was used, for example, in Lanfranc's rebuilding of Canterbury, but at Battle abbey, where there appeared to be a shortage of stone so that William was prepared to import from Caen, a miraculous discovery of good quality stone nearby made that unnecessary.[18] Barnack stone was used for the rebuilding of many of the Fenland houses, and Henry I issued a writ in favour of Bury St Edmunds obliging Peterborough abbey to allow the monks free passage of Barnack stone.[19]

Fashion and architecture are indicators of acculturation, language is another, perhaps more sensitive. Indeed, much of the evidence relating to cultural assimilation is linguistic. The relationship between the language of government and of administration and political hegemony is a complex one. In the empires of the Ancient

World, legal and governmental texts were seldom translated into the tongues of subject peoples. In the New World, the Spanish language was both an instrument and a symbol of empire. It has recently been observed, in the debate over bilingualism in Wales, that 'societal bilingualism – where all people speak two languages for all occasions – does not exist. Languages do not co-exist; they compete for speakers.' In England, the change from English to Latin as the language of government was more than a matter of administrative convenience – indeed, it may actually have decreased efficiency – but it set up long-lasting cultural resonances. But cultural, and linguistic, change is extremely difficult to calibrate. Undoubtedly it proceeded at different paces in different circumstances. Developments in the cloister were not always matched by those in the market-place, those in the aristocracy were clearly not paralleled amongst the peasantry. Different languages in a multi-lingual culture can be used for different functions. Norman-French was used at court and on the battlefield; Latin, increasingly, in the Church and law (though lawyers probably spoke French in court); English remained the language of the majority of the population. We must also remember that the settlement itself was far from homogeneous: substantial Breton and Flemish immigration added to the linguistic mix. Moreover, the multiplicity of English dialects confused communication between natives from different regions: as late as the end of the twelfth century, Abbot Samson, of Bury St Edmunds, was said to speak a Norfolk dialect. In this new linguistic world it is hardly surprising to find interpreters figuring as modest Domesday lords, for such men were necessary. One, Edric, was a tenant of Bury St Edmunds abbey and may have been retained by the monks for his skills.[20]

Twelfth-century evidence from hagiographical sources suggests that there was a deep linguistic divide between native English speakers and Norman colonisers, which it still required interpreters or divine intervention to bridge.[21] The *Life* of the twelfth-century Somerset anchorite Wulfric of Hazelbury tells how he cured a dumb man so that he was able to speak both English and French, to the annoyance of the English parish priest, who complained that he was unable to understand the (French-speaking) bishop and archdeacon when they came on visitation.[22] Though a few conscientious prelates might attempt to learn, or use, the language of the conquered – the addition of some contemporary English sermons to a Pontifical owned by the bishop of Salisbury in the late-eleventh century is suggestive – few of the lesser clergy could understand their masters.[23] How far bilingualism was common in the higher strata of society is hard to determine. On the one hand, it is likely that many aristocratic children would have had English nurses, on the other, that their training in baronial households and at the royal court would have ensured they were fluent in French. Anglo-Norman, which was itself coming under criticism for its 'barbarity' by the end of the twelfth century, remained the tongue of a largely alien aristocracy. If Normans needed to speak English on occasion, if only to their servants, what of the English? For as long as it remained an indicator of social status, an upwardly mobile English man or woman would require French, but though there is evidence of this in the twelfth century there is none from the generations immediately following the Conquest.

Assimilation and integration could most readily be achieved through intermarriage.[24] Indeed this was probably the channel though which the native language was best transmitted to the new rulers. It is no coincidence, either, that the early twelfth-century chroniclers most sympathetic to native culture were of mixed race. William of Malmesbury claimed impartiality specifically because he carried 'the blood of both races'; Henry of Huntingdon's father was probably a clerical immigrant, whilst the best-documented case of all, Orderic Vitalis, was the son of a clerk of the earl of Shrewsbury and an English mother, who knew no Norman-French till sent to St Evroul at the age of ten. Orderic condemns the Normans for their behaviour towards native women: 'noble maidens were exposed to the insults of low-born soldiers . . . matrons . . . mourned the loss of their loving husbands and almost all their friends, and preferred death to life'.[25] Certainly some women fled to nunneries 'through fear of the French', as a letter of Lanfranc to Bishop Gundulf makes plain. These were allowed to depart if their community accepted that this was their motive. This might indicate that life was now (the letter is dated 1077–1089) returning to normal and that it was now safer for the women to re-enter secular society. It may also be, as Eleanor Searle suggests, that these women were regarded as more useful outside the cloister, where they could be given in marriage to legitimise the settlement, than within it.[26] For marriage also served to validate Norman claims to English lands. Though this practice may have been most widespread at relatively humble levels of society – typically, the Lincolnshire monastic reformer, Gilbert of Sempringham, was the son of an English mother and a knightly tenant of Alfred of Lincoln – intermarriage was also not infrequent amongst the wealthier aristocracy, and Henry I himself married Edith, niece of Edgar *aetheling* and daughter of Malcolm Canmore. The political function of marriage was recognised on both sides of the Channel, and royal sanction of aristocratic marriage was recognised, if not explicitly stated. To ignore a prohibition, as did the earls of Norfolk and Hereford in 1075, could lead to irretrievable disseisin. Where it was licensed, however, it could firmly cement tenurial transfers, oil the transition of power at local levels, and lead to great wealth. Some marriage alliances pre-dated the Conquest; William Malet, who was prominent at Hastings, had an English mother and may have held lands in England prior to 1066. The majority of these marriages occured later, however. Lucy, the English heiress of Bolingbroke, married successively: Ivo Taillebois, Roger fitzGerold, and Ranulf Meschin, earl of Chester; while Robert d'Oilly married the daughter of Wigot of Wallingford, and Geoffrey de la Guèrche obtained Aelgifu and, through her, his estates in Leicestershire.[27] How far the king actively intervened to make these marriages cannot be ascertained, though we know from Domesday that he gave the widow of the English sheriff, Aelfwine, to Richard, 'a young man'.[28] Eleanor Searle has shrewdly observed that the leading survivors of the old English nobility left only heiresses. In other words, they could safely be left in control of their estates, so long as their daughters were married to Normans, who would then assume their lands. Such a policy was less brutal than conquest, it was no less effective.

Yet even if, as most would agree, post-Conquest England and Wales (and, in different measure, Scotland) possessed many colonial characteristics, it does not inevitably follow that there was a

Norman Empire. There certainly was a rhetoric of empire. Contemporary eulogies of William I praised him as Caesar, and Dr English has recently made the interesting suggestion that the crown, which the *Carmen de Hastingae Proelio* describes as having been commissioned for the new king from a Greek goldsmith, is based on Ottonian imperial models.[29] The early Anglo-Norman *laudes* refer to William's *imperium* and hail him as *serenissimus*, an imperial attribute; these *laudes* were probably written in the circle of Archbishop Ealdred of York, who had close ties with the German imperial court. One or two charters also designate William as *basileus* (emperor), but whether we can argue from all this that contemporaries really saw the Anglo-Norman state as an *imperium*, rather than merely ascribing 'unofficial' imperial status to the king, is debatable.[30]

The colonisation of England proceeded along a different course from that pursued in Wales (and later in Ireland). There was never an attempt at territorial demarcation between the races: no area was defined as *pura Anglia*, there were no Englishries. Neither was there anything like the tenth-century Danelaw, an area racially, socially and legally distinct. Nor should we expect it, for by the mid-eleventh century the theoretical unity of the English kingdom was such as to ensure that its conquerors took all or nothing. And here may lie the clue to the emergence of a colonial, but not an imperial, Anglo-Norman society. In 1066 a duke conquered a king. The seizure of England not only brought great wealth and prestige, but the assumption of the crown gave Duke William powers and resources his ancestors could only have dreamt of. The 'colony' of England was in most respects more vital to William's interests than his homeland. This is not to deny that William continued to think of himself as a Norman. He spent far more time in Normandy than in England – though he took good care to defend his new kingdom in person, or through his agents, when it was threatened – and he chose to be buried in his abbey of Caen, not in Westminster or Winchester. But his enhanced power and prestige was grounded in his kingship. And herein lay the most dangerous of the tensions which shot through the Conquest. Ducal prerogative was subsumed in the royal, and, though William I was never styled *rex Normanno-*

rum, he obviously ruled over his Norman subjects in England as fully as over the English. In other words, William's supreme authority was derived from his rule (which he claimed as legitimate, and which was in any case validated by conquest) over the English. The 'colony' was not only wealthier than the 'homeland', it also conveyed more power. This largely defined the new king's relations with his new subjects. Dr Garnett has recently demonstrated that legal distinctions between Normans and English were only short-lived, a consequence of the immediate problems of security after Hastings.[31] Writs and charters addressed to 'French and English' were merely formulaic, and carried no legal connotations of difference. Norman settlers were subject to English laws and to the king of England, who happened to be a Norman.

There has often been an assumption that all the Norman conquerors were colonisers. Their historians were anxious to promote a myth of solidarity amongst an homogeneous aristocracy in support of Duke William in his foreign adventure and eager for reward. Yet, for all their provision of ships and men, it is not hard to detect tensions and debate behind the apparent unanimity. After Hastings, divisions were more intrusive. Not all who fought in 1066 stayed on. Many, perhaps especially the lesser lords, but including such prominent figures as the count of Evreux, were paid off and returned home. Others followed, and though they might have retained small estates in England, these yielded little, and were seemingly little regarded. There were comparatively few genuinely cross-channel magnates. While many had estates in both England and Normandy, few were willing or able to be equally active in both. England (and later, Wales and Scotland too) opened up opportunities for the ambitious of moderate means, above all perhaps for younger sons, like William de Warenne. How much did these think of their homeland? Very few followed the example of the families of Montgomery or Corbet, who named their new *capita* Montgomery (as it is already styled in Domesday) and Cause (Shropshire), after their origins in the Pays de Caux. Rather, those who rooted themselves in England identified themselves more and more with the colony, not the motherland. Here they tended to choose their wives, here increasingly they were buried. If these settlers had a group-solidarity it was based on their claim to have fought at Hastings, to hold their lands *a conquestu* ('by conquest'). In the new land, where the establishment was dominated by *arrivistes* and men rose rapidly by military or administrative service, it was conquest and settlement that validated status, not family origins. On the other hand, there were many Norman lords whose interests in England were minimal or non-existent. The very nature of settlement increased the potential for division. Typically, Norman lands went to the elder, the English to the younger son. Cross-channel tenurial integrity was fractured by inheritance or forfeiture. Between 1087 and 1106 the division of the kingdom from the duchy can only have exacerbated these tendencies. If England was a colony, the colonists, as so often in more recent centuries, discovered different interests from those of the motherland. In these growing political, cultural and political disparities were the faultlines producing future Anglo-Norman disputes that were to recur for generations, and which would ultimately lead to the 'loss of Normandy'.

William's coronation as king of the English inevitably exalted his status in Normandy, but to what extent? The relationship between kings of France and dukes of Normandy had long been subtle, and the nature of the latter's vassalage ambiguous.[32] The fragmentation of Carolingian France and the assumption of royal prerogatives by rulers of the French principalities was suggested in the latter's occasional description as *regna* (kingdoms). Though such a term had no constitutional connotations, it did reflect political realities, which ensured that however much the French kings might wish to treat the Norman dukes as vassals like any other, this was impossible. Only once (1060) did Duke William apparently render homage, and it is far from certain what either side understood by the act.[33] In truth, the implications of homage varied according to the ever-shifting political balance of power to which the performance of homage, of course, in itself contributed. In the everyday government of the duchy, the French king confirmed no charter, imposed no law, though this did not prevent him from meddling in the political affairs of the duchy when opportunity arose. In many respects William's rule in Normandy was already quasi-regal, and within the pre-Conquest duchy even the *laudes regiae*, the ceremonial acclamations of the king, associated his own name with that of the French monarch.[34]

After 1066, though for practical and military reasons England and Normandy had to be regarded as a unity, there is little evidence to suggest that unity had any theoretical underpinning before at least 1100. Now, when the *laudes* were sung at Winchester they proclaimed William as suzerain king, while at Rouen the name of the French king continued to be glorified as before, in association with the duke, but not supplanted by him. Many historians have drawn attention to the Conqueror's double- sided seal.[35] On one side he is shown in majesty, just as was Edward, his predecessor on the English throne; on the other he is shown as a mounted warrior, the very model of a model French lord. There is also a one-sentence inscription, on the 'English' side describing William as king, on the 'French', as 'patron' of the Normans. Though le Patourel argued that this inscription was 'intended to unite the two dignities', it seems, rather, to stress symbolic duality. This is also suggested in the post-Conquest charters. Though they have no fixed diplomatic formula, they almost universally distinguish between William's status as *rex Anglorum* and *princeps Normannorum* – the most usual appellation, though *patronus* and *dux* are also found.

In any discussion of contemporary perceptions of William's kingship and William's self-perception, we must distinguish between theoretical definitions of royal and ducal authority, which are rarely articulated, and only worked through in any detail during this period by the 'Norman Anonymous' (*c.* 1100); expressions of that authority in administrative records, where, as we have seen, there appears no standard expression; and, perhaps most importantly, the views of chroniclers and other writers. A contemporary eulogy of William tells how 'he changed himself from duke into king'.[36] This was undoubtedly how contemporaries on both sides of the Channel saw his reign, and, when reporting William's activities in Normandy, chroniclers like William of Poitiers or Orderic Vitalis regularly style him *rex*, ignoring any constitutional niceties or problems. What was important was that William acted as a king in all of the territories subject to him.

On William's death there were, of course, changes. Whatever the dead king had really wanted, the fact that England and Normandy were now disengaged removed some of the ambiguities. William Rufus issued charters solely as *rex Anglorum*, and the same designation was carried on his seal. Robert Curthose was *dux Normannorum*, and even after 1096, when he left the duchy under William II's control he did not relinquish his title. Conversely, Rufus continued to style himself *rex Anglorum* in Normandy as well.

It may be possible to suggest two contemporary readings of the 'Anglo-Norman state'. In the sphere of the formal structures of government and administration, England and Normandy moved on different tracks – though in the same direction. In part this was inevitable. Long-established frontiers and jurisdictions could not be overturned. It was not possible, nor contemplated, to amalgamate the provinces of Canterbury and Rouen; local administrative methods remained intact, hundreds were not exported to Normandy nor did the *vicomte* find a home in England; legal and judicial systems, though undoubtedly cross- fertilising each other, continued distinct; coins minted in England were not current in Normandy and *vice versa*, and taxes paid in these coins went to the treasury either at Winchester or at Rouen. If the inertia of custom and administrative convenience combined to keep Normandy and England apart, there may, too, have been political advantage in separateness. If England were subsumed into a 'greater Normandy', then logically the king of France could demand homage for both territories. It is noteworthy that Robert Curthose did perform homage for Normandy, and conversely appealed to the French king for aid against Rufus.

At the same time, Normandy and England were subject to the same ruler from 1066 to 1087 and again from 1096. The very fact that William I was obliged to be constantly on the move through all his lands, using, for example, English forces in his Maine campaign of 1073, and bringing large French and Breton forces to England to counter the invasion threat in 1085, contributed to a unity that was predicated on personal rule not institutional assimilation, that was *de facto* not *de iure*. But there was a fundamental, and ultimately unresolvable, paradox. The king of England was an autonomous ruler, militarily and economically powerful. He owed his authority to what he perceived to be legitimate succession. The duke of

Normandy was a vassal of the king of France, and however much this was resented it could not be gainsaid. This dilemma was to determine Anglo-French relations for centuries. Such a theoretical division ensured that, however much Anglo-Norman kings and their followers appreciated the practical advantages of union, the Channel could never be bridged.

NOTES

Abbreviations Used in the Notes

ASC	Anglo-Saxon Chronicle
ANS	*Proceedings of the Battle Conference on Anglo-Norman Studies,* continued from 1983 as *Anglo-Norman Studies*
BAR	British Archaeological Reports
DB	*Domesday Book, seu Liber Censualis Willelmi Primi Regis Angliae,* ed. A. Farley and H. Ellis (4 vols, London, 1783–1816)
EHD	*English Historical Documents, ii: 1042–1189,* ed. D. C. Douglas and G. W. Greenway (2nd edn, London, 1981)
EHR	*English Historical Review*
GR	William of Malmesbury, *Gesta Regum Anglorum: The History of the English Kings,* ed. R. A. B. Mynors, R. M. Thomson and M. Winterbottom, 2 vols (Oxford, 1998)
OV	*The Ecclesiastical History of Orderic Vitalis,* ed. M. Chibnall (6 vols, Oxford, 1969–80)
TRE	*tempore Regis Eadwardi* ('in the time of King Edward')
TRHS	*Transactions of the Royal Historical Society*
VCH	*Victoria County History*

1 THE SOURCES

1. The best introduction to the sources is A. Gransden, *Historical Writing in England, c.550–c.1307* (London, 1974), pp. 87–185.
2. *EHD, ii*, no. 1, p. 147.
3. J. Campbell, 'Some Twelfth-Century Views of the Anglo-Saxon

Past', in *Essays in Anglo-Saxon History* (London, 1986), pp. 209–28; R. W. Southern, 'Aspects of the European Tradition of Historical Writing, 4: the Sense of the Past', *TRHS*, 5th series, 23 (1973), pp. 246-56.

4. G. A. Loud, 'The Gens Normannorum: Myth or Reality?', *ANS*, 4 (1981), pp. 104–16.

5. *The Gesta Normannorum Ducum of William of Jumèiges*, ed. and trans. E. M. C. van Houts (Oxford, 1992), vol. i, esp. pp. xix–xxxv.

6. See R. H. C. Davis, 'William of Poitiers and his History of William the Conqueror', in R. H. C. Davis and J. M. Wallace-Hadrill (eds), *The Writing of History in the Middle Ages* (Oxford, 1981), pp. 71–100.

7. *The Carmen de Hastingae Proelio of Guy, Bishop of Amiens*, ed. F. Barlow (2nd edn, Oxford, 1999).

8. R. H. C. Davis, 'The *Carmen de Hastingae Proelio*', *EHR*, 93 (1978), pp. 241–61.

9. E. M. C. van Houts, 'Latin Poetry and the Anglo-Norman Court, 1066–1135: the *Carmen de Hastingae Proelio*', *Journal of Medieval History*, 15 (1989), pp. 39–62, with full bibliography.

10. S. A. Brown, *The Bayeux Tapestry: History and Bibliography* (Woodbridge, 1988). The best edition is D. M. Wilson, *The Bayeux Tapestry* (London, 1985).

11. See N. P. Brooks and H. E. Walker, 'The Authority and Interpretation of the Bayeux Tapestry', *ANS*, 1 (1977), pp. 1–34.

12. Notably by C. R. Dodwell, 'The Bayeux Tapestry and the French Secular Epic', *Burlington Magazine*, 108 (1966), pp. 549–60.

13. H. E. J. Cowdrey, 'Towards an Interpretation of the Bayeux Tapestry', *ANS*, 10 (1987), p. 65.

14. D. J. Bernstein, *The Mystery of the Bayeux Tapestry* (Chicago and London, 1986).

15. Cowdrey, 'Towards an Interpretation', p. 64.

16. See M. Chibnall's monumental edition, *The Ecclesiastical History of Orderic Vitalis* (6 vols, Oxford, 1969–80). Her *The World of Orderic Vitalis* (Oxford, 1984) provides an excellent context.

17. *OV*, vi. pp. 550–7.

18. Ibid., iv. pp. 80–95.

19. R. Thomson, *William of Malmesbury* (Woodbridge, 1987), esp. ch. 2.

20. I. Short, 'Patrons and Polyglots: French Literature in Twelfth-Century England', *ANS* 14 (1991), pp. 229–50.

21. *GR*, p. 425. For William's prefaces see GR, pp. 15–17, 152–3, 425, 542–3, 709.

2 PRELUDE TO THE CONQUEST

1. S. Keynes, 'The Aethelings in Normandy', *ASC,* 13 (1990), pp. 173–206, provides the best account.

2. *OV,* vi, p. 169; R. L. G. Ritchie, *The Normans in England Before Edward the Confessor* (Exeter, 1948); E. Searle, 'Emma the Conqueror', in C. Harper-Bill, C. J. Holdsworth and J. L. Nelson (eds), *Studies in Medieval History presented to R. Allen Brown,* (Woodbridge, 1989), pp. 281–8, is also of value; P. Stafford, *Queen Emma and Queen Edith* (London, 1997), pp. 211–20, discusses Emma's Norman origins.

3. *VCH, Warwickshire,* i, p. 275 from Hemming's Cartulary.

4. P. Stafford, *Unification and Conquest* (London, 1989), pp. 88–9.

5. *OV,* ii, p. 43.

6. Keynes, 'The Aethelings', esp. pp. 188–93.

7. A. Williams, 'The King's Nephew: the Family and Career of Ralph, Earl of Hereford', in *Studies in Medieval History presented to R. Allen Brown,* pp. 327–44.

8. For fitzWimarch, see *The Life of King Edward who Rests at Westminster,* ed. and trans. F. Barlow (2nd edn, Oxford, 1992), p. 76, n. 4.

9. *OV,* iv, p. 139.

10. The best study of Eustace is now H. J. Tanner, 'The Expansion of the Power and Influence of the County of Boulogne under Eustace II', *ANS,* 14 (1991), pp. 251–86.

11. V. H. Galbraith, *Domesday Book: Its Place in Administrative History* (Oxford, 1974), p. 175.

12. G. Garnett, 'Coronation and Propaganda: Some Implications of the Norman Claim to the Throne of England in 1066', *TRHS,* 5th series, 36 (1986), p. 107.

13. D. C. Douglas was certainly sceptical. See his 'Edward the Confessor, Duke William, of Normandy and the English Succession', *EHR,* 68 (1953), pp. 526–45.

14. *Eadmer's History of Recent Events in England,* trans. G. Bosanquet (London, 1964), pp. 5–9.

15. A. Williams, 'Some Notes and Considerations on Problems connected with the English Royal Succession, 860–1066', *ANS,* 1 (1977), pp. 144–7 and 225–33.

16. See Williams, op. cit., and J. S. Beckerman, 'Succession in Normandy, 1087, and in England, 1066: the Role of Testamentary Custom', *Speculum,* 47 (1972), pp. 258–60.

17. E. John, 'Edward the Confessor and the Norman Succession', *EHR* 94 (1979), pp. 241–67, esp. 254–5.

18. See N. Hooper, 'Edward the Aetheling: Anglo-Saxon Prince, Rebel and Crusader', *Anglo-Saxon England*, 14 (1985), pp. 197–214.
19. P. Grierson, 'A Visit of Earl Harold to Flanders in 1056', *EHR*, 51 (1936), pp. 90–7.
20. *EHD, ii,* no. 1, p. 137.
21. Stafford, *Unification and Conquest,* p. 94.
22. *The Life of King Edward who Rests at Westminster*, ed. and trans. F. Barlow (2nd edn, Oxford, 1992), pp. 51, 81.
23. F. Barlow, *Edward the Confessor* (London, 1970), p. 222.
24. Staffird, *Unification and Conquest,* p. 97.
25. G. Garnett, 'Coronation and Propaganda: Some Implications of the Norman Claim to the Throne of England in 1066', *TRHS* 5th series, 36 (1986), pp. 91–116.

3   THE NORMAN CONQUEST

1. GR, p. 445.
2. The fullest study of Edgar is now N. Hooper, 'Edgar the Aetheling: Anglo-Saxon Prince, Rebel and Crusader', *Anglo-Saxon Studies*, 14 (Cambridge, 1985), pp. 197–214.
3. E. Mason, *St Wulfstan of Worcester, c. 1008–1095* (Oxford, 1990), pp. 102–4.
4. E. van Houts, 'The Ship List of William the Conqueror', *ANS*, 10 (1987), pp. 159–83.
5. For two examples, see *EHD, ii,* nos 236–7, pp. 982–3.
6. G. Garnett, 'Coronation and Propaganda: Some Implications of the Norman Claim to the Throne of England in 1066', *TRHS,* 5th series, 36 (1986), p. 110.
7. The clearest account is R. A. Brown, 'The Battle of Hastings', *ANS*, 3 (1980), pp. 1–21.
8. DB, ii, f. 14b.
9. A. Williams, 'Land and Power in the Eleventh Century: the Estates of Harold Godwineson', *ANS*, 3 (1980), pp. 178–80; F. M. Stenton, 'St Benet of Holme and the Norman Conquest', *EHR*, 37 (1922), p. 233. The abbot appears to have been allowed to return later.
10. D. C. Douglas, 'Companions of the Conqueror', *History*, 28 (1943), pp. 130–47.
11. Eustace's part in the battle is discussed by S. A. Brown, 'The Bayeux Tapestry: Why Eustace, Odo and Williarn', *ANS*, 12 (1989), pp. 7–28.

12. For the Bretons, see K. S. B. Keats-Rohan, 'William I and the Breton Contingent in the Non-Norman Conquest 1060–1087', *ANS*, 13 (1990), pp. 157–72; and for the Aquitanians, J. Martindale, 'Aimeri of Thouars and the Poitevin Connection', *ANS*, 7 (1984), pp. 224–45 and G. Beech, 'The Participation of Aquitanians in the Conquest of England, 1066–1100', *ANS*, 9 (1986), pp. 1–24.

13. J. Nelson, 'The Rites of the Conqueror', *ANS*, 4 (1981), pp. 117–18.

14. G. Garnett, 'Coronation and Propaganda', esp. pp. 95–9.

15. C. P. Lewis, 'The Early Earls of Norman England', *ANS*, 13 (1990), pp. 216–18.

16. *OV*, ii, p. 203.

17. G. Garnett, '*Franci et Angli*: the Legal Distinctions Between Peoples after the Conquest', *ANS*, 8 (1985), pp. 116–28.

18. For Eadric see S. Reynolds, 'Eadric Silvaticus and the English Resistance', *BIHR*, 54 (1981), pp. 102–5; and for Hereward, J. Hayward, 'Hereward the Outlaw', *Journal of Medieval History*, 14 (1988), pp. 293–304 is the most recent account.

19. H. Tanner, 'The Expansion of the Power and Influence of the Counts of Boulogne under Eustace II', *ANS*, 14 (1991), pp. 272–4.

20. J. H. Round, 'The Conqueror at Exeter', in *Feudal England* (London, 1895), p. 450.

21. Of the copious literature on the northern rebellions the fullest account, though not uncontroversial, is W. Kapelle, *The Norman Conquest of the North: the Region and its Transformation, 1000–1135* (London, 1979), chs 4–6.

22. H. E. J. Cowdrey, 'Bishop Erminfrid of Sion and the Penitential Ordinance following the Battle of Hastings', *Journal of Ecclesiastical History*, 20 (1969), pp. 225–42. See below, p. 174.

23. K. S. B. Keats-Rohan, 'William I and the Breton Contingent in the Non-Norman Conquest, 1060–1087', *ANS*, 13 (1990), p. 167.

24. *OV*, ii, pp. 311–23.

25. *OV*, ii, p. 315; Lewis, 'The Early Earls', p. 221.

26. C. P. Lewis, 'The Norman Settlement of Herefordshire under William I', *ANS*, 7 (1984), pp. 195–213.

27. As suggested in one of Lanfranc's admonitory letters to Roger (*The Letters of Lanfranc Archbishop of Canterbury*, ed. and trans. H. Clover and M. Gibson (Oxford, 1979), pp. 120–1 and n. 5.

28. *The Text of the Book of Llan Dâv*, ed. J. G. Evans (Oxford, 1893), pp. 277–8; C. J. Spurgeon, 'Mottes and Castle-ringworks in Wales', in J. R. Kenyon and R. Avent (eds), *Castles in Wales and the Marches* (Cardiff, 1987), p. 39.

29. Kapelle, *The Norman Conquest of the North*, pp. 134–7.
30. For the best introduction to Anglo-Welsh relations during this period, see R. R. Davies, *Conquest, Coexistence, and Change: Wales, 1063–1415* (Oxford, 1987), chs 1–4. See also D. Walker, *Medieval Wales* (Cambridge, 1990), ch. 2.
31. The best discussion is K. L. Maund, *Ireland, Wales and England in the Eleventh Century* (Woodbridge, 1991), pp. 129–40.
32. Pre-Conquest relations between Wales and England are conveniently summarised by W. Davies, *Wales in the Early Middle Ages* (Leicester, 1982), pp. 112–6.
33. Davies, *Conquest, Coexistence and Change, p.* 27.
34. J. Hillaby, 'The Norman New Town of Hereford', *Transactions of the Woolhope Naturalists' Field Club*, 44 (1982–4), pp. 185–95.
35. I. W. Rowlands, 'The Making of the March: Aspects of the Norman Settlement of Dyfed', *ANS*, 3 (1980), pp. 142–57.
36. *Brut y Twywysogyon*, ed. T. Jones (Cardiff, 1955), p. 31.
37. A. P. Smyth, *Warlords and Holymen: Scotland AD 80–1000* (London, 1984), ch. 7.
38. For a clear overview see G. W. S. Barrow, 'The Anglo-Scottish Border', in *The Kingdom of the Scots* (London, 1973), pp. 139–64.
39. J. Green, 'Anglo-Scottish Relations, 1066–1174', in M. Jones and M. Vale (eds), *England and her Neighbours* (London, 1989), pp. 53–72.
40. G. W. S. Barrow, *Kingship and Unity* (London, 1981), p. 28.
41. See G. W. S. Barrow, *The Anglo-Norman Era in Scottish History* (Oxford, 1980), for an excellent account.

4 SETTLEMENT AND COLONISATION

1. *OV*, iii, pp. 255–7.
2. For Guitmond, see *OV* ii, pp. 273–9.
3. *GR*, p. 737.
4. See W. J. Corbett, 'The Development of the Duchy of Normandy and the Norman Conquest of England', *Cambridge Medieval History*, 5 (Cambridge, 1926), pp. 505–13; and C. W. Hollister, 'The Greater Domesday Tenants in Chief', in J. C. Holt (ed.), *Domesday Studies* (Woodbridge, 1987), pp. 219–48.
5. For Hollister, see n. 4; D. Bates, *Normandy before 1066* (London, 1982), esp. chs 3 and 4.
6. Hollister, 'The Greater Domesday Tenants in Chief', pp. 227–8.

7. D. Greenway, 'Conquest and Colonization: the Foundation of an Alien Priory, 1077, in John Blair and Brian Golding (eds), *The Cloister and the World* (Oxford, 1996), p. 55.

8. 0 V, iv, p. 100.

9. OV, ii, p. 265.

10. See H. Tanner, 'The Expansion of the Power and Influence of the Counts of Boulogne under Eustace II', *ANS*, 14 (1991) pp. 270–7.

11. K. S. B. Keats-Rohan, 'William I and the Breton Contingent in the Non-Norman Conquest, 1060–1087', *ANS* 13 (1990), pp. 157–72, and 'The Bretons and Normans of England, 1066–1154: the Family, the Fief and the Feudal Monarchy', *Nottingham Medieval Studies*, 36 (1992), pp. 42–78.

12. See B. E. English, *The Lords of Holderness, 1086–1260* (Oxford, 1979), pp. 6–9; R. H. George, 'The Contribution of Flanders to the Conquest of England', *Revue belge de philologie et d'histoire*, 5 (1926), pp. 81–97.

13. J. Martindale, 'Aimeri of Thouars and the Poitevin Connection', *ANS*, 7 (1984), pp. 224–45; G. Beech, 'The Participation of Aquitanians in the Conquest of England, 1066–1100', *ANS*, 9 (1986), pp. 1–24, esp. 20–4.

14. J. H. Round, 'The Family of Ballon and the Conquest of South Wales', in *Studies in Peerage and Family History* (London, 1901), pp. 181–215.

15. *OV*, ii, p. 267.

16. The fullest discussion is now R. Fleming, *Kings and Lords in Conquest England* (Cambridge, 1991), chs 4–7.

17. *DB, i, f.* 158b.

18. A useful summary of the English baronage under Rufus is F. Barlow, *William Rufus* (London, 1983), pp. 163–75.

19. Fleming, *Kings and Lords*, p. 229. See also her 'Domesday Estates of the King and the Godwines: A Study in Late Saxon Politics', *Speculum*, 58 (1983), pp. 987–1107, esp. 1007.

20. J. Green, 'William Rufus, Henry I and the Royal Demesne', *History*, 64 (1979), pp. 337–52.

21. *Regesta Regum Anglo-Normannorum: the acta of William I (1066–1087)*, ed. D. Bates (Oxford, 1998), nos 120–1, pp. 423–7.

22. J. Campbell, 'Some Agents and Agencies of the Late Anglo-Saxon State', in J. C. Holt (ed.), *Domesday Studies* (Woodbridge, 1987), p. 214.

23. E.g. *DB*, i, ff. 35a, 36a, 50a, 21 la, 21 lb, 218b.

24. D. Bates, 'The Origins of the Justiciarship', *ANS*, 4 (19811), pp. 3–4.

See *DB*, i, f. 216a, for an example of Odo's seizure of land for one of his household.

25. See *DB*, i, f. 50a, for a possible indication of fitzOsbern's activities.
26. *DB*, i, f. 162a.
27. D. C. Douglas, *Feudal Documents from the Abbey of Bury St Edmunds* (Oxford, 1932), pp. xcv–c, 47.
28. *DB*, i, f. 62a.
29. *DB*, i, f. 148b; ii, f. 1b.
30. *VCH, Hampshire*, i, p. 428; B. Golding, *The Hampshire Domesday* (London, 1989), p. 25.
31. See above, p. 67; *DB*, i, f. 50a. In the same shire another English tenant claimed to hold Oakhanger 'by purchase from the king' (*DB*, i, f. 49a).
32. H. P. R. Finberg, *Tavistock Abbey* (Newton Abbot, 1969), pp. 4–12.
33. R. Mortimer, 'The Beginnings of the Honour of Clare', *ANS*, 3 (1980), pp. 124–7.
34. Ibid., pp. 128–31. See *DB*, ii, f. 102b (Wihtgar), f. 329a (Finn).
35. Campbell, 'Some Agents and Agencies', p. 210. For Edward, see *VCH, Wiltshire*, ii, p. 99.
36. A. Williams, 'A Vice-Comital Family in Pre-Conquest Warwickshire', *ANS*, 11 (1988), pp. 286–92.
37. *DB*, ii, f. 38b.
38. *DB*, i, f. 208b.
39. *Chronicon Monasterii de Abingdon*, ed. J. Stevenson (Rolls Series, London, 1858), vol. i, pp. 484, 490.
40. F. M. Stenton, 'St Benet of Holme and the Norman Conquest', *EHR*, 37 (1922), pp. 233–4.
41. *Chronicon Abbatiae de Evesham*, ed. W. D. Macray (Rolls Series, London, 1863), p. 90.
42. E. Mason, *St Wulfstan of Worcester, c. 1008–1095* (Oxford, 1990), pp. 14–7, where the steersman is tentatively identified with Eadric 'the wild'.
43. *DB*, ii, f. 87a.
44. Le Patourel, *The Norman Empire*, ch. 2, pp. 28–48.
45. *OV*, ii, pp. 195, 203.
46. *OV*, ii, pp. 203, 221.
47. *OV*, ii, p. 221.
48. Fleming, *Kings and Lords*, esp. ch. 5, pp. 145–82.
49. J. F. A. Mason, *William the First and the Sussex Rapes* (Historical Association, Hastings Branch, 1966); and E. Searle, 'The Abbey of the

Conqueror: Defensive Enfeoffment and Economic Development in Anglo-Norman England', *ANS*, 2 (1979), pp. 154–64.

50. P. Sawyer, '1066–1086: A Tenurial Revolution', in *Domesday Book: A Re-Assessment* (London, 1985), pp. 71–85.

51. Fleming, *Kings and Lords*, esp. pp. 123–5.

52. *VCH, Norfolk*, ii, pp. 18–9.

53. B. Golding, 'Robert of Mortain', *ANS*, 13 (1990), pp. 135–8; R. Mortimer, 'The Beginnings of the Honour of Clare', *ANS*, 3 (1980), pp. 135–6.

54. See below, p. 169.

55. For Holderness, see B. English, *The Lords of Holderness, 1086–1260* (Oxford, 1979), p. 8.

56. *OV*, ii, p. 263.

57. *Cartulary of Oseney Abbey*, ed. H. E. Salter (Oxford Historical Society, 97, 1934), vol. iv, p. 1; *VCH, Oxfordshire*, i, p. 383; *VCH, Buckinghamshire*, i, pp. 213–4; *VCH, Berkshire*, i, pp. 290–1.

58. See below, pp. 141–2.

59. *Chronicon Abbatiae Ramseiensis*, ed. W. D. Macray (Rolls Series, London, 1886), pp. lxxx–lxxxi.

60. A full study of the Conquest's impact on the towns is still awaited, but see S. Reynolds, 'Towns in Domesday Book', in *Domesday Studies*, pp. 295–310.

61. *A God's House Miscellany*, ed. J. M. Kaye (Southampton Record Series, 27, 1984), p. xx.

62. M. Biddle *et al.* (eds), *Winchester in the Early Middle Ages* (Oxford, 1976), esp. pp. 187–91, 474–6.

63. C. Clark, 'Battle *c.*1110: An Anthroponymist Looks at an Anglo-Norman New Town', *ANS*, 2 (1979), pp. 21–41.

64. *DB*, ii. f. 117b.

65. H. G. Richardson, *The English Jewry under Angevin Kings* (London, 1960), ch. 1, pp. 1–22.

66. See Barlow, *William Rufus*, pp. 110–12, 115–16.

67. The best introduction is G. W. S. Barrow, *The Anglo-Norman Era in Scottish History* (Oxford, 1980).

68. *DB*, i, f. 296a.

69. *OV*, v, p. 203; vi. p. 17. See E. Mason, 'Magnates, Curiales and the Wheel of Fortune, 1066–1154', *ANS*, 2 (1979), pp. 118–40.

70. *The Chronicle of Battle Abbey*, ed. and trans. E. Searle (Oxford, 1980), p. 179.

5 GOVERNING THE CONQUERED

1. See J. Campbell, 'The Age of Arthur', in *Essays in Anglo-Saxon History* (London, 1986), pp. 121–30 and references there cited.
2. For a useful introduction, see A. Williams, *Kingship and Government in Pre-Conquest England, c. 500–1066* (Basingstoke, 1999), pp. 88–96.
3. See P. A. Stafford, 'The "Farm of One Night" and the Organisation of King Edward's Estates in Domesday', *Economic History Review*, 33 (1980), pp. 491–502.
4. The best introduction is M. T. Clanchy, *From Memory to Written Record* (2nd edn, Oxford, 1993), esp. pp. 26–32. S. Keynes, 'Royal Government and the Written Word in Late Anglo-Saxon England' R. McKitterick (ed.), *The Uses of Literacy in Early Medieval Europe* (Cambridge, 1990), pp. 226–57 is also indispensable.
5. See J. Campbell, 'Observations on English Government from the Tenth to the Twelfth Century', in *Essays in Anglo-Saxon History*, pp. 157–8.
6. F. E. Harmer, *Anglo-Saxon Writs* (Manchester, 1952). Two important works, taking different approaches, are P. Chaplais, 'The Origin and Authority of the Royal Anglo-Saxon Diploma and the Anglo-Saxon Chancery: from the Diploma to the Writ', *Journal of the Society of Archivists*, 3 (1965–6), pp. 48–61; and S. Keynes, *The Diplomas of King Aethelred the Unready, 978–1016* (Cambridge, 1980), pp. 160–76.
7. J. Campbell, 'The Significance of the Anglo-Norman State in the Administrative History of Western Europe', in *Essays in English History*, p. 178, and 'Observations on English Government', pp. 157–8.
8. There is a brief account in E. Mason, *Norman Kingship* (Bangor, 1991), and see Loyn, *Governance*, ch. 4, pp. 81–90.
9. See C. W. Hollister and J. W. Baldwin, 'The Rise of Administrative Kingship: Henry I and Philip Augustus', *American Historical Review*, 83 (1978), pp. 870–905.
10. *DB*, i, f. 48b; *English Lawsuits from William I to Richard I*, ed. R. C. van Caenegem (Selden Society, 106, 1990), no. 12, p. 35.
11. D. Bates, 'The Origins of the Justiciarship', in *ANS*, 4 (1981), pp. 1–12.
12. For Ranulf's career see R. W. Southern, 'Rannulf Flambard and Early Anglo-Norman Administration', in *Medieval Humanism and Other Studies* (Oxford, 1970), pp. 183–205, and Barlow, *William Rufus*, esp. pp. 193–205.
13. Loyn, *Governance, p.* 194.
14. Bates, *Normandy before 1066, pp.* 160–1.

15. The best introduction is J. Nelson, 'The Rites of the Conqueror', *ANS*, 4 (1981), pp. 117–32.
16. See H. E. J. Cowdrey, 'The Anglo-Norman *Laudes Regiae*', *Viator*, 12 (1981), pp. 37–78.
17. M. Biddle, 'Seasonal Festivals and Residence: Winchester, Westminster and Gloucester in the Tenth to Twelfth Centuries', *ANS*, 8 (1985), pp. 51–72.
18. Le Patourel, *Norman Empire*, pp. 233–6.
19. *Walter Map, De Nugis Curialium*, ed. and trans. M. R. James, revised C. N. L. Brooke and R. A. B. Mynors (Oxford, 1983), p. 3.
20. See above, n. 17.
21. J. Nelson, 'The Rites of the Conqueror', *ANS*, 4 (1981), pp. 131–2 (and refs.) is illuminating.
22. Le Patourel, *The Norman Empire*, ch. 5, 'The Practical Problems of Government', pp. 121–72, is essential reading here.
23. J. A. Green, *The Government of England under Henry I* (Cambridge, 1989), ch. 2, pp. 19–37.
24. See Barlow, *William Rufus*, ch. 3, pp. 91–155. For d'Aincurt see pp. 133–4.
25. The standard accounts are J. O. Prestwich, 'The Military Household of the Norman Kings', *EHR*, 96 (1981), pp. 1–35, and M. Chibnall, 'Mercenaries and the *Familia Regis* under Henry I', *History*, 62 (1977), pp. 15–23.
26. J. O. Prestwich, 'War and Finance in the Anglo-Norman State', *TRHS*, 5th series, 4 (1954), p. 36.
27. Ibid., pp. 19–43.
28. *OV*, ii, p. 267.
29. J. A. Green, 'The Last Century of Danegeld', *EHR*, 96 (1981), pp. 241–58 is the best survey.
30. *EHD*, ii, no. 19, pp. 432–4.
31. C. W. Hollister, 'The Origins of the English Treasury', *EHR*, 93 (1978), pp. 262–75.
32. Green, *Government of England*, pp. 34–5.
33. See above, n. 6, and S. Keynes, 'Regenbald the Chancellor (*sic*)', *ANS*, 10 (1987), pp. 185–222.
34. See below, p. 104. D. Bates, 'The Earliest Norman Writs', *EHR*, 100 (1985), 266–84. For a characteristically more optimistic view, see R. A. Brown, 'Some Observations on Norman and Anglo-Norman Charters', in D. Greenway, C. Holdsworth, and J. Sayers (eds), *Tradition and Change* (Cambridge, 1985), pp. 145–64.

35. *EHD*, ii, no. 30, pp. 54–60; Green, *Government of England*, pp. 27–30.

36. Barlow, *William Rufus*, pp. 195, 201–3.

37. J. H. Round, 'Bernard the King's Scribe', *EHR*, 14 (1899), pp. 417–30; Green, *Government of England, p.* 235.

38. *Calendar of Documents Preserved in France*, no. 326, p. 111; *EHD*, ii, no. 1, pp. 167–175.

39. *EHD*, ii, no. 52, pp. 485–6.

40. *Regesta Regum Anglo-Normannorum: the Acta of William I (1066–1087)*, ed. D. Bates (Oxford, 1998), no. 235, pp. 728–9.

41. J. E. A. Jolliffe, *Angevin Kingship* (London, 1955), pp. 166–88.

42. R. Bartlett, *Trial by Fire and Water* (Oxford, 1986), is the fullest discussion of the ordeal in its western European context.

43. *EHD*, ii, no. 18, pp. 431–2.

44. See Green, *Government of England, pp.* 124–30.

45. E.g. *DB, i*, ff. 49a–50b.

46. For the park of Earl Roger of Shrewsbury, in Hampshire, see *DB*, i, f. 49a.

47. D. J. A. Matthew, *The Norman Conquest* (London, 1966), pp. 150–2.

48. B. Golding, *The Hampshire Domesday* (London, 1989), pp. 15–8 and references there cited.

49. These changes are summarised in *Facsimiles of English Royal Writs to AD 1100*, ed. T. A. M. Bishop and P. Chaplais (Oxford, 1957), pp. xiii-xv. See also Clanchy, *Memoqv to Written Record*, pp. 211-2.

50. *EHD*, ii, no. 40, p. 464.

51. R. C. van Caenegem, *The Birth of the English Common Law* (2nd edn, Cambridge, 1988), ch. 2, pp. 29–61.

52. See above, n. 34.

53. There is no full-length recent study of the pre-Conquest sheriff, but see W. A. Morris, *The Medieval English Sheriff to 1300* (Manchester, 1927), chs 1 and 2, and J. Green, 'The Sheriffs of William the Conqueror', *ANS*, 5 (1982), pp. 129–45.

54. The status of the earls is discussed by C. P. Lewis, 'The Early Earls of Norman England', *ANS*, 13 (1990), pp. 208–23.

55. *EHD*, ii, no. 38, p. 463.

56. Green, *Government of England*, p. 110.

57. Barlow, *William Rufus, pp.* 208–9. See also H. A. Cronne, 'The Office of Local Justiciar in England under the Norman Kings', *University of Birmingham Historical Journal*, 6 (1958), pp. 18–38.

58. E. Miller, 'The Land Pleas in the Reign of William I', *EHR*, 62 (1947), pp. 438–56; D. Bates, 'The Land Pleas of William I's Reign: Penenden

Heath Revisited', *BIHR*, 51 (1978), pp. 1–19, usefully reviews recent scholarship.

59. H. R. Loyn, 'The Hundred in the Tenth and Early Eleventh Centuries', in H. Hearder and H. R. Loyn (eds), *British Government and Administration* (Cardiff, 1974), pp. 1–15; J. Campbell, 'Observations on English Government', pp. 161–2.

60. The best survey is Campbell, 'Some Agents and Agencies', esp. pp. 205–8.

61. *English Lawsuits from William I to Richard I*, no. 4, pp. 6–7.

62. W. L. Warren, 'The Myth of Norman Administrative Efficiency', *TRHS*, 5th series, 34 (1984), pp. 118–9.

63. *English Lawsuits from William I to Richard I*, no. 12, p. 35.

64. See Campbell, 'Some Agents and Agencies', esp. pp. 205–18.

65. As argued by J. Green, 'William Rufus, Henry I and the Royal Demesne', *History*, 64 (1979), esp. pp. 347–9. See also her 'The Last Century of Danegeld', *EHR*, 96 (1981), pp. 241–58.

66. The clearest account is R. H. M. Dolley, *The Norman Conquest and the English Conquest* (London, 1966).

67. Bates, *Normandy before 1066*, pp. 164–5; L. Musset, 'A-t-il existé une aristocratie d'argent?', *Annales de Normandie*, 9 (1959), pp. 285–99.

68. C. J. Spurgeon, 'Mottes and Castle-Ringworks in Wales', in J. R. Kenyon and R. Avent (eds), *Castles in Wales and the Marches* (Cardiff, 1987), pp. 40–1.

69. Discussed by D. M. Metcalf, 'The Taxation of Moneyers under Edward the Confessor and in 1086', in J. C. Holt (ed.), *Domesday Studies*, (Woodbridge, 1987), pp. 279–95.

70. For the Winchester moneyers, see M. Biddle (ed.), *Winchester in the Early Middle Ages* (Oxford, 1976), pp. 396–422.

71. P. Nightingale, 'Some London Moneyers and Reflections on the Organisation of English Mints in the Eleventh Century', *Numismatic Chronicle*, 142 (1982), pp. 35–50.

72. As hinted by J. Campbell, 'Some Agents and Agencies', pp. 209–10.

73. Keynes, 'Regenbald the Chancellor', pp. 185–222.

74. Warren, 'The Myth of Norman Administrative Efficiency', pp. 113–32.

75. Lewis, 'The Early Earls of Norman England', pp. 208–23.

76. F. M. Stenton, *The First Century of English Feudalism* (2nd edn, Oxford, 1961), ch. 2, pp. 42–83.

77. R. Lennard, *Rural England, 1086–1135* (Oxford, 1959), pp. 34–6.

78. See J. F. A. Mason, 'Barons and their Officials in the Later Eleventh Century', *ANS*, 13 (1990), pp. 243–62.

79. See Lennard, *Rural England*, p. 50.
80. *OV*, ii, p. 263; Golding, 'Robert of Mortain', *ANS*, 13 (1990), pp. 138–9.
81. *OV*, ii, p. 263.
82. S. Harvey, 'The Extent and Profitability of Demesne Agriculture in the Later Eleventh Century', in T. H. Aston et al. (eds), *Social Relations and Ideas* (Cambridge, 1983), pp. 45–72.
83. Harvey, 'Extent and Profitability', p. 57. See also Lennard, *Rural England*, pp. 210–12.
84. As suggested by Robin Fleming, 'Domesday Book and the Tenurial Revolution', *ANS*, 9 (1986), esp. pp. 91–3, 101.
85. Golding, 'Robert of Mortain', pp. 133–5.
86. *EHD*, ii, no. 18, p. 431.

6 MILITARY ORGANISATION

1. The classic account is J. Prestwich, 'War and Finance in the Anglo-Norman State', *TRHS*, 5th series, 4 (1954), pp. 19–43.
2. 'The Military Household of the Norman Kings', *EHR*, 96 (1981), p. 32. See also his 'Anglo-Norman Feudalism and the Problem of Continuity', *Past and Present*, 26 (1963), pp. 39–57.
3. See especially M. Chibnall, 'Military Service in Normandy before 1066', *ANS*, 5 (1982), pp. 65–77; D. C. Bates, *Normandy before 1066*, pp. 122–8; and E. Z. Tabuteau, 'Definitions of Feudal Military Obligations in Eleventh-Century Normandy', in M. S. Arnold et al. (eds), *On the Laws and Customs of England: Essays in Honor of S. E. Thorne* (Chapel Hill, NC, 1981), pp. 18–59.
4. As hinted by E. van Houts, 'The Ship-List of William the Conqueror', *ANS*, 10 (1987), pp. 170–2.
5. The best introduction is now R. Abels, *Lordship and Military Obligation in Anglo-Saxon England* (Berkeley, Cal., 1988).
6. N. P. Brooks, 'Arms, Status and Warfare in Late-Saxon England', in D. Hill (ed.), *Ethelred the Unready* (BAR, British Series, 59, 1978), p. 87.
7. See J. Kiff, 'Images of War: Illustrations of Warfare in Early Eleventh-Century England', *ANS*, 7 (1984), pp. 177–94.
8. R. H. C. Davis, *The Medieval Warhorse* (London, 1989), pp. 70–8; R. Abels, *Lordship and Military Obligation*, pp. 176, 234, n. 47.
9. *DB*, i, ff. 179a, 189b.
10. As would C. W. Hollister, *The Military Organisation of Norman England* (Oxford, 1965), ch. IV, for example.

11. *English Historical Documents*, i, *c. 500–1042*, ed. D. Whitelock (2nd edn, London, 1979), no. 51, pp. 468–9.
12. See N. Hooper, 'The Housecarls in England in the Eleventh Century', *ANS*, 7 (1984), pp. 161–76. For a rather different interpretation, see J. Campbell, 'Some Agents and Agencies of the Late Anglo-Saxon State', in J. C. Holt (ed.), *Domesday Studies* (Woodbridge, 1987), pp. 201–4.
13. Abels, *Lordship and Military Obligation*, p. 169 and refs there cited.
14. Hollister, *The Military Organisation of Norman England*, p. 219.
15. The fullest treatment is N. Hooper, 'Some Observations on the Navy in Late Anglo-Saxon England', in C. Harper-Bill et al. (eds), *Studies in Medieval History presented to R. Allen Brown* (Woodbridge, 1989), pp. 203–13. See also C. W. Hollister, *Anglo-Saxon Military Institutions on the Eve of the Norman Conquest* (Oxford, 1962), ch. VI, and *The Military Organisation of Norman England*, pp. 248–9.
16. Hollister, *Military Organisation of Norman England*, p. 15.
17. The best introductions are R. A. Brown, *English Castles* (3rd edn, London, 1976), ch. 1, and D. F. Renn, *Norman Castles in Britain*, (2nd edn, London, 1973).
18. *OV*, ii, p. 219.
19. Le Patourel, *The Norman Empire*, pp. 316–8.
20. C. G. Harfield, 'A Handlist of Castles recorded in the Domesday Book', *EHR*, 106 (1991), pp. 371–92.
21. D. J. Cathcart King, *The Castle in England and Wales* (London, 1988).
22. Bates, *Normandy Before 1066*, pp. 114–15 and references there cited.
23. A. Williams, 'A Bell-house and a Burh-geat: Lordly Residences in England before the Norman Conquest', in C. Harper-Bill and R. Harvey (eds), *Medieval Knighthood, IV* (Woodbridge, 1992), pp. 221–40.
24. B. Golding, 'Robert of Mortain', *ANS*, 13 (1990), pp. 134–5.
25. Discussed by Hollister, *Military Organisation of Norman England*, ch. V, and F. M. Stenton, *The First Century of English Feudalism* (2nd edn, Oxford, 1961), ch. VI.
26. J. F. A. Mason, 'Barons and their Officials in the Later Eleventh Century', *ANS*, 13 (1990), pp. 243–62.
27. J. Bradbury, 'Battles in England and Normandy, 1066–1154', *ANS*, 6 (1983), pp. 1–12.
28. The fullest account is J. O. Prestwich, 'The Military Household of the Norman Kings', *EHR*, 96 (1981), pp. 1–37. Also see above, pp. 95–6.
29. *OV*, ii, pp. 261–3.

30. *EHD*, ii, no. 223, p. 967.
31. In J. H. Round, *Feudal England* (London, 1895), pp. 225–316.
32. J. C. Holt, 'The Introduction of Knight Service in England', *ANS*, 6 (1983), pp. 89–106.
33. By M. Hollings, 'The Survival of the Five-Hide Unit in the West Midlands', *EHR*, 63 (1948), pp. 453–87, and E. John, *Land Tenure in Early England*, (Leicester, 1960), pp. 80–139.
34. J. Gillingham, 'The Introduction of Knight Service into England', *ANS* 4 (1981), pp. 53–64.
35. Tabuteau, 'Feudal Military Obligations', p. 59.
36. See above, p. 121.
37. See Hollister, *The Military Organisation of Norman England*, ch. VII.
38. For two examples, see *EHD*, ii, nos 220, 221, pp. 961–3. A context is provided by M. T. Clanchy, *From Memory to Written Record* (2nd edn, Oxford, 1993), pp. 52–6.
39. Stenton, *The First Century*, pp. 170–2.
40. See W. Kapelle, *The Norman Conquest of the North* (London, 1979), p. 194.
41. *DB*, i, f. 173a.
42. *DB*, ii, f. 18b.
43. *DB*, i, f. 210b; J. A. Raftis, *The Estates of Ramsey Abbey* (Toronto, 1957), p. 25.
44. B. F. Harvey, *Westminster Abbey and its Estates in the Middle Ages* (Oxford, 1977), pp. 70–77.
45. *EHD*, ii, no. 224, p. 971.
46. *EHD*, ii, no. 220, p. 961; *DB*, i, f. 66a.
47. *Chronica Monasterii de Abingdon*, ed. J. Stevenson (Rolls Series, London, 1858), vol. ii, pp. 6–7.
48. *DB*, i, f. 222a.
49. The most sensitive recent discussion is D. Fleming, 'Landholding by *Milites* in Domesday Book: a Revision', *ANS*, 13 (1990), pp. 83–98.
50. See, for example, his 'The Status of the Norman Knight', in J. Gillingham and J. C. Holt (eds), *War and Government in the Middle Ages: Essays in Honour of J. O. Prestwich*, (Woodbridge, 1984), pp. 18–32.
51. S. Harvey, 'The Knight and the Knight's Fee in England', *Past and Present*, 49 (1970), pp. 3–43.
52. *EHD*, ii, no. 222, pp. 963–4.
53. Fleming, 'Landholding by *Milites*', p. 97.
54. P. Coss, 'Literary and Social Terminology: the Vavasour in England', in T. H. Aston et al. (eds), *Social Relations and Ideas* (Cambridge, 1983), pp. 109–50.

55. See Hollister, *Anglo-Saxon Military Institutions*, pp. 81–2.
56. M. Chibnall, *Anglo-Norman England, 1066–1166* (Oxford, 1986), p. 30.
57. Kapelle, *Norman Conquest of the North*, ch. 7.
58. D. R. Roffe, *The Nottinghamshire Domesday* (London, 1990), p. 13.
59. J. Bradbury, *The Medieval Archer* (Woodbridge, 1985), esp. chs 2 and 3.
60. At Shaftesbury Ann Williams has identified several of the nunnery"s military tenants as English, see 'The Knights of Shaftesbury Abbey', *ANS*, 8 (1985), esp. pp. 231–2.

7   A COLONIAL CHURCH?

1. *Eadmer's History of Recent Events in England*, trans. G. Bosanquet (London, 1964), p. 10. For a useful, if somewhat unsympathetic, account of the post-Conquest church, see F. Barlow, *The English Church, 1066–1154* (London,1979).
2. The most recent overview is provided by C. Morris, *The Papal Monarchy: The Western Church from 1050 to 1250* (Oxford, 1989), chs 4 and 5.
3. M. Gibson, *Lanfranc of Bec* (Oxford, 1978), esp. pp. 139–40.
4. The most concise account is H. E. J. Cowdrey, 'Pope Gregory VII and the Anglo-Norman Church and Kingdom', reprinted in *Popes, Monks and Crusaders* (London, 1984), IX, pp. 79–114.
5. I. S. Robinson, *The Papacy, 1073–1198* (Cambridge, 1990), p. 309.
6. Discussed in Gibson, *Lanfranc of Bec*, pp. 131–40.
7. Several of the more important of William, Gregory and Lanfranc's letters are translated in *EHD*, ii, nos 96–106, pp. 688–97, and *The Letters of Lanfranc Archbishop of Canterbury*, ed. and trans. H. Clover and M. Gibson (Oxford, 1979), nos 38–9, pp. 128–33.
8. See below, p. 158.
9. For the Canterbury version, see *Eadmer's History of Recent Events in England*, pp. 11–2, 17, 43; and for York's case Hugh the Chanter, *The History of the Church of York, 1066–1127*, ed. and trans. C. Johnson, revised M. Brett, C. N. L. Brooke and M. Winterbottom (Oxford, 1990). The introduction to this text is the clearest recent guide to the dispute.
10. Davies, *Conquest, Coexistence and Change*, pp. 188–9.
11. M. T. Flanagan, *Irish Sociey, Anglo-Norman Settlers, Angevin Kingship* (Oxford, 1989), ch. 1, is a useful introduction.
12. *Eadmer's History of Recent Events in England*, pp. 79–81.
13. See *Hugh the Chanter*, pp. xlv–xlix for an excellent introduction.
14. Ibid., p. 50.
15. For a useful introduction, see H. R. Loyn, 'William's Bishops: Some

Further Thoughts', *ANS*, 10 (1987), pp. 223–6.

16. London, Dorchester (later Lincoln), and Worcester were the wealthiest of the secular sees, all with incomes of around £600. See W. J. Corbett, 'The Development of the Duchy of Normandy and the Norman Conquest of England', in *Cambridge Medieval History* (Cambridge, 1926) v. 511.

17. One of the moneyers at Hereford belonged to the bishop; the bishop of Winchester farmed the mint of Colchester.

18. M. Ruud, 'Monks in the World: The Case of Gundulf of Rochester', *ANS*, 11 (1988), p. 248.

19. *EHD*, ii, no. 39, p. 463.

20. *EHD*, ii, no. 50, pp. 482-3.

21. F. Barlow, *William Rufus* (London, 1983), pp. 182–5.

22. A useful, brief introduction, with special reference to York, is by R. Hill and C. N. L. Brooke, in G. E. Ayimer and R. Cant (eds), *A History of York Minster* (Oxford, 1977), pp. 20–8.

23. *History of the Church of York, pp.* 18–21.

24. C. N. L. Brooke, 'The Composition of the Chapter of St Paul's, 1086–1163', *Cambridge Historical Journal*, 10 (1951), esp. p. 125.

25. *EHD*, ii, no. 78, pp. 646–7.

26. See D. Owen, 'The Norman Cathedral at Lincoln', *ANS*, 6 (1983), pp. 188–99.

27. C. Brooke, 'The Archdeacon dnd the Norman Conquest', in D. Greenway, C. Holdsworth and J. Sayers (eds), *Tradition and Change* (Cambridge, 1985), pp. 1–19.

28. *EHD*, ii, no. 79, pp. 647–8; C. Morris, 'William I and the Church Courts', *EHR*, 82 (1967), pp. 449–63.

29. *Gesta Pontificum, p.* 282, cited in E. Mason, St *Wulfstan of Worcester, c. 1008–1095* (Oxford, 1990), pp. 139–40.

30. For a sceptical reappraisal, see J. Barrow, 'How the Twelfth-Century Monks of Worcester Perceived Their Past', in *The Perception of the Past in Twelfth-Century Europe,* ed. P. Magdalino (London, 1992), pp. 60–9. See also Mason, *Wulfstan*, pp. 213–16.

31. The most useful studies on this topic are contained in J. Blair (ed.), *Minsters and Parish Churches: The Local Church in Transition 950–1200* (Oxford University Committee for Archaeology Monograph, 17, 1988).

32. M. J. Franklin, 'The Secular College as a Focus for Anglo-Norman Piety: St Augustine's, Daventry', in *Minsters and Parish Churches*, pp. 97–104.

33. J. Blair, 'Secular Minster Churches in Domesday Book', in P. Sawyer (ed.), *Domesday Book. A Reassessment* (London, 1987), pp. 134–5.

34. P. H. Hase, 'The Mother Churches of Hampshire', in *Minsters and Parish Churches*, esp. pp. 49–50.

35 See Blair, 'Local Churches in Domesday Book and Before', in J. C. Holt (ed.), *Domesday Studies* (Woodbridge, 1987), pp. 265–78.

36 T. Tatton-Brown, 'The Churches of Canterbury Diocese in the 11th Century', in *Minsters and Parish Churches*, pp. 105–18.

37 See R. Gem, 'The English Parish Church in the 11th and Early 12th Centuries: A Great Rebuilding', in *Minsters and Parish Churches*, pp. 21–30.

38 R. Lennard, *Rural England, 1086–1135* (Oxford, 1959), pp. 327–38, remains a useful guide to the social status of the village priest.

39 M. Brett, *The English Church under Henry I* (Oxford, 1975), pp. 219–20.

40 For a useful, brief (and fully annotated) introduction, see J. Gillingham, 'The Introduction of Knight Service into England', *ANS*, 4 (1981), pp. 59–60 and 184–5.

41 See *EHD*, ii, no. 38, p. 463.

42 For Harold, see A. Williams, 'Land and Power in the Eleventh Century: the Estates of Harold Godwineson', *ANS*, 3 (1980), pp. 181–4.

43 Gillingham, 'The Introduction of Knight Service', esp. pp. 57–8. See above, pp. 135–6.

44 *EHD*, ii, no. 223, p. 967; D. C. Douglas, *Feudal Documents from the Abbey of Bury St Edmunds* (Oxford, 1932), pp. xcv–c.

45 M. Gibson, *Lanfranc of Bec* (Oxford, 1978), pp. 174–5.

46 Ibid., p. 188.

47 R. W. Southern, 'Aspects of the European Tradition of Historical Writing: 4. The Sense of the Past', *TRHS*, 5th series, 23 (1973), pp. 246–56.

48 S. J. Ridyard, '*Condigna Veneratio*: Post-Conquest Attitudes to the Saints of the Anglo-Saxons', *ANS*, 9 (1986), pp. 179–206; D. Rollason, *Saints and Relics in Anglo-Saxon England* (Oxford, 1989), pp. 215–39.

49 A. W. Klukas, 'The Architectural Implications of the *Decreta Lanfranci*', *ANS*, 6 (1983), pp. 136–71.

50 See C. Clark, 'People and Language in Post-Conquest Canterbury', *Journal of Medieval History*, 2 (1976), pp. 1–34.

51 *EHD*, ii, no. 81, pp. 649–50.

52 The fullest study remains D. J. A. Matthew, *The Norman Monasteries and their English Possessions* (Oxford, 1962).

53 See E. Searle, *Lordship and Community: Battle Abbey and its Banlieu, 1066–1538* (Toronto, 1974), pp. 21–36, and *The Chronicle of Battle Abbey*, ed. and trans. E. Searle (Oxford, 1980), pp. 15–23.

54 B. Golding, 'The Coming of the Cluniacs', *ANS*, 3 (1980), pp. 65–87.

55 K. Cooke, 'Donors and Daughters: Shaftesbury Abbey's Benefactors, Endowments and Nuns, c.1086–1130', *ANS*, 12 (1989) pp. 29–46; D. Bates, 'The Building of a Great Church: the Abbey of St Peter's,

Gloucester, and its Early Norman Benefactors', *Transactions of the Bristol and Gloucestershire Archaeological Society*, 102 (1984), pp. 129–32.

56 B. Golding, 'Anglo-Norman Knightly Burials', in C. Harper-Bill and R. Harvey (eds), *The Ideals and Practice of Medieval Knighthood* (Woodbridge, 1986), pp. 35–48.

57 Le Patourel, *The Norman Empire*, pp. 317–8

8 ANGLO-NORMAN ENGLAND

1. Le Patourel, *Norman Empire*, esp. ch. 9, pp. 208–18.

2. See J. Gillingham, *The Angevin Empire* (London, 1984).

3. D. Bates, 'Normandy and England after 1066', *EHR*, 104 (1989), pp. 851–76. An earlier and valuable contribution to the debate is C. W. Hollister, 'Normandy, France and the Anglo-Norman *Regnum*', *Speculum*, 51 (1976), pp. 202–42, reprinted in *Monarchy, Magnates and Institutions in the Anglo-Norman World* (London, 1986), pp. 17–58.

4. B. Bartel, 'Comparative Historical Archaeology and Archaeological Theory', in S. L. Dyson (ed.), *Comparatives Studies in the Archaeology of Colonialism* (British Archaeological Reports, International Series, 233, 1985), p. 9.

5. G. Loud, 'The "Gens Normannorum": Myth or Reality', *ANS*, 4 (1981), pp. 104–16, a convincing critique of R. H. C. Davis, *The Normans and their Myth* (London, 1976).

6. As shown by le Patourel, *Norman Empire*, pp. 331–4.

7. Particularly by M. K. Lawson, 'These Stories Look True: Levels of Taxation in the Reigns of Aethelred II and Cnut', *EHR*, 104 (1989), pp. 389–90.

8. For London, see S. Reynolds, 'The Rulers of London in the Twelfth Century', *History*, 57 (1972), pp. 339–40.

9. As indicated in his charter founding Neath abbey (*Cartae et Munimenta de Glamorgan*, ed. G. L. Clark (6 vols, Cardiff, 1910), vol. i, pp. 74–5.

10. *OV*, ii, p. 257.

11. C. Clark, 'Women's Names in Post-Conquest England: Observations and Speculations', *Speculum*, 53 (1978), esp. pp. 240–51. This is an article of considerable resonance, with implications far more wideranging than its title suggests.

12. E. Searle, *Lordship and Community: Battle Abbey and its Banlieu, 1066–1538* (Toronto, 1974), pp. 69–78; C. Clark, 'An Anthroponymist Looks at an Anglo-Norman New Town', *ANS*, 2 (1979), pp. 21–41.

13. C. Clark, 'People and Languages in Post-Conquest Canterbury', *Journal of Medieval History*, 2 (1976), pp. 1–34, esp. 8–26.

14. See Barlow, *William Rufus*, pp. 105–8.

15. For a clear overview, see E. Fernie, 'The Effect of the Conquest on Norman Architectural Patronage', *ANS*, 9 (1986), pp. 71–85, and references there cited.

16. For Bishop Herman of Lotharingia's cathedral, at Old Sarum, see R. Gem, 'The First Romanesque Cathedral at Old Sarum', in E. Fernie and P. Crossley (eds), *Medieval Architecture and its Intellectual Context* (London, 1990), pp. 9–18.

17. Fernie, 'The Effect of the Conquest', p. 85.

18. *Chronicle of Battle Abbey*, p. 45. For the use of Caen stone see Bates, 'England and Normandy', pp. 869–70 and references there cited.

19. F. E. Harmer, *Anglo-Saxon Writs* (Manchester, 1952), p. 480.

20. *Feudal Documents from the Abbey of Bury St Edmunds*, ed. D. C. Douglas (Oxford, 1932), no. 172, p. 154.

21. I. Short, 'On Bi-lingualism in Anglo-Norman England', *Romance Philology*, 33 (1980), pp. 467–79.

22. H. Mayr-Harting, 'The Functions of a Twelfth-Century Recluse', *History*, 60 (1975), p. 344.

23. I owe this information to Dr Tessa Webber.

24. See Clark, 'Women's Names', esp. pp. 223–30.

25. *OV*, ii, p. 269.

26. *The Letters of Lanfranc*, no. 53, p. 167; E. Searle's 'Women and the Legitimization of Succession at the Norman Conquest', *ANS*, 3 (1980), pp. 159–70, is essential reading.

27. Searle, 'Legitimization of Succession', p. 164; Clark, 'Women's Names'.

28. *DB*, i, f. 167.

29. B. English, 'William I and the Anglo-Norman Succession', *Historical Research*, 64 (1991), p. 234.

30. See above, pp. 92–3 for the *laudes*.

31. G. Garnett, '*Franci et Angli*: the Legal Distinctions Between Peoples after the Conquest', *ANS*, 8 (1985), pp. 109–37.

32. Hollister, 'The Anglo-Norman *Regnum*'.

33. Ibid., p. 18 and refs.

34. As suggested by Cowdrey, see above, pp. 92–3.

35. Hollister, 'The Anglo-Norman *Regnum*', pp. 21–2; le Patourel, *Norman Empire*, pp. 233–5.

36. Cited in Bates, 'Normandy and England', p. 863.

SELECT BIBLIOGRAPHY

No other period of medieval British history has given rise to more than a fraction of the literature devoted to the Norman Conquest. It remains one of the most vibrant areas of medieval English historical research, and consequently generates a bibliography of almost unmanageable proportions. The published bibliographies of Domesday Book and the Bayeux Tapestry are themselves substantial works as long as this study. The following can be no more than a brief selection of the more useful, recent, and accessible works. More specific works can be pursued through the footnotes. It should also be supplemented by constantly updated bibliographies such as the Royal Historical Society's annual *Bibliography of British and Irish History* and the biannual *International Medieval Bibliography* of the University of Leeds. No student of Anglo-Norman history can ignore the annual publication of *Anglo-Norman Studies* (and its predecessor till 1983, *Proceedings of the Battle Conference on Anglo-Norman Studies*) which have since 1979 been the showcase of Anglo-Norman scholarship, under the editorship first of Allen Brown and latterly of Marjorie Chibnall and Christopher Harper-Bill.

Primary Sources

The Bayeux Tapestry, ed. D. M. Wilson (London, 1985).

The Carmen de Hastingae Proelio of Guy, Bishop of Amiens, ed. and trans. F. Barlow (2nd edn, Oxford, 1999).

Domesday Book: a Facsimile, eds A. W. Williams, R. W. H. Erskine and G. Martin (London, 1986–92).

Eadmer's History of Recent Events in England, trans. G. Bosanquet (London, 1964).

English Historical Documents II 1042–1189, ed. D. C. Douglas and G. W. Greenaway (2nd edn, London,1981).

The Chronicle of John of Worcester: vol. ii. The Annals from 450 to 1066, ed. and trans. R. R. Darlington and P. MacGurk (Oxford, 1995) and *vol. iii. The Annals from 1066 to 1140*, ed. P. McGurk (Oxford, 1998).

Select Bibliography

The Life of King Edward who lies at Westminster, ed. and trans. F. Barlow (2nd edn, Oxford, 1992).

The Ecclesiastical History of Orderic Vitalis, ed. and trans. Marjorie Chibnall (6 vols, Oxford, 1969–80).

Regesta Regum Anglo-Normannorum: the Acta of William I (1066–1087), ed. D. Bates (Oxford, 1998).

William of Jumièges, *Gesta Normannorum Ducum*, ed. and trans. E. van Houts (2 vols, Oxford, 1992–5).

William of Malmesbury, *Gesta Regum Anglorum: The History of the English Kings*, ed. and trans. R. A. B. Mynors, R. M. Thomson, and M. Winterbottom, 2 vols, (Oxford, 1998).

William of Poitiers, *Gesta Guillelmi*, ed. and trans. R. H. C. Davis and Marjorie Chibnall (Oxford, 1998).

Secondary Sources

R. Abels, *Lordship and Military Obligation in Anglo-Saxon England* (Berkeley, 1988) is a convincing study of pre-Conquest arrangements.

F. Barlow, *Edward the Confessor* (London, 1970) remains the standard interpretation.

F. Barlow, *William Rufus* (London, 1983) is a sympathetic and wide-ranging examination of the reign.

F. Barlow, *The English Church 1000–1066* (2nd edn, London, 1979) is valuable for secular as well as ecclesiastical developments. So, too, is its sequel, *The English Church, 1066–1154* (London, 1979).

G. W. S. Barrow, *The Anglo-Norman Era in Scottish History* (Oxford, 1980), though concentrating on the twelfth century, has much of value.

D. Bates, *Normandy before 1066* (London, 1982) is the clearest and most detailed study in English.

D. Bates, 'Normandy and England after 1066', *EHR* 104 (1989), 851–76, is a major reassessment of cross-Channel relations, with far-reaching implications.

W. J. Blair, (ed), *Ministers and Parish Churches: the Local Church in Transition, 950–1200* (Oxford, 1988) is the best introduction to ecclesiastical organisation at the grass-roots.

E. A. R. Brown, 'The Tyranny of a Construct: Feudalism and Historians of Medieval Europe', *American Historical Review* 79 (1974), 1063–88, is an invigorating corrective to over-glib use of 'feudal' concepts.

R. A. Brown, *Origins of English Feudalism* (London, 1973) – with a useful appendix of documents – is the most forceful statement of structural change in post-Conquest military organisation.

R. A. Brown, *English Castles* (3rd edn, London, 1976), ch. 1, is the best introduction to this subject.

R. C. van Caenegem, *The Birth of the English Common Law* (2nd edn, Cambridge, 1988) examines legal developments during this period.

J. Campbell, *Essays in Anglo-Saxon History* (London, 1986) conveniently reprints most of the relevant articles of this most incisive historian.

M. Chibnall, *Anglo-Norman England* (Oxford, 1986) is a clear and thoughtful analysis.

M. T. Clanchy, *From Memory to Written Record* (2nd edn, Oxford, 1993) is a brilliant account of changes in governmental practice.

H. C. Darby, *Domesday England* (Cambridge, 1977) is a useful abridgement of the same author's earlier regional studies of Domesday geography.

R. R. Davies, *Conquest, Coexistence, and Change: Wales, 1063–1415* (Oxford, 1987), chs 1–4, is the best introduction to developments in Wales.

R. H. M. Dolley, *The Norman Conquest and the English Conquest* (London, 1966) is the clearest account of changes in the coinage.

Domesday Book: a Reassessment, P. Sawyer, ed. (London, 1985) is a valuable collection of essays.

Domesday Studies, J. C. Holt, ed. (Woodbridge, 1987) contains an excellent range of papers, not all of which are specific to Domesday.

D. C. Douglas, *William the Conqueror*, (London, 1964), though now somewhat dated, is still an excellent account.

R. Faith, *The English Peasantry and the Growth of Lordship* (London, 1997) includes a major re-evaluation of the impact of the Conquest on rural society.

R. Fleming, *Kings and Lords in Conquest England* (Cambridge, 1991) is a compelling analysis of the Norman settlement.

R. Fleming, *Domesday Book and the Law: Society and Legal Custom in Early Medieval England* (Cambridge, 1998).

E. A. Freeman, *The History of the Norman Conquest of England* (5 vols, Oxford, 1867–79) is a narrative on the grand scale, a monument of Victorian historiography.

V. H. Galbraith, *The Making of Domesday Book* (Oxford, 1961) and *Domesday Book: Its Place in Administrative History* (Oxford, 1974) are fundamental analyses.

M. Gibson, *Lanfranc of Bec* (Oxford, 1978) is the fullest study of Lanfranc, though less good on his archiepiscopal career than on other aspects.

J. A. Green, *The Government of England under Henry I* Cambridge, 1986) contains much of value for the reigns of William I and II.

J. A. Green, *The Aristocracy of Norman England* (Cambridge, 1997) is a masterly and wide-ranging study of the Anglo–Norman elite.

C. W. Hollister, *Anglo-Saxon Military Institutions on the Eve of the Norman Conquest* (Oxford, 1962) and *The Military Organisation of Norman England* (Oxford, 1965), together comprise an important interpretation.

J. Hudson, *Land, Law and Lordship in Anglo–Norman England* (Oxford, 1994)

E. Kapelle, *The Norman Conquest of the North: the Region and its Transformation 1000–1135* (Chapel Hill, 1979) is an important, though not uncontroversial, regional account.

D. M. Knowles, *The Monastic Order in England, 943–1216* (Cambridge, 1949) is the fullest, though rather dated, account.

G. Loud, 'The "Gens Normannorum": Myth or Reality', *ANS* 4 (1981), pp. 104–16, is an excellent analysis of Norman 'self-awareness'.

H. R. Loyn, *Harold, son of Godwin* (Historical Association, 1966) is the only modern (though brief) study.

H. R. Loyn, *The Governance of Anglo-Saxon England, 500–1087* (London, 1984) presents a clear introduction.

J. le Patourel, *The Norman Empire* (Oxford, 1976). The most stimulating interpretation of Normandy and England from the tenth to the mid-twelfth century in recent times.

J. O. Prestwich, 'War and Finance in the Anglo-Norman State', *TRHS* 5th ser., 4 (1954), 19–43, 'Anglo-Norman Feudalism and the Problem of Continuity', *Past and Present* 26 (1963), 39–57 and 'The Military Household of the Norman Kings', *EHR* 96 (198 1), pp. 1–35 – sequence of articles which still constitute the most convincing analysis of Anglo-Norman military organisation.

S. Reynolds, *Fiefs and Vassals* (Oxford, 1994).

D. Roffe, *Domesday: the Inquest and the Book* (Oxford, 2000) is a controversial and far-ranging reappraisal.

E. Searle, *Predatory Kinship and the Creation of Norman Power, 840–1066* (Berkeley, 1988) is a controversial work which stresses the Scandinavian elements of the Norman polity.

R. W. Southern, *Saint Anselm: a Portrait in a Landscape* (Cambridge, 1990) is a masterly illumination.

F. M. Stenton, *The First Century of English Feudalism* (2nd edn, Oxford, 1962); an influential, though now much challenged, interpretation.

F. M. Stenton, *Anglo-Saxon England* (3rd edn, Oxford, 1971) is a classic, and takes the narrative up to the Conqueror's death.

W. L. Warren, 'The Myth of Norman Administrative Efficiency', *TRHS* 5th ser., 34 (1984), pp. 113–32, is thought-provoking, important, and very controversial.

W. L. Warren, *The Governance of Norman and Angevin England, 1087–1272* (London, 1987) provides a lucid overview.

A. Williams, *The English and the Norman Conquest* (Woodbridge, 1995) is important both as a study of post-1066 political and cultural developments and as an investigation of native 'winners' and 'losers'.

INDEX